Introduction to Advertising

D0147281

This book is an introductory roadmap to the advertising process. Advertising is explored as a creative communication message from a brand, created by advertising agencies and distributed across different media to target the right consumers.

The book provides an understanding of the benefits of advertising, its role in the economy and, even more so, acknowledges that advertisements are not only about selling but also about effectively communicating a message. The creative and conceptual approach towards the communication process is discussed, and insight is presented into the dynamics within the industry and the different stakeholders involved, while recognising how different creative elements in advertisements are consciously selected to make them appealing. Finally, it considers how to analyse and measure an advert's effectiveness and looks ahead to future ideas and technologies arising in advertising. Effectively combining theory with practical insight, each chapter begins with learning objectives and ends with key learnings. International case studies feature throughout, including insights from British Gas, WPP, Audi and KFC, as well as other examples from smaller organisations and the non-profit sector.

Taking students step by step through the advertising process, it is important reading for undergraduate and postgraduate students studying Advertising, Brand Management, Marketing Communications and Media Planning.

Emmanuel Mogaji is a Senior Lecturer in Advertising and Marketing Communications at the University of Greenwich, UK. His research interests include artificial intelligence, digital marketing and brand management. Emmanuel has previously worked as a marketing communication executive, responsible for designing and managing campaigns.

Introduction to Advertising

Understanding and Managing the
Advertising Process

Emmanuel Mogaji

Routledge
Taylor & Francis Group

LONDON AND NEW YORK

First published 2021
by Routledge
2 Park Square, Milton Park, Abingdon, Oxon OX14 4RN

and by Routledge
605 Third Avenue, New York, NY 10158

Routledge is an imprint of the Taylor & Francis Group, an informa business

British Library Cataloguing-in-Publication Data
A catalogue record for this book is available from the British Library

Library of Congress Cataloging-in-Publication Data
Names: Mogaji, Emmanuel, author.
Title: Introduction to advertising : understanding and managing the
    advertising process / Emmanuel Mogaji.
Description: Abingdon, Oxon ; New York, NY : Routledge, 2021. | Includes
    bibliographical references and index.
Identifiers: LCCN 2020052443 (print) | LCCN 2020052444 (ebook)
Subjects: LCSH: Advertising. | Branding (Marketing) | Communication in
    marketing.
Classification: LCC HF5823 .M47 2021 (print) | LCC HF5823 (ebook) |
    DDC 659.2—dc23
LC record available at https://lccn.loc.gov/2020052443
LC ebook record available at https://lccn.loc.gov/2020052444

ISBN: 978-0-367-44278-1 (hbk)
ISBN: 978-0-367-44199-9 (pbk)
ISBN: 978-1-003-00872-9 (ebk)

Typeset in Galliard
by Apex CoVantage, LLC

To my wife, Temitope and children, Praise, Precious and Hephzibah. Thank you for your support, understanding and patience while I was writing this book.

To my students at the University of Greenwich. Thank you for motivating and challenging me to improve the quality of my teaching.

Contents

Figures

Acknowledgements

Writing a book can be a daunting and lonely experience, yet the help of numerous people along this solitary journey cannot be underestimated. Upon reflection in writing this acknowledgement, it is surprising to see how many people have contributed in one way or the other to making it a success.

Firstly, I am most grateful to the Almighty God, the giver of life, wisdom, knowledge and understanding. I acknowledge that God has given me the skills, strength and expertise needed to complete this book. It was never my doing. He surrounded me with people to make this work a success; I appreciate his grace, mercy and kindness throughout this process.

I want to acknowledge the immeasurable support of my wife – Temitope and children – Praise, Precious and Hephzibah for their love, care and sharing my enthusiasm throughout this period of writing. I appreciate their understanding when I was running late to make lunch, and they reassured me: "Daddy don't worry, Mummy has fed us." Thank you for your sacrifice of love.

Special thanks to extended family and friends, for their support and encouragement. Pastor Femi and Lady Evangelist Rodah Mogaji, Dr Ola and Mrs Tobi Madamidola, Ebenezer and Vanessa Mogaji and Elizabeth Mogaji. Thank you, Pastor Christopher, and Mrs Sola Farinloye, for the interest you showed in my progress. I would also like to acknowledge the moral support of Pastor Azeez Ayege, Mr Damilola Olowookere and Mr Ayo and Omowunmi Ajanaku. Thank you for your spiritual, virtual and physical support.

I acknowledge my students at the University of Greenwich for their tenacity and motivation, especially my Personal Development Group in the 2017/18 Session, MARK 1192 Introduction to Advertising of 2018/19 and 2019/20. You motivated me to develop myself, carve a niche for my teaching style and improve my student engagement.

I would also like to acknowledge the scholars that paved the way and provided shoulders for me to stand on while I was writing this book. I acknowledge the producers of the existing body of knowledge. Special mention to my academic colleagues and friends who have supported me through this process. Thank you Professor Liz Warren, Professor Jillian Farquhar, Professor Varsha Jain, Professor Robert Ebo Hinson, Professor Felix Maringe, Dr Barbara Czarnecka, Dr Annie Danbury, Dr Taiwo Soetan, Dr Arinze Nwoba, Dr Monique Charles, Dr Nenadi Adamu and Dr Claudette Kika. I appreciate your feedback, insight and advice.

Sincere appreciation goes to those who have assisted with the data, images and information to enhance the students' learning experience in this book. Finally, I acknowledge the staff at Routledge, Sophia Levine and Emmie Shand. Thank you for your support through this process. You believed in me, supported me and always reassured me. I appreciate your prompt answers to my technical questions.

Introduction

It is my pleasure to welcome you aboard this journey as I introduce you to *Introduction to Advertising*.

Advertising is a process that needs to be effectively managed and coordinated to produce an engaging and effective advertisement. Advertisements have become an integral part of our daily lives; we encounter and engage with them every day and on different media. Studies suggest we are exposed to thousands of advertisements every day. Coupled with the growing interest in social media, advertising is even more conspicuous.

I want to believe many advertisements have popped up on your social media feed today and you have ignored them. The advertisers have spent a huge sum of money in creating and promoting that advert, so why skip it? Perhaps it was for a product you are not interested in, it featured a song you dislike or it was the wrong timing. These are the understandings that shape how advertisements are conceptualised and developed.

This highlights the need for a better understanding and process of developing an engaging campaign. Understanding how these advertisements work is important for businesses and those who have a vested interest in their success. Also, understanding the impacts of advertisements on businesses, brands and people is essential. Therefore, in this book, I will introduce you to the basic concepts of advertising by adopting a structure flow between the **brands**, sending the advertisements, the **advertisers** working on the message and the **consumers** engaging with the advertisement. Though there are many books out there on advertising, adopting this structure makes this book different and engaging.

The positioning of the book

From an academic point of view, it is important to acknowledge that there are different ways of approaching the study of advertising. These are some of the approaches:

1. Reading advertisement: This is more applicable for cultural studies, critical theory, audience studies, media; it belongs to Humanities and/or Social Sciences. Reading advertisement explores meaning embedded in advertisement and how it tells the story about cultural norms.
2. Making advertisement: This is the more practical side of advertising as it involves creativity, graphic designers, creative advertising. It belongs to Arts Schools where students are taught to design print advertisement and direct and produce video advertisement.

3.   Managing advertisement: This is the management side of the advertising process. It involves advertising practitioners working within the frame of marketing, sales, branding and promotions. It belongs to the business school. These individuals may not know how to design an advertisement on Adobe Photoshop or Adobe Illustrator but they know how to coordinate the process.

This book specifically focuses on the third strand which is Managing Advertisement. This management recognises the process of creating an advertising campaign and sociological approach that look at the role of advertising communications from a cultural production perspective within a consumer-driven society. In addition, an understanding of the creative process will also be embedded. This is to expand your knowledge. By understanding how other professionals (within the advertising industry) create what they want to be managing, you will be able to widen your horizon and gain more knowledge. This approach of teaching advertising fits with the pedagogical approach adopted for studying Advertising in the Business Schools.

Even though you may not have the design skills to develop advertisements now (though it would be an added advantage), you will gain an understanding about different creative approaches. You will understand different creative processes and elements. If you cannot design, you will need the basic understanding of the designer's language and then be able to work with designers and other practitioners. This knowledge will aid the working relationship between the makers and managers of advertisement. The managers can discuss feedback from the brand, engage in the designing process and make contributions to the development of the advertisements. This understanding will position you for a career in advertising and marketing generally.

The book overview

This book provides an overall "basic roadmap" of the theory and practice of advertising. It takes you down the route of understanding advertisement as a message. The message may not always be about selling, but communication. Brands are the main reasons for advertising. If brands do not have any message or need to inform the public about a phenomenon (product, service, event etc.), there will be no need for an advertisement. The book is structured to start with brands. These are the entities that are willing to send a message to their target audience, the role of the advertising agencies, with a focus on the creative design of the advertisement, the advertising regulators and the consumers engaging with the advertisements.

To explain better, let us start with a story.

I was planning a birthday party for my child and I needed a beautiful cake. I could have baked it myself, but I wanted something special. So, I asked for recommendations for cake makers and, after collecting a few names, I checked their portfolios to see examples of their past work and what skills they possessed. I had a spending budget, which also meant that I was limited in my options. It is important to note that there is an art in cake making – ensuring the right mix of ingredients and the creative design of the decoration, which is why I hired a cake maker. On the day of the celebration, the cake maker brought a big beautiful cake and we had to find a table strong enough to support it. Everyone liked the cake, apart from my neighbour's daughter, who wished it had been coloured red. Unfortunately, one of the guests reported a case of food poisoning to the public health department after eating the cake, but that was found to be a hoax as no problem was eventually found with the cake. On a positive note, the cake maker even submitted the design for an award, and it was awarded the best cake in its category.

To break down this story, the cake maker here is the advertising practitioner who is charged with the responsibility of creating the advertisement. While many people can make an advert, like the homemade cake, it is better and more reasonable to leave it to the professional who understands the art and science of creating an advert.

Figure 0.1 presents an overview of the book:

- Chapter 1 explains the concept of advertising as a message, a necessity for businesses and organisations, like cakes that are needed for occasions.
- Chapter 2 explores the art and science of advertisement. The chapter discusses the theories behind advertisement, like the cake maker, the understanding of the right mix of flour and eggs to make the right cake.
- Chapter 3 describes the professionals responsible for making the adverts. These are the cake makers from the story who have different skills and expertise.
- Chapter 4 delves into the creative elements of the advertisement. This chapter shows how advertising practitioners are incorporating different creative elements like images, text and audio to create an engaging advertisement.
- Chapter 5 and 6 recognise that the media is essential for disseminating the advertisement. Like the cake table, certain media such as newspapers and radio are not strong enough to carry the creative output of the advertisers, which is why digital media may be more appropriate for some adverts. Many people are no longer reading newspapers as national newspaper circulation in the United Kingdom has decreased from 22 million in 2010 to 10.4 million in 2018, a decline of 52.5%. Newspaper as an advertising medium is getting weak and, instead, advertisers are using social media because that's where people engage better. Even with social media, there are specific creative elements that need to be considered, like the idea of swiping left on Instagram, which is not available on YouTube.
- Chapter 7 recognises that advertisement should reflect the values of the target audience. Just like the fact that not everybody will like the cake at a party, the cake maker recognises that a birthday cake is different from a wedding cake, therefore advertisers are aware of their role and the expectations of their clients.
- Chapter 8 explores the possibilities of finding advertisement offensive. Just like the cake story, one of the guests reported a case of food poisoning to the public health department after eating the cake at the party, but this was not my fault. Still, it has to be investigated, so likewise some people may find an advertisement offensive, they find it "poisonous", irritating and angry, and report it to the regulatory body, which has to investigate and decide whether or not the advertisement should be banned or not.
- Chapter 9 looks at the measure of effectiveness of an advertisement, a sense of accomplishment and achievement. On a positive note, advertisers can submit their works for different advertising awards so they can evaluate their creativity and take pride in their achievements. This chapter explores the concept of an effective advertisement.
- Chapter 10 is the concluding chapter of the book. It looks at what is ahead for the student, practitioners and the industry. It highlights the role of technology, data and insight for creating and disseminating advertisement.

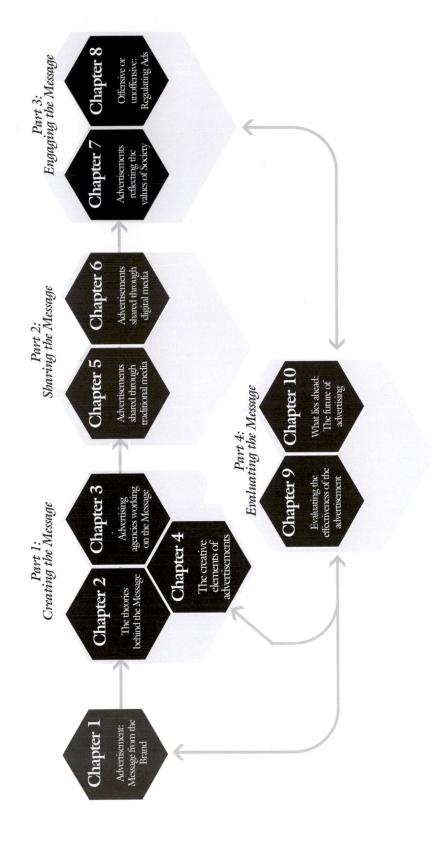

Figure 0.1 The overview of the book

Source: author.

Overall learning objectives

After completion of all chapters in this book, you will be able to:

- Demonstrate an understanding of the importance and nature of advertisement and marketing communications;
- Apply various models of advertising theory to practical situations;
- Illustrate advertising strategies using various advertising appeals;
- Demonstrate an understanding of the professionals responsible for making advertisements;
- Discuss different aspects of advertising functionality in developing creative strategy/ tactics;
- Describe what can make people find an advertisement offensive;
- Describe the concept of effective advertisement.

The expectations

This book is here to support you on your quest for knowledge; however, there are key expectations from you to make the best use of it.

- You are expected to take responsibility for your learning. This book will provide the information and theoretical underpinning; it is, however, essential for you to explore beyond what has been provided.
- Engage your senses. Look around, watch advertisement (do not skip it). Engage with the advertisements.
- You should get familiar with www.adsoftheworld.com which is a website that features creative advertisement. Advertisements on this website can be filtered according to medium, industry and country. In addition, subscribe to news updates from the following industry news sources: Campaign Live, Advertising Age, Marketing Week, Drum. Muse by Clio is a good website for coverage of the best in creativity in advertising and beyond. You should also familiar yourself with academic journals like *Journal of Advertising*, *Journal of Advertising Research* and *International Journal of Advertising*.
- Do not look at advertisements just for the sake of looking, be critical and evaluate each advertisement that comes your way. What do you like about it? The story, the creative elements or the media that was used. What do you dislike about it? What can you do better? What will you do differently? What can you adopt in your own design (for another product)?
- It is expected that you will move from being an "advertisement viewer" to an "advertisement developer". You are not just watching advertisement but engaging with it on a different level.
- Be creative. Do not ignore your pen and paper, scribble ideas down, graphically illustrate your thoughts, document your thoughts (on blog post or social media), engage in design competition and start building your portfolio. Volunteer (and or intern) with small businesses or charity organisations to practise what you have learnt.

1 Advertisement

Message from the brand

This chapter offers a different and unique approach to advertising. It recognises that brands who want to send out a message to their target audience are the reasons why advertising keeps on growing. The chapter starts with insight as to why a brand may want to communicate. Brands communicate not just to increase sales but to perform corporate social responsibility or show their reaction towards a behavioural change as a form of social marketing. The chapter gives an overview of advertising from the brand's perspective, the type of products they are advertising and the advertising strategy they might want to adopt as they approach their advertising agency.

Learning outcome

At the conclusion of this teaching, students will be able to:

- Explain the role of brands in the advertising process;
- Recognise that advertising is more than just creating awareness about products and services;
- Give examples of different types of brand messages beyond just selling;
- Summarise the concept of messaging with a purpose;
- Describe the challenges and factors that may influence the message.

Introduction

Communication is an essential feature of our daily lives. As we communicate with families and friends, sharing messages on social media and seeing the blue tick as an indication that they have read the message, likewise brands are trying to communicate with customers regularly, sometimes to inform us about their new product or to advise us about any closure on the transportation network. That is the basic concept of advertising.

The concept of advertising, however, may differ for different people. Kerr and Schultz (2010) noted that advertising has been defined in many ways as the industry evolved and moved from the days of print media to digital media. A survey of advertising and marketing textbooks makes it obvious there is no widely adopted definition (Dahlen & Rosengren, 2016), but the most recent and commonly used definition of advertising was provided by Richards and Curran (2002) where they defined advertisement as a paid, mediated form of communication from an identifiable source, designed to persuade the receiver to take some action, now or in the future. As this definition has been in existence for almost two decades and with recent changes in media formats, consumer behaviour and advertising effects (Eisend, 2016), there has been a call for an updated definition that reflects the evolving nature of the industry.

In recognising that the definition provided by Richards and Curran (2002) is outdated and in need of refinement, Dahlen and Rosengren (2016) provided an alternative working definition which includes the following terms:

(1) brand-related/brand-initiated/incentivised (instead of paid, mediated and identifiable source) communication (targeted at),
(2) people/participants (instead of the receiver) (designed to), and
(3) impact/effect (instead of persuading . . . to take some action).

While this definition captures the essence of advertisement, I believe creatively communicating this brand-related message is also important. The creativity sets the message apart from the media cluster and allows the target audience to engage better and take action. I agree with the idea of Eisend (2016) that "Advertising is communication whose meaning is always brand related" (p. 354) but I will define advertising as

> *The process of creatively communicating a message with a purpose to a target audience through media.*

There are five key points that need to be explored to better understand and appreciate this definition.

First, advertisement is not solely from a corporate brand as we know it. It is not only big corporations that place advertisements on social media, TV or Billboards as small brands and individuals also place advertisements and publicise a product so people can be aware of it. While Dahlen and Rosengren (2016) and Eisend (2016) agree that advertising is "brand communication", I posit that this is not just limited to corporate brands. Humans are brands and therefore anyone can create an advertisement. Therefore, it is essential to move beyond the mindset that big brands are the only ones who do advertising. Individuals can place their advertisements on social media, put a notice on the notice board or write out their message and put it in their shop window. Figure 1.1 is an image I found in a local shop window; the individual is selling some used items including a ballet outfit. Even though the message is not from Amazon or eBay, would you not consider this an advertisement? Brands, in this case, do not necessarily mean big cooperation, and it could mean a charity organisation or an individual who is placing a message on Facebook to sell a car.

Second, advertising is not all about selling or convincing people to buy a new product. There is a difference between advertising and marketing communications. An advertisement may inform you about the Marathon happening in the city or a road to be closed for repairs, these are communications from the organiser of the events and the local authority, they are not necessarily selling you anything. As earlier indicated, advertising is about communications, but when the message being communicated is for marketing purposes, then you have marketing communications. Marketing communication is a subset of advertising (different from integrated marketing communications which is a strategic combination of various communication forms like advertising, public relations and sales promotions (Grove et al., 2007). So, as you read on, you must understand that the scope of advertising is wider than that of marketing communication. Figure 1.2 illustrates the intersection between advertising (which could be a communication about anything from anybody), marketing communication (a form of advertising with the

Figure 1.1 Shop window advertisement
Source: author.

purpose of selling) and integrated marketing communications (a combination of market-ing strategies which may include marketing communications).

Third, the purpose makes a difference in advertising. Following from the second point, the purpose of communication may not necessarily be to sell. The purpose could be to change behaviour or to invite people to an event. As far as advertising is concerned, there is always a purpose and objectives for deciding to send a message. The brand that is responsible for the message has a purpose. This purpose will influence the media to use the target audience and other creative elements to be considered in the message.

Fourth, creatively communicating the advertisement is also crucial. You can imagine why some messages with emojis are more positively received than others. Deciding to send a message to a friend, you might choose to use emojis instead of a text. That is a creative decision you have made to select an emoji, out of the numerous options you have. You

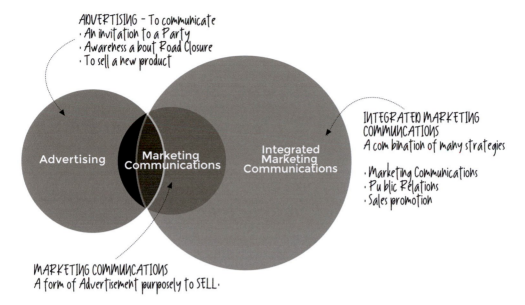

Figure 1.2 The intersection between advertising, marketing communications and integrated marketing communications

Source: author.

knew your friend would be able to associate with it and it can touch the right emotional string. Likewise, as you are communicating intending to appeal, brands are making a creative effort to deliver their messages in a very creative and unique way.

☺ or Love

Figure 1.3 shows an advertisement for a sales event being organised by a charity. This advertisement was handwritten, and you wonder whether they could not afford to type this out in a word processing program and print it out or perhaps hire a designer to design the advertisement for them. This is where the idea of creatively communicating a message comes in – for a brand to do something that makes the advertisement stand out and be more inviting. Figure 1.4 is a redesigned version of the same advertisement by one of my students, Ingrid Ionita. She did this design in her first year and I like the idea of retaining that handwritten font but also the choice of images to complete the message. I consider Ingrid's design to be more creative, appealing and engaging. Remember the two advertisements are still communicating the same message but one is more appealing.

Lastly, the target audience for that message is significant. How did you feel when you sent a message to the wrong person by mistake? The fact remains the message has been sent and, possibly, it has been received, but there is a sense of wasted effort since the person reading it might not make use of it or find the information relevant. This further highlights the need to understand the target audience and how to position the communications to meet them at the right time and in the right place. There are possibilities of sending the message to a specific member of the target audience – that is, direct marketing – and there could be mass marketing through traditional mass media. Digital marketing and social media, in particular, can aid the possibilities of sending the right message to the right person and at the right time.

Figure 1.3 Advertisement for a sales event being organised by a charity
Source: author.

Figure 1.4 Redesigned advertisement for a sales event being organised by a charity
Source: Ingrid Ionita.

Engaging with this advertisement and reciprocating is, however, uncontrollable. There is no guarantee that all creatively presented advertisements will appeal to the reader, or that the reader will act. A message has been sent to invite people for an event; the members of the targeted audience have seen it, they have engaged with it, liked it and shared it but there is no guarantee that everyone who saw the advertisement will come for the event.

This highlights why studying advertising becomes essential – to be able to deliver a message that generates results; to understand what appeals to people and how they can be nudged to act and fulfil the purpose of the message. Understanding factors that will hinder this achievement is also crucial for students of advertising.

Advertising, advertisement and advertiser

Advertising, advertisement and advertiser are three words that will regularly appear in this book; though they look the same, it is important not to confuse them.

Advertising. This is a verb. It is a process and an action word (Cluley, 2017). Consider it a process of creating an advertisement. Advertising involves working with the brands, advertising practitioners, media houses and getting the intended message to the customer. To create an effective and engaging advertisement, you need to understand and manage the advertising process.

Advertisement. This is also known as **Advert** or **Ad**. It is a noun, it is physical, it can be touched and experienced. After the sleepless night, the briefing and the hard work, the advertisement is the finished creative product. This is what you see on your mobile phone, on billboards, and on TV. It could be a poster or a 30-second clip on TV. This can be summarily said to be an announcement or notice that is intentionally put in a public medium to promote a service, a product, an event or vacancy etc. It is simply an entity that is used to publicise a phenomenon.

Advertiser. This is a noun. Advertisers are the people responsible for advertising and delivering the advertisement. They are responsible for carrying out the research, working with the clients to understand what they need and creating the advertisement, either as a graphic designer or art director. It is important that you do not mix an advertiser with a company or individual that pays for an event product or job to be advertised in a newspaper, on social media, on television, online, in a handbill or on a poster. You must understand that, in this book, advertisers are simply those professionals who ensure a company's intention to inform people about a product event, service etc. is achieved through advertisement. Hence, these advertisers can also be considered as advertising practitioners. That is, they are professionals that practise advertising. I anticipate you will be one very soon.

Case study 1.1

Advertising my tutorial class

I teach Introduction to Advertising at the University to first-year students. Often, they get confused about the timetable, the venue for their tutorial group or the time.

I consider creating a form of reminder for the students. I see this as a need to create an advertisement. As illustrated in Figure 1.5, my key message was for them to come to their tutorial and engage with other students. I came up with different layouts and ideas for my design. Like many other brands, they are creating a message, in the form of an advertisement to reach out to prospective customers – to inform them

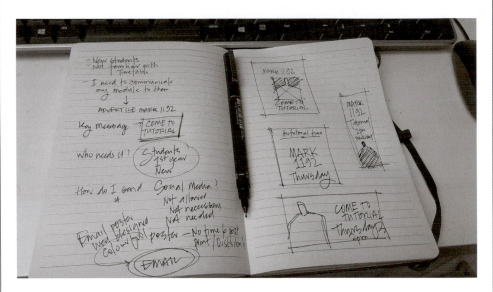

Figure 1.5 The advertising and conceptualising stage
Source: author.

Figure 1.6 Initial poster design
Source: author.

what is on offer, the services they offer or an invitation to an event. While many of these brands may have the resources to employ an advertiser, I was solely responsible for the conceptualisation and design. If it was a bigger brand/campaign, this would have involved many teams and not just me (more in Chapter 3). This solo approach is also relevant for many small businesses and individuals.

Figure 1.6 illustrates my advertisement. This is the noun. This is the thing that will be printed. If you notice, the text/copy (more in Chapter 5) has changed between the advertising/conceptualising stages to the final design stage. The idea was to say "Come to Tutorial" but at the time of the design, the idea was modified. This could be a discussion between the copywriter and designer in advertising but because I am the only one working on this, it was easy for me to decide and act. Take note of the image as well: I had to decide which image suits this advertisement. I would have loved to use the image of a celebrity, maybe Snoop Dogg, but I cannot afford it. I would have loved to use the image of my students, maybe the social media influencers among them, but I don't know if they would be willing to front my campaign, so I had to use my own image. That way, I didn't have to incur any unnecessary expenses.

I had to consider many other options during the advertising stage – remember it's a process. I considered changing the image – I did not want the students to be distracted by my picture; I considered changing the colour in case I had to print it from my office printer. I also considered the layout – I thought a portrait orientation

Figure 1.7 Alternative poster design
Source: author.

Figure 1.8 Selected advertisement design, printed and disseminated
Source: author.

would be better since I may share it as an email attachment and we often read in portrait (newspaper, mobile phones, reports). Figure 1.7 presents an updated design for the invite. If you notice, the text (copy) is the same, I simply rearranged it to suit the design layout. Importantly, I also changed the image and replaced it with cartoon illustrations. I did not have to pay any model or social media influencers; I believe I can communicate with my students using these images. Figure 1.8 presents the final advertisement design, which was printed and disseminated.

So now we have:

1. The advertising – the process of selecting the image, coordinating the design and sourcing for relevant images;
2. The advertisement – the poster and handbill that I will be sharing; and
3. The advertiser – that is, me! I am the tutorial leader (the host/the brand) sending a message (invitation to attend tutorials) to my target audience (MARK 1192 students at my University).

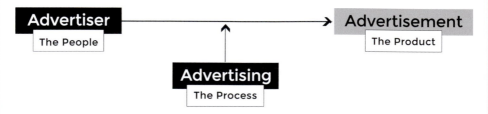

Figure 1.9 Conceptual illustration of the advertiser, advertisement and advertising
Source: author.

Figure 1.9 illustrates the relationship between the advertiser, advertisement and advertising.

Reflective questions

1. Considering I am not selling any product, would you consider this invite an advertisement?
2. What is the main message this advertisement aims to communicate?
3. Sometimes, as seen in this case, it is possible for the advertiser (designing the message), to also be the brand (sending out the message). In what other situation do you see this happening?

Why a brand may want to communicate

There are many reasons why a brand will want to communicate. There is always something always going on – there are new products being developed, and a new date is being announced for the artist's world tour. While it may not be possible to list all the reasons for advertising, it will be appropriate to have a definite guide and typology. Fill and Turnbull (2019) discuss a model in their textbook on marketing communications, which can be used to plan a communications strategy. They called the model DRIP, which is an acronym meaning differentiate, reinforce, inform and persuade. This model has been used in marketing communication, but it can be applied in the primary context of Advertising.

Differentiate

Some messages are being sent to differentiate a brand from others. This could be in terms of competing brands. They send out an advertisement highlighting how they are different from others. They often use statistics, facts and figures to show they are better than the others. This type of messaging is done to make the brand stand out from the category. As seen with the example from Aldi in Figure 1.10, they are communicating the fact that shoppers will get better value for money when they shop in their store. They are using the advertisement to differentiate themselves from Tesco and possibly other retail stores.

Reinforce

Brands that are well established may no longer be interested in differentiating themselves but in reinforcing customers' knowledge about their brand. The advertisements are presented to remind and reassure the customer that the brand still exists and is still doing great. They are created to consolidate and integrate previous messages that have been sent (Manser Payne et al., 2017). A prominent example is the Coca Cola truck at Christmas. Everyone knows that Coca Cola cans are red and white, but that has not stopped the brand associating their truck with Santa Claus at Christmas (Mochama, 2020).

Inform

Literally, when you inform, you are giving someone facts or information about something. In advertising management, this (informing) could be for a new product being advertised –

Figure 1.10 Advertisement from Aldi
Source: Aldi UK.

to let the target audience know that there is something new on the shelves and they should go and try it. This could also be an advert for a movie, informing viewers that the movie is now in the cinema and they should go and watch it. This may not necessarily mean selling a product but, rather, educating people, informing people about an event, train delays or the effects of Brexit. In a time of uncertainty because of Brexit, the government has created advertisements to communicate with the citizens about different scenarios, how it may affect them and actions which they must take. These are all about providing the needed information. Likewise, organisations can use advertisement to communicate what they are doing to protect the environment (Schmuck et al., 2018). It is critical to note that this is not about selling but using the advertisement to position the brand as a socially responsible company. Figure 1.11 is a National Rail advertisement informing passengers about service changes.

Persuade

Ultimately, the purpose of the communications is for the receiver to take some actions. This could be to buy the product that is being advertised or to make an enquiry, but as earlier stated, there is more to advertisement than selling. Persuasive advertisements can also be in the form of a social campaign to nudge people towards making changes. This could be informing people about the benefits of recycling, washing hands after going to the toilet or the benefits of donating blood or organs to save a life. Figure 1.12 shows a

Figure 1.11 National Rail advertisement informing passengers about service changes
Source: National Rail.

Figure 1.12 Senior copywriter vacancy advertisement from Fuel Communications
Source: Fuel Communications, copywriter: Dimtang Bishmang, associate creative director/art director/illustrator: Olalekan Akinyele.

vacancy advertisement from Fuel Communications advertising agency for the role of senior copywriter. This is an advert created to persuade interested candidates to apply for the role. This suggests again that advertising is not just about selling but to communicate with a purpose.

Case study 1.2

Budweiser relief efforts

During the 2018 Super Bowl, Budweiser decided to create a 60-second advertisement focusing on their relief efforts to help people in need after major natural disasters that took place in the United States. The advertisement showed a man waking up in the middle of the night to go to a Budweiser factory. At the factory, they stopped their normal beer production line and started using their facilities to produce clean water instead. These cans of water were distributed to those in need of relief and they ended the advertisement with the slogan: "Whenever you need us, we'll stand by you."

The advertisement was promoting the corporate social responsibility that Budweiser takes part in. The brand message they wanted to send out was that they cared about their customers. This is a form of social marketing that is tailored towards raising awareness of the "social good" that Budweiser takes part in.

Advertising on Super Bowl is not a cheap or easy feat. Brands have one of the biggest platform to sell and reach out to audiences around the world (Hatzithomas et al., 2016). But here we see there is more to advertising than just selling. Budweiser's switch to social marketing, especially since they are known for their Super Bowl commercials, is important to consider because they are effectively switching to raising awareness instead of trying to sell their beer. This is a form of brand communication that has been well crafted to appeal to people's emotions (Czarnecka & Mogaji, 2019). They see Budweiser beyond beer as a brand doing good. No doubt, this switch is also beneficial for their profits as people are moved by their emotions and want to help a company that is helping others.

Reflective questions

1. Discuss the benefits and drawbacks of switching to social marketing.
2. What do you think are the most important aspects of social marketing? Consider the emphasis shown on helping those in need and the emotions connected to that.
3. Why would Budweiser choose one of the biggest sport events of the year to premiere an advertisement with such an important message?
4. Do you think focusing on corporate social responsibility is a good advertising idea?
5. List the most important parts of a social marketing advertisement. What do you need in the advertisement for it to be effective? Is profit the most important outcome?

Contributed by Jacqueline Millisits.

Factors influencing brand communication

As earlier indicated, the effective delivery of the message is not always guaranteed, and many factors can influence how effective the delivery of the messages will be. Understanding these factors helps in conceptualising and developing communications plans that appeal to the audience and one which they can engage with.

The brand

As individuals are different, so likewise, are brands. Some brands do not like to use emoji in their text messages; they are straightforward and appear sophisticated while some brands can send a whole email in emojis. Some brands, like fashion brands, do not have much text in their advertisement. They often use models and simple text about the price while some brands like financial services may give you much information about the loans, mortgages and credit cards they have to offer. The nature of the brand will influence the way they will choose to communicate (Keller, 2016). This illustration aligns with the high vs low involvement type of products. Some advertisements are high involving because the brand is communicating a very serious message and therefore the reader needs to be involved, while some messages are low involving, just a few words and the message is conveyed (Mogaji, 2018).

The way you will process an invitation to a birthday party will be different from processing the information about going on holiday. Some information are presented with more details because of the expected level of involvement and information needed to make an informed decision by the audience (Belanche et al., 2017). This communication strategy is more like aligning the purpose of the message with the values and positioning of the company. The advertising agency they choose to work with (this will be discussed in Chapter 3) needs to be aware of this as they develop their campaign.

The message

Following on from the DRIP model, it is essential to recognise the purpose of sending a message. Brands need to identify the purpose of sending the message – perhaps its more than just making sales and rather towards corporate social responsibility. It is not surprising to see brand appearing "woke", addressing social issues and appealing to a diverse audience. Even as millennials are embracing corporate social responsibility campaigns (Polizzotto, 2015), it is becoming essential to understand and properly execute these campaigns. An example is the Gillette #MeToo advert to address on "toxic masculinity" (Topping et al., 2019). The video released in January 2019 urges men to hold each other to a higher standard and to step up when they see fellow men acting inappropriately towards women. Gillette had both praise and abuse after launching the advertising campaign; some even called for a boycott, thus, it is not surprising to see that the brand is "shifting the spotlight from social issues to local heroes" after the toxic masculinity caused a customer backlash (Green, 2019). A new advertisement, developed by Havas Sports & Entertainment, featured an Australian firefighter and personal trainer, Ben Ziekenheiner. It was released in August 2019. This change in direction suggests that while brands may want to communicate, the content and social context of the message may hinder the effective delivery and hurt the brand. Another example is from Simply Be, a fashion retailer specialising in fashion that fits all that cares about inclusivity for everyone and everybody. The brand created a campaign seeking new icons in the fashion industry. They argued that despite the fact that over 50% of the female population are a size 16 or above, the majority of the fashion industry still considers curve bodies a niche, warranting only a small part of their attention.

The audience

With a purpose in mind, understanding the target audience is essential. This understanding involves research from the brand to understand with whom they want to engage, the type of messages they like and the platform they like for getting the information. Some students will send an email to their tutor but send a text message to a friend. That is understanding the target audience of the message and the right medium to use in sending the message across to the target audience. This information will be useful when they are engaging with advertising agencies to develop their campaign. The understanding of this target audience will influence the media to be used, the creative elements to be embedded and also the media planning. That is why some messages will not be communicated to those under 18 years old, some advertisements will not be communicated during a particular time of the day, and some disclaimers need to be included in advertisements to inform the target audience. There are instances where vaping companies are facing ASA scrutiny over targeting children and misinformation (Bold, 2019). The ASA has a code of practice that contains specific requirements for targeting children and young people (ASA, 2018a). Influencers sending messages to the audience through the brands are also factors that can influence the brand communication (Jin et al., 2019). Getting this wrong can have a negative influence on the brand and the influencer. Johnson & Johnson, a Listerine brand, found itself in the eye of a social media storm as the sponsored image, a paid-for Instagram post from Scarlett Dixon (aka Scarlett London) promoting Listerine, went viral on Twitter for all the wrong reasons (Stewart, 2018). The influencer even said she had received "death threats" over the sponsored post. The audience felt the message they had received was not credible – it was staged and the audience recognised this; the intended purpose of the message was thereby not achieved.

The creativity

As advertisements are considered a creatively communicative message, creativity plays an essential role in brand communication. It makes the difference in how the audience perceives the advertisement. As illustrated in Figure 1.13, the same message – "Come, explore with us" – has been presented in four different formats.

   Creativity makes the message different and unique, but it also comes with a price. Brands pay an enormous amount of money for creative designs to set their message apart from the media clusters. Brewdog had a billboard advert with a single beer can set against the word "ADVERT". Imogen Watson of *The Drum* described it as the brand's most honest and transparent advertisement (Watson, 2019). You would expect a brand to be more

Figure 1.13 The creativity in arranging text in an advertisement
Source: author.

colourful and convincing in their approach but Brewdog took a different direction which was creative enough to surprise people.

Many brands will want to achieve a high level of creativity, and that is why they are more likely to engage the service of an advertising agency. While some may not be able to afford a design agency, they can give their design to a family friend or get it done by a freelancer from an online marketplace such as Fiverr, Upwork, PeoplePerHour etc. The output of these advertisements will vary. The creative capabilities could also involve having the right connections in order to have a celebrity on the advertisements, using a unique location or having a partnership with another brand.

The finances

The financial implication of creativity and its impact on brand communication cannot be overemphasised. Following on from the previous point, with the creative capabilities come the financial commitments. This requires advertising financial commitment to hire an advertising agency and distribute the intended messages (Bold, 20). Many brands may want to advertise but do not have the financial capabilities. As seen with social media advertising on Facebook, brands can tailor their advertisements to their target audiences based on their financial capabilities. Just imagine you want to send a message on WhatsApp, but you do not have an internet connection on your mobile phone; you might need to go and use free Wi-Fi at a café to have your message sent. Though the message is eventually sent after using the free Wi-Fi at the café, there were some commitments on your part which included you walking down to the café, thus, forsaking your comfort at that moment. This can be likened to financial commitment which brands must make. This financial factor can also influence having the right celebrity or influencer. Companies may have to pay more than a million US dollars to get access to Kim Kardashian's 149 million Instagram followers as of September 2019. Companies pay an average of $5 million to run a 30-second ad during the 2019 Super Bowl (Nittle, 2019). Not all brands can afford this, therefore, looking for a cheaper alternative becomes an important creative decision.

Samuel L. Jackson led the #ShareTheOrange campaign for Alzheimer's Research, which aims to get people to think differently about dementia. It may have been expensive to have such a Hollywood star in an advertisement, but Alzheimer's Research UK did not pay Samuel L. Jackson or any other celebrity or influencer for their support for the campaign (Samuel generously offered his time and experience free of charge, having seen six members of his family affected by Alzheimer's disease). In fact, it is part of their policy not to pay celebrities for supporting their work. Though a celebrity-fronted advert for a commercial brand may incur a huge financial commitment, working for a charity may offer a different arrangement.

Case study 1.3

Kingdom Heritage Christian Fellowship: reaching out to prospective worshippers

UK Church membership has been declining in recent times, and it is projected that by 2025, membership will fall to 8.4% of the population. According to the British

Social Attitudes report in 2018, only 38% of Britons described themselves as Christian, down from 50% in 2008. In 1983, when this survey was first conducted, 66% of the population described themselves as Christian. Over the period 2005–2010, the major Christian denominations such as Anglican, Catholic and Presbyterian all saw falls in membership; however, Pentecostal churches saw an increase in membership.

Kingdom Heritage Christian Fellowship is a Pentecostal church in South West London; they have just moved into a bigger auditorium and are keen to increase the number of their worshippers. While acknowledging that UK Church membership is declining, they have the aspiration of sharing their Pentecostal approach with many others, and they decided to design a leaflet to advertise and invite people to worship with them (Figure 1.14). These leaflets were shared with passers-by around their new location and distributed at different supermarkets and given to members to share with their friends and families.

The fact that Kingdom Heritage Christian Fellowship is a church, a religious organisation and a charity organisation does not stop them from advertising. Here the message is not to sell any product or to provide any service in return for money but to reach out to the targeted audience who may be willing to worship. They have a message they want to communicate, to invite people. It is also essential to recognise there is an attitude towards the brand – a church – which may make people ignore the message and even discard the leaflet. Still, the point is the message has been communicated and, like any advertisement, some may decide to skip it (on YouTube), flip it over in the newspaper, while some may choose to process it and make a decision.

Figure 1.14 Flyer for Kingdom Heritage Christian Fellowship
Source: author.

Moving on

When the need for communication has been identified, it is essential to strategise and put the action in place to achieve the objectives. This action plan depends on many factors, many of which have been discussed earlier. Despite these limitations and challenges, the message needs to be communicated in one form or the other. The size of the brand may depend on whether they need to work with a design agency or hire a freelancer; the nature of the message can also influence the creative process and media planning. So, while considering making an advert, many things must be put into consideration. Those things include budget, size of the brand, the population of the target audience, the medium through which they can be easily reached and the right time to send the message to the target audience. Notwithstanding, there are other vital points to consider.

Conceptualising the message

Sometimes the idea is just abstract, the message is still in the head of the Marketing Director and it is still being thought through. Moving on, the message needs to be conceptualised and developed into a brief. This sometimes depends on the size of the brand. For some smaller brands, it could just be putting up a message on Fiverr, asking for a designer or it could be sitting with a freelancer who is asking the questions or developing a brief that highlights the message, target audience and how it should be conveyed. These are more like blueprints that are prepared for whoever is expected to work on the message.

Commissioning the message

Now that the brief has been prepared, it is essential to commission and ask an organisation or someone to help with the implementation. This is sometimes a competitive process whereby advertising agencies are invited to bid and pitch their ideas. Some have described this as a beauty pageant for advertising agencies. The brands will want to see who is most capable of interpreting their message and bringing it to life (this will subsequently be covered in Chapter 3).

MullenLowe won the Co-operative Bank account in 2018. Leo Burnett has previously handled the Co-operative Bank's advertising. PlayStation began a search for a creative agency to work on its advertising across Europe, the Middle East and Africa, and Adam & Eve/DDB became PlayStation's new global creative agency of record following a six-month review in May 2019 after Incumbent Bartle Bogle Hegarty (BBH) New York who had partnered with PlayStation for six years decided not to participate in the global pitch process. Take note of these advertising agencies, and you need to know their works as you plan for your career.

For agency selection, brands may have to use a consultant (or intermediary) as the selection process might be very tedious. Brands may need assistance with crafting a brief, producing a shortlist of suitable agencies, guiding the pitching delivery, fee benchmarking, contract negotiations and onboarding new agency partners. This is where the intermediaries come in. These consultants help brands and agencies to find each other, work together and get the best out of their partnership with each other. These consultants can help make the right decision when appointing a new agency or reviewing a current agency. One of these is AAR Group; they describe themselves as the original matchmaker, established in 1975, were the first intermediary service in the world and have pioneered best practice approach for four decades (AAR, n.d.). Another is

Creativebrief, bringing brands and agencies together to make the industry's most powerful and recognisable work (Creativebrief, n.d.). The Oystercatchers is another intermediary working with the brands and agencies (The Oystercatchers, n.d.). Moonpig, a UK online cards, gifts and flowers retailer, appointed Creature as creative agency following a competitive pitch run by Oystercatchers.

Creating the message

When the message has been commissioned, the creation is left to the advertising agencies. They are expected (as promised during pitching) to bring the conceptualised message into reality. The creation, however, does not lie with the advertising agency as this could be a business owner uploading images on Facebook and paying for it to be boosted. On an agency level, the creation will involve working with the in-house creative team, going on location to shoot and produce the advertisement. This could also involve working with other creatives (Douglas, 2019).

Advertising campaign

Brands have many reasons to communicate with audiences. Often, they align with the DRIP models and many of these advertisements are sent out more than once. The advertising campaign is an overarching message from a brand that is sent through advertisements that feature different creative elements and through different media to form an integrated communication strategy. As illustrated in Figure 1.15, the campaign is often made of up of a series of advertisement messages all sharing the same overarching ideas, but there is also the possibility of a campaign having just one advertisement (Parente & Strausbaugh-Hutchinson, 2014). This depends on the financial capabilities of the brand or the extent to which they want to send the message. So, in this book, we might be focusing on an advertisement but you should be aware that that advertisement could be a part of many advertisements that form a campaign or it could also be a stand-alone.

As illustrated in Figure 1.16, the brand has a campaign – to raise awareness about the need for people to wash their hands to prevent the spread of coronavirus. That is the overarching message of the brand and they can commission an advertising agency to develop this campaign. In developing the campaign, the advertising agencies come up with different

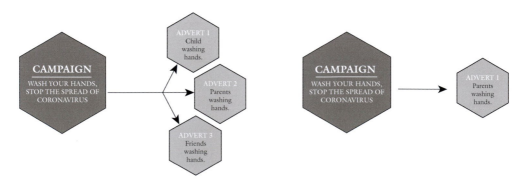

Figure 1.15 Conceptualising advertising campaign
Source: author.

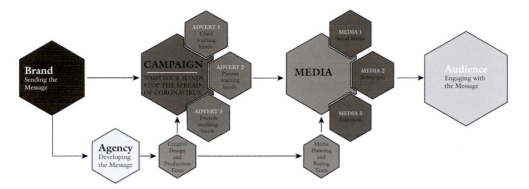

Figure 1.16 Conceptualising advertising campaign around different creative elements and media

Source: author.

ideas and creative elements (to be further discussed in Chapter 4) and this could mean creating three different scenes, all reinforcing the idea of washing hands, to be shared across three different media. These three scenes are created through the creative design team, comprising the art director, designers and copywriters (Chapter 3). On the other hand, these scenes are disseminated through different media to reach the audience (more to be discussed in Chapter 5 and 6) with the support of the media planning team (Chapter 3). This can generate a matrix of nine different advertisements, as presented in Figure 1.17, through a cross-tabulation of the media and creative elements.

MEDIA

	Social Media	Newspaper	Billboard
Child	**ADVERT 1** Child washing hands on Social Media.	**ADVERT 2** Child washing hands on Newspaper.	**ADVERT 3** Child washing hands on Billboard.
Parent	**ADVERT 4** Parents washing hands on Social Media.	**ADVERT 5** Parents washing hands on Newspaper.	**ADVERT 6** Parents washing hands on Billboard.
Friends	**ADVERT 7** Friends washing hands on Social Media.	**ADVERT 8** Friends washing hands on Newspaper.	**ADVERT 9** Friends washing hands on Billboard.

CREATIVE ELEMENT

Figure 1.17 Generated matrix of different advertising through cross-tabulation of the media and creative elements

Source: author.

Figure 1.18 "Imperfection", part of campaign titled *Uncut*
Source: designed by 42 Ltda for plastic surgeon Dr Rafael Anlicoara.

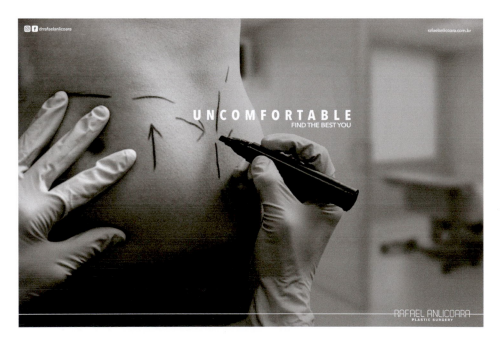

Figure 1.19 "Uncomfortable", part of campaign titled *Uncut*
Source: designed by 42 Ltda for plastic surgeon Dr Rafael Anlicoara.

Figures 1.18 and 1.19 show a campaign titled *Uncut*, aimed at publicising the work of Plastic Surgeon Dr Rafael Anlicoara. The print advertisement created by 42 Ltda, Brazil seeks to show that plastic surgery has the power to modify one's perception of one's body to give a sense of perfection, satisfaction and fullness. This is a campaign with two different advertisements that can stand on their own. You can see both advertisement sharing the same layout and design, albeit different images and words were used.

Same message, different channel

While the message has been created and ready for distribution, it is essential to note that, in some cases, the messages might be sent by a third party instead of the brand who commissioned the message. To illustrate, if you do not have credit on your phone, you might want to use a friend's phone to send a message, and at the end of the message, you may indicate that you are using a friend's phone. The message is still coming from you, but perhaps through a different person. There are various examples of such a scenario in real life. Hence, a particular message could be sent through different channels

Political advertisements

The campaigning candidate may not necessarily send an advertisement – supporters or friends could have sent it (Sohal & Kaur, 2018). These supporters paid for the advertisements to be created and delivered. This may or may not be with the knowledge of the candidate. This includes public communications coordinated with a political candidate (i.e., in-kind contributions or coordinated party expenditures) that are paid for by a political committee or that contain express advocacy or a solicitation. Crucial information regarding the sponsor must be declared to inform prospective voters about who is really behind the message.

Disclaimers are a legal requirement in some cases, as a political advertisement. According to the Special Notices on Political Ads and Solicitations document prepared by the United States' Federal Election Commission Disclaimer, notice is defined as "a statement placed on a public communication that identifies the person(s) who paid for the communication and, where applicable, the person(s) who authorised the Communication" (FEC, 2020). These disclaimers, often at the bottom of the print advert, end of the TV advert or a link on a social media advert can look like "*Paid for by the Sheridan for Congress Committee*", "*Paid for by the XYZ State Party Committee and authorized by the Sheridan for Congress Committee*". It is important to note that this is not just limited to mass media; it is also applicable on social media. Facebook has provided information on how disclaimers work for ads about social issues, elections or politics (Facebook, 2020). This disclaimer will appear at the top of any ads that you run on Facebook or Instagram and include information on the entity that paid for the advertisement.

Social media influencers

This is becoming an essential feature in advertising and marketing communications. This communication strategy has become predominantly centred around social media, creating an opportunity for brands to market through social media influencers. According to a study by Freberg et al. (2011), social media influencers (SMIs) represent a new type of independent third-party endorser who shapes audience attitudes through blogs, tweets and the use of other social media. With influencers on YouTube, Instagram and many other social media profiles, they can be paid by brands to communicate their messages. The trust consumers have in these influencers and the brands are often contentious; there is a blurred line in understanding whether the influencers are truly using a brand or have been paid to advertise the brand and only claiming to use the brand when actually they are not.

This lack of trust and confusion has also necessitated the need for disclaimers. It is expected that declaimers should accompany sponsored contents. While hashtags like #spon and #ad are becoming prominent, the United Kingdom Advertising Standards Agency (ASA) has created a guide on the rules of sponsored content, and this is to address the ambiguity surrounding sponsored advertisement on social media. ASA noted that brands engage with people who are popular on social networks to discuss, photograph and recommend a product, and this has necessitated the need for the guidelines (ASA, 2018b).

Carriers and partnership

This is different from the previous two types of arrangement where a disclaimer is necessary. This type of communication arrangement involves two different brands working together to reach their target audience. To understand this better, each of the brands can advertise on their own, but this arrangement allows one brand to be the conveyor of the message. A prominent one is the mobile phones market where we have the carrier (telecommunication service providers) and mobile phone manufacturers. For example, different telecommunication companies advertise the Apple iPhone (Mogaji, 2014). The telecommunications companies send the message to:

1. Inform prospective customers that they have a new phone
2. Persuade them to use their services.

Remember, Apple will still run its advertisements, but the telecommunication companies serve as another medium to convey the message about the iPhone (the product) and their services. Often, the same images supplied by Apple are used in all the advertisements, but the brand (telecommunication company) message is different. Importantly, as well, the same telecommunication company will also advertise for Samsung when a new version is released. The downside is that someone seeing the advert by EE, for example, may be attracted to the phone but not necessarily to the carrier as they get their contract from Vodafone.

Another example of this arrangement is in the automobile sector. A partnership between car manufacturers and engine oil producers. For example, "Hyundai Recommend Shell as Preferred Aftermarket Oil Supplier For Another Five Years". In their agreement, Shell is recommended as the preferred aftermarket motor oil supplier for Hyundai vehicles worldwide, so, when Hyundai is advertising, they are also conveying a message about Shell. Likewise, there is a global strategic relationship between the PSA Peugeot Citroën Group and the Total Group spanning over 20 years. The partnership includes the global endorsement of Total lubricants for the maintenance of Citroën ("Citroën prefers Total") and Peugeot ("Peugeot recommends Total") vehicles.

Another example is in retail. This involves big supermarkets creating an advertisement, shared on different media about another product. Often this is about raising awareness for both brands, as seen with the Iceland advert featuring Flora in Figure 1.20; however, Iceland could produce their advert using any brand, and likewise Flora could do their advertisement. Notwithstanding, there are possibilities for partnership, such as Iceland using Flora to convey a message to attract customers to their stores. ASDA have adopted this same

Figure 1.20 Iceland advert for Flora
Source: Iceland.

approach as they advertise different products as well. However, a different approach has been adopted by Wilkinson – they advertise a product which is theirs. This suggests that brands can advertise on their own and likewise share their message through another brand.

Summary

The chapter gives an overview of advertising from the brand's perspective, recognising that the basis of advertising is shaped by the brand's need to communicate a message. As illustrated in Figure 1.21, the summary of the chapter is to recognise the brand as the person, organisation or company that wants to send out a message to the audience. Often these brands may not be able to creatively communicate their message, so they hire an advertising agency to develop a message that would creatively communicate the brand's message to the audience who will later engage with the message.

The chapter conveys the notion that advertising is all about communication. The message being communicated may not necessarily be a marketing communication (as this is the general notion of advertising) but could be to *differentiate* from another political candidate; to *reinforce* a message so that people will not forget to pay their dues; to *inform* the community about an event happening at the sports centre; or to *persuade* drivers to reduce their speed around the primary school because of the children. Advertising is more than just marketing communication, but it starts with communication.

Figure 1.21 Summary of advertisement as a message from a brand to an audience
Source: author.

Limitations to this communication have been discussed as well, and they include the brand, the message and even the financial commitment. Notwithstanding these limitations, it is essential to move on – to conceptualise the idea and develop a brief, commission the project to a competent professional and watch it being created. Upon creating the project, different directions of communication were also explored, such as political marketing, social media influences and carriers.

Revision questions

1. What is the main essence of advertising?
2. Can you explain the relationship between the audience, advertising agencies and brand in the advertising process?
3. How would you describe the DRIP model? Can you give examples of each scenario?
4. What is your understanding of the concept of messaging with a purpose?
5. What are the challenges and factors that may influence an advertising process?

Student activity

Understanding the advertisement as brand communication

- Visit www.adsoftheworld.com
- Filter advertisement using these filters – medium (print), industry (beauty) and country (Brazil).
- Select 4 advertisements that get your attention and interest you.
- For each selected advertisement, identify (1) the brands sending the message, (2) the message that is being sent in the advertisement and, (3) the target audience of the message.
- Discuss this with your group members, do they agree with you, or do they have alternative ideas about the advert?

References

AAR, n.d. [Online] Avaialble at: https://aargroup.co.uk.

ASA, 2018a. *Children: Targeting.* [Online] Available at: www.asa.org.uk/advice-online/children-targeting.html [Accessed 7.7.2020].

ASA, 2018b. *New guidance launched for social influencers.* [Online] Available at: www.asa.org.uk/news/new-guidance-launched-for-social-influencers.html [Accessed 9.9.2020].

Belanche, D., Flavián, C. & Pérez-Rueda, A., 2017. Understanding interactive online advertising: Congruence and product involvement in highly and lowly arousing, skippable video ads. *Journal of Interactive Marketing*, 37, pp. 75–88.

Bold, B., 2019. *Vaping companies face ASA scrutiny over targeting children and misinformation.* [Online] Available at: www.campaignlive.co.uk/article/vaping-companies-face-asa-scrutiny-targeting-children-misinformation/1661071 [Accessed 7.7.2020].

Bold, B., 2020. *Goodstuff wins £5m Tia Maria and Disaronno media business.* [Online] Available at: www.campaignlive.co.uk/article/goodstuff-wins-5m-tia-maria-disaronno-media-business/1660879 [Accessed 7.7.2020].

Cluley, R., 2017. *Essentials of advertising.* London: Kogan Page.

Creativebrief, n.d. [Online] Available at: www.creativebrief.com/about-us/.

Czarnecka, B. & Mogaji, E., 2019. How are we tempted into debt? Emotional appeals in loan advertisements in UK newspapers. *International Journal of Bank Marketing*, 38(3), pp. 756–776.

Dahlen, M. & Rosengren, 2016. If advertising won't die, what will it be? Toward a working definition of advertising. *Journal of Advertising*, 45(3), pp. 334–345.

Douglas, F., 2019. *Kraken enlists horror director for spooky cinematic experience.* [Online] Available at: www.campaignlive.co.uk/article/kraken-enlists-horror-director-spooky-cinematic-experience/1661029 [Accessed 8.8.2020].

Eisend, M., 2016. Comment: Advertising, communication, and brands. *Journal of Advertising*, 45(3), pp. 353–355.

Facebook, 2020. *How disclaimers work for ads about social issues, elections or politics.* [Online] Available at: www.facebook.com/business/help/198009284345835?id=288762101909005 [Accessed 9.9.2020].

FEC, 2020. *Advertising and disclaimers.* [Online] Available at: www.fec.gov/help-candidates-and-committees/advertising-and-disclaimers/ [Accessed 7.7.2020].

Fill, C. & Turnbull, S., 2019. *Marketing communications: Touchpoints, sharing and disruption.* London: Pearson.

Freberg, K., Graham, K., McGaughey, K. & Freberg, L., 2011. Who are the social media influencers? A study of public perceptions of personality. *Public Relations Review*, 37(1), pp. 90–92.

Green, R., 2019. *Gillette shifts focus after 'toxic masculinity' backlash with new Australian Tvc via Havas S&E.* [Online] Available at: https://campaignbrief.com/gillette-shifts-focus-after-toxic-masculinity-backlash-with-new-australian-tv-campaign/ [Accessed 4.4.2020].

Grove, S., Carlson, L. & Dorsch, M., 2007. Comparing the application of integrated marketing communication (IMC) in magazine ads across product type and time. *Journal of Advertising*, 36(1), pp. 37–54.

Hatzithomas, L., Boutsouki, C. & Ziamou, P., 2016. A longitudinal analysis of the changing roles of gender in advertising: A content analysis of Super Bowl commercials. *International Journal of Advertising*, 35(5), pp. 888–906.

Jin, S., Muqaddam, A. & Ryu, E., 2019. Instafamous and social media influencer marketing. *Marketing Intelligence & Planning*, 37(5), pp. 567–579.

Keller, K., 2016. Unlocking the power of integrated marketing communications: How integrated is your IMC program?. *Journal of Advertising*, 45(3), pp. 286–301.

Kerr, G. & Schultz, D., 2010. Maintenance person or architect? The role of academic advertising research in building better understanding. *International Journal of Advertising*, 29(4), pp. 547–568.

Manser Payne, E., Peltier, J. & Barger, 2017. Omni-channel marketing, integrated marketing communications and consumer engagement: A research agenda. *Journal of Research in Interactive Marketing*, 11(2), pp. 185–197.

Mochama, A., 2020. Interpretations of television aesthetics: A mise-en-scène analysis in audiovisual Coca-Cola commercials. *International Journal of Research and Scholarly Communication*, 3(1), pp. 14–30.

Mogaji, E., 2014. Print Advertisement of iPhone by UK Carriers. *SSRn Electronic Journal.* SSRN. Available at: https://ssrn.com/abstract=2536639.

Mogaji, E., 2018. *Emotional appeals in advertising banking services.* London: Emerald.

Mogaji, E., Badejo, F., Charles, S. & Millisits, J., 2020. To build my career or build my brand? Exploring the prospects, challenges and opportunities for sportswomen as human brand. *European Sport Management Quarterly*, [Online] Available at: https://doi.org/10.1080/16184742.2020.1791209, pp. 1–19.

Nittle, N., 2019. *What makes a Super Bowl ad successful? An ad exec explains.* [Online] Available at: www.vox.com/the-goods/2019/1/25/18197609/super-bowl-ads-commercials-doritos-sprint-skittles [Accessed 8.8.2020].

Parente, D. & Strausbaugh-Hutchinson, K., 2014. *Advertising campaign strategy: A guide to marketing communication plans.* Boston, MA: Centage.

Polizzotto, P., 2015. *Millennials are embracing corporate social responsibility campaigns.* [Online] Available at: https://adage.com/article/digitalnext/ways-marketers-create-smarter-csr-campaigns/301796 [Accessed 3.3.2020].

Richards, J. I., & Curran, C. M. (2002). Oracles on "advertising": Searching for a definition. *Journal of Advertising,* 31(2), pp. 63–77.

Schmuck, D., Matthes, J., Naderer, B. & Beaufort, M., 2018. The effects of environmental brand attributes and nature imagery in green advertising. *Environmental Communication,* 12(3), pp. 414–429.

Sohal, S. & Kaur, H., 2018. A content analysis of YouTube political advertisements: Evidence from Indian parliamentary elections. *Journal of Creative Communications,* 13(2), pp. 133–156.

Stewart, R., 2018. *Influencer featured in "ridiculous" Listerine ad condemns "nasty" response.* [Online] Available at: www.thedrum.com/news/2018/09/02/influencer-featured-ridiculous-listerine-ad-condemns-nasty-response [Accessed 2.2.2020].

The Oystercatchers, n.d. [Online] Available at: www.theoystercatchers.com/pages/pitch-partnership.

Topping, A., Lyons, K. & Weaver, M., 2019. *Gillette #MeToo razors ad on "toxic masculinity" gets praise – and abuse.* [Online] Available at: www.theguardian.com/world/2019/jan/15/gillette-metoo-ad-on-toxic-masculinity-cuts-deep-with-mens-rights-activists [Accessed 6.6.2020].

Watson, I., 2019. *Brewdog punks Game of Thrones with its most honest ad yet.* [Online] Available at: www.thedrum.com/news/2019/05/13/brewdog-punks-game-thrones-with-its-most-honest-ad-yet [Accessed 7.7.2020].

Theme 1
Creating the message

2 The theories behind the message

This chapter introduces you to the theories behind advertisement. The chapter discusses the theories and explains how they work with different advertisements around the world. They includes the DAGMAR model which presents four phases that potential customers pass through as they are made aware of a brand message: unaware, aware, comprehension, conviction; the AIDA model, an acronym for attention, interest, desire and action, which are the four phases of the psychological process that people pass through as they decide whether to buy something or not; the FCB grid which recognises the consumers' level of involvement and helps us understand where a product stands in the mind of a consumer. The communications theory and ELM are also discussed.

Learning outcome

At the conclusion of this teaching, students will be able to:

- Describe and explain the role of brands in the advertising process;
- Recognise the importance of theory in advertisement design and development;
- Give examples of different theories related to advertising;
- Describe how the theories can be applied to advertisements;
- Summarise the concept of the theory behind the message.

Introduction

As discussed in Chapter 1, advertising is about communicating a message. The message is conceived by the brands, developed by the advertising agencies and engaged with by the audience. The previous chapter recognised the brands' role in the communication process. The book will explore the role of advertising agencies and customers engagement with advertisement. However, before we get into the practical and creative side of things, it is essential to understand the theories behind advertising.

In some cases, this might not be discussed at all or discussed as part of the creative process, but I consider it essential to dedicate a chapter to the theoretical aspects of advertising – better still, how advertising works or should work. This theoretical understanding is vital as it prepares you to engage better with the advertisements as you progress further in your studies.

The chapter introduces you to different theories, backed up by research which has been known to shape advertisements. It will provide a brief insight into theories, highlighting their importance and why they are being studied. Subsequently, the chapter will cover the role of advertising theories in academia and practice. Importantly, though the list is inexhaustible, different types of theories which are familiar, easy to understand and relevant will be presented. These theories will be further explored with some relevant examples. You will be expected to use various advertisements to illustrate your understanding of these theories.

What are theories

This is an attempt to go beyond advertising and have a holistic understanding of theory; then, with that understanding, a focus on advertising theories will be discussed. A theory can be defined as a logical, rational or contemplative mode of thinking that is aimed at a generalising view on a certain phenomenon. Most times, theories are results of rigorous observations, studies, research and interrogations. At this point, we are going to take an in-depth look at different advertisement theories.

There are many theories going on around us, and often we take them for granted. Gravity is most accurately described by the general theory of relativity (proposed by Albert Einstein in 1915). We know that if anything is thrown up, the gravitational force pushes it down. If you are not into science or astrophysics, this might not interest you. It is important to note that theories exist in different fields as this suggests why advertising students need to recognise the different theories that operate in their field and engage with them as they may affect their practice.

According to Dictionary.com (n.d.), a theory is

> a coherent group of **tested general propositions**, commonly regarded as correct, that can be used as **principles of explanation** and **prediction** for a class of phenomena
>
> a **particular conception** or view of something to be done or of the **method of doing it;** a system of rules or principles:
>
> a **proposed explanation** whose status is still conjectural and **subject to experimentation**, in contrast to well-established propositions that are regarded as reporting matters of actual fact.

The Cambridge Dictionary (n.d.) also described it as "a **formal statement** of ideas that are **suggested to explain a fact or event,** or how something works".

With these definitions, there are vital points to note:

A theory is a **formal statement** – it has been written out, explained and can be said to be set in stone. It is more of a definition. The statement has been **tested**. Here, we recognise the role of academic researchers in developing theories. The test of these formal statements provides **conception** and **explains how things work**; in addition, it can also be used to **make a prediction** because it has been tested in many other contexts and situations. However, the statements are still **subject to experimentation** as researchers continually challenge, revise, replace and propose new statements.

From an advertising perspective, there are formal statements (like DRIP, as discussed in Chapter 1) that have been tested and researched, which explain how brands may decide to conceptualise their advertisements. The theory can also be used for predictions as with the student activities where you were challenged to identify how the advertisements fit into the DRIP model. However, as we noted during the activities, the theory might not always fall into those four classifications. These theories may have been developed years ago; things are changing, and therefore there is always a need to develop and research to identify whether there are newer explanations which have not been previously observed. Von Nordenflycht (2010) presents an example of how new theories are developed to explain situations and occurrences.

Why theories?

- **Theories are essential for explaining how things work**. As earlier indicated, theories provide a background knowledge which explains how things work. It can be reassuring when you know that things will happen when you do something in a certain way. For the beginner, theories give the initial insight into how advertising works, what needs to be done to get an appropriate response and simplify complex advertising processes into an easily recollected model. For more experienced people, theories are there to be challenged. They are looking for ways to stretch the theories, have a better understanding and make impact.
- **Theories are vital for academic work and theoretical advancement**. As theories are often developed by academics, it is essential to feed that knowledge into the education system. Theories are developed and are further tested by other researchers to confirm their validity, and this is about theoretical advancement, which also feeds into practice. I have developed two theories as part of my research. My theory of emotional appeal recognises that when consumers are exposed to emotional appeal in advance, they acknowledge it but filter it through their personal filtration mechanism which is based on their personal experiences (Mogaji, 2018).
- **Theories are essential for practice**. Advertisers may often think that they know how things work but theory explains the concept behind it. As theories get developed by academics (in universities), these are applicable in the industry to make a practical impact.
- **Theories are evolving**. There is new knowledge every day as human behaviours evolve, so likewise the explanation for things around us. What was happening previously about how the consumer engages with advertisements may no longer be relevant to advertisements in society today. The theories are therefore changed or replaced if they are no longer able to explain the situation of things. More theories are being developed and shared with researchers and practitioners to test and further validate them (Hazarika & Zhang, 2019).
- **Theories are often graphically illustrated**. Though not compulsory, it is often the case that theories have images that graphically illustrate the statement and how the variables are interrelated. Most times, images used for advertisement explain the statement and message of an advert better than words could. This could be in the form of a linear connection, multiple connections with correlation and causal effects or grids. This is why some are called "frameworks" or "models". Look at the examples that will be shared and consider their graphical representation, as this may assist in a better explanation of the situation.

The place of theory in the message

Advertising theories are essential for advertisers to have a better understanding of and justifications for the approach they want to take as they engage with their customers. The

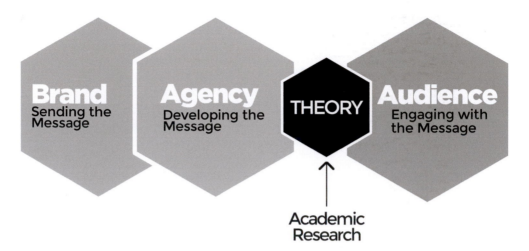

Figure 2.1 The place of theory in advertising as a brand communication strategy
Source: author.

brands commission the message, and it is essential for advertisers to creatively develop the message and allow the audience to engage with it. In between this relationship comes the theory.

As illustrated in Figure 2.1, the theory takes an important place in advertising as a brand communication strategy. It is important to both the advertisers and the audience. They are the ones exchanging the messages and, also, we cannot ignore the brands which are in the background. Academic research has a significant influence on theory development. Researchers work with both parties to understand how consumers engage with advertisements, analyse their findings and make their results available to practitioners, often through journals and business reports. The theories can be used by advertisers to develop their campaigns. As advertisers, you must understand that, to reach an audience, there is a specific approach to consider based on the theory that has been developed.

It is important to note, however, that theories are not only developed by academics. Remember, theories provide explanation, and it is not surprising to see that advertisers, over time, can come up with their own explanations and theories. An example is the Foote, Cone and Belding grid (FCB grid) (which will be discussed later in this chapter). The grid is also called the Vaughn Grid. It was developed by Richard Vaughn, the Senior Vice President of Foote, Cone and Belding. The first paper was published as "How Advertising Works: A Planning Model" (Vaughn, 1980) and the model was revised in a paper titled "How Advertising Works: A Planning Model Revisited" (Vaughn, 1986).

Advertising theories

There are many advertising theories. Many are obsolete, outdated and no longer relevant. Many are still being developed to explain the evolving human engagement with advertisements; at the last count, Kim et al. (2014) identified the top 30 theories in advertising

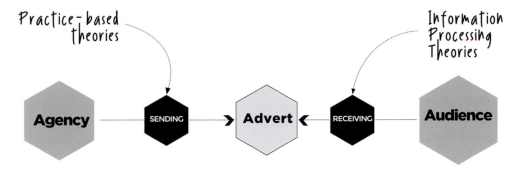

Figure 2.2 Practice-based theories for agencies when sending the advertisement and information-processing theories for the audience receiving the advertisement

Source: author.

research between 1980 and 2010. While you may know all these theories, their application varies, and their explanation may not fit all criteria.

As illustrated in Figure 2.2, these theories can be from the perspective of both the agency with practice-based theories that shape their creative decisions in developing the advertisements, and the audience with the information processing theories engaging with the advertisement.

- **For the agency**. These are the theories that shape their creative approach. These are also called *practice-based theories*. Advertisers can adapt the theory to shape how they will develop their advertising. The agencies' understanding of the theory influences how they will decide to communicate the brands' message (Melewar & Nguyen, 2014). An example is *FCB grids* which advise the agency to develop an advertisement in a way because of the level of involvement customers have when deciding to buy the product. *Communications theory* also puts the onus on the brand to encode their message and send it through the media while *congruency theory* expects the agency to adopt creative elements that their audience will engage with because it is in congruence with their personality.
- **For the Audience**. These are theories that explain how the audience deals with the advertisements when they receive them. These are also called information processing theories. Information processing is the way an observer of an event or phenomenon engages with the information and the decisions they make thereafter (Gong & Cummins, 2020). As such, it is a process that describes everything that happens to a phenomenon. In advertising, this theory recognises that the engagement with the advertisement is relative to individuals. Brands and advertisers do not have control over how their messages are being processed, but they can make an effort to make them unique. The information processing model alludes to the fact that the audience is getting the information which they must process at their own pace before deciding (Kazakova, et al., 2016). The brands will have to recognise this and anticipate the delivery of the information well in time for the right processing. Schema

has to do with a pattern of thought or behaviour that organises categories of information and the relationships among them. *Schema theory* in advertising recognises that customers have a perception about things around them and store it in their memory; Advertisements featuring any of these stored elements could trigger a response which could be positive or negative. Again, brands do not have control over things. Instead, they rely on consumers' feedback to shape their creative effort (Kujur & Singh, 2018).

Examples of advertising theories

Now it is essential to explore the main contents of the chapter to identify various advertising theories and see how they are being used and whether they are relevant. Previously, there has been an underlying assumption that one universal model could embrace all types of purchase and communication situations, but with theoretical advancement there are many more theories that have been developed. These theories recognise the cognitive–affective–conative sequence of attitude formation.

Communications theory

The communication theory can be described as one of the simplest theories for advertising. It is so easy to comprehend as it explains the essential elements of the advertising process. The theory is also often referred to as linear communication theory, and it highlights the communication between the brand and the consumers (Cluley, 2017). The brands are described as the senders, and consumers as the receivers. The brands try to encode their message and send it through the media. The consumers (receivers) make an effort to decode the advertisement and then decide on the form of feedback. The theory also recognises that noise that can interfere in the linear communication between both parties.

For example, Samsung wants to make you aware of their new mobile phone; they have decided to encode the message by using a social media influencer to unbox the phone and explain the different features. The concept of selecting an influencer is a creative effort to encode the advertisement in a manner that their target audience can engage with. The advertisement is then shared on YouTube and other social media. This then allows the consumers to engage with and decode the advertisement; perhaps if you like the influencers that have been used, you have a more positive attitude towards the advertisements, and your feedback could be to share the advertisements with your network or carry on and buy the new mobile phone. There are also possibilities for you not to decode the advertisement, and perhaps you may not be bothered because you are an Apple fan. Even though the advertisement got to you through the process of decoding, you have ignored the message sent by Samsung. The noise that can interfere with the communication is also acknowledged. This could be the text message you were reading on your phone or the distraction around the crucial time when you got the message which may have hindered you from effectively processing the advertisement. Figure 2.3 presents a graphical explanation of the communication theory.

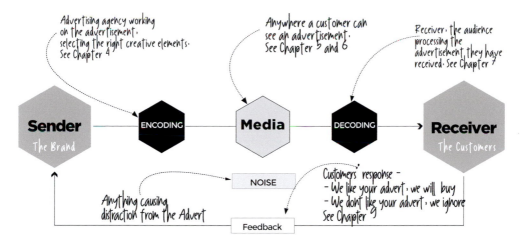

Figure 2.3 An explanation of the communication theory
Source: author.

DAGMAR

DAGMAR is a marketing expression that stands for "defining advertising goals for measured advertising results". It was developed by Russell Colley in 1961. Colley (1961) advocated that effective advertising seeks to communicate rather than to sell. The DAGMAR model assumes that company advertising must be informative enough so that the consumers become fully aware of the product or service. The theory is also integrated with the ACCA model which is an acronym for awareness, comprehension, conviction and action.

This suggests that consumers must be aware of the product that is being advertised. Awareness involves the creative design and position of the advertisements (Weilbacher, 2001). Upon awareness, consumers should be able to comprehend the information presented. This could mean using related images and copy that can quickly convey the message in simple terms. When consumers can comprehend the information, they should be convinced to take action. The action taken is, therefore, a measurement of the advertising results.

For example, if the Health Ministry wants people to change their health behaviour – maybe start doing more exercise – it is crucial to create awareness for this change in behaviour. To make people comprehend, they may want to include some health benefits, show images of those who have changed their behaviour and present some testimonials. It is left to individuals to process this information and be convinced to act. Their conviction will lead them to start jogging and be more active. The impacts of this campaign can be measured from the feedback from doctors and health professionals, and the general wellbeing of the citizen.

AIDA

This theory describes the steps a customer goes through in the process of deciding. Advertisers need to be aware of this in order to shape their design practices. The theory is an acronym for attention, interest, desire, action. It is essential to know that this also relates closely to the DAGMAR ACCA. With awareness, consumers get to know the product exists and this arouses their interest in reading more about it to see if it is something they will need. This interest should lead to the desire to buy the product; just like the conviction in ACCA, consumers develop interest and a positive attitude towards the product which will make them take action to buy it (Lee & Hoffman, 2015).

From an advertisers' point of view, it is essential to create attention in the advertisement. This could be the positioning of the advertisement on a huge billboard, the model that was used in the advertisement or the length of the advertisement. There should be some form of creative elements to create that attention. An advertisement from First Direct Bank was placed at a train station and the copy aligns well with the situation of the advert – "Move down to allow others onto the platform". Another one was from Lloyds TSB with the copy "Platform one. The perfect spot to catch up on your banking". These advertisements may not work elsewhere, but on the platform of this station they received attention. This aroused interest – therefore, information needs to be provided to buttress the interest of the consumers. This is where integrated marketing communications comes in. The advertisement caught the attention of the viewers, and information can be further provided through different media, perhaps through radio, TV or direct marketing. This information should make them act. At least that is how the theory expects it to work.

Means–end chain

The theory considers the steps and hierarchy of processes that a person must pass through for them to achieve their intended objectives and goals. It also looks at potential identities of the actions necessary for the person to reach his or her goal in life. In advertising, this has to do with the advertisers looking at the emotions, consequences, feelings, objectives and worldviews of a potential customer and projecting the advert onto those recognisable factors (Xiao et al., 2017). Furthermore, the theory uncovers the underlying emotions, consequences and personal values that drive consumer choice. The means–end approach is based on a theory that product and service attributes are associated with consequences, or product benefits and risks, and the product can even help consumers fulfil personal values (Zhou et al., 2020). The result is a value chain linking a product attribute to its functional consequence, to the psychosocial (or emotional) consequence, to the underlying personal value.

Hierarchy of effects

A consumer moves through a series of six steps to be convinced of the purchase. Hierarchical models are linear sequential models built on an assumption that consumers move through a series of cognitive and affective stages, beginning with brand awareness (or category awareness) and culminating in the purchase decision (Hazel & Kang, 2018). The hierarchy of effects developed by Lavidge and Steiner (1961) is one of the original hierarchical models. It proposes that customers progress through a sequence of six stages from brand awareness to the purchase of a product.

- Stage 1: Awareness – the consumer becomes aware of a category, product or brand (usually through advertising).
- Stage 2: Knowledge – the consumer learns about the brand (e.g. sizes, colours, prices, availability etc).
- Stage 3: Liking – the consumer develops a favourable/unfavourable disposition towards the brand.
- Stage 4: Preference – the consumer begins to rate one brand above other comparable brands.
- Stage 5: Conviction – the consumer demonstrates a desire to purchase (via inspection, sampling, trial).
- Stage 6: Purchase – the consumer acquires the product.

Elaboration likelihood model

The elaboration likelihood model (ELM) was developed by Cacioppo and Petty (1984). The model provides two different ways of forming attitudes. First, the careful consideration of information through the central route. The elaboration likelihood is high, and this explains that the consumer is hugely involved with the purchase and they are making an effort to decide (links with the involvement theory and the FCB grid). On the other hand, there is a short cut through the peripheral route whereby the consumer is not really engaging, and there is low involvement and motivation. Advertisers need to be aware of the type of message they want to send and how to creatively meet the need of the consumers who are looking for the information in order to make a decision.

Attitude towards the advert

There are five variables that explain viewers' attitude towards the advertisement they have been exposed to.

1. Ad cognitions (Ad_c) – i.e., recipients' perceptions of the ad itself (e.g., its execution);
2. Brand cognitions (B_c) – i.e., recipients' perceptions of the brand being advertised (e.g., brand attributes);
3. Attitude towards the ad (A_{ad}) – i.e., recipients' affective reactions (e.g., like-dislike) to the ad itself;
4. Attitude towards the brand (A_b) – i.e., recipients' affective reactions towards the advertised brand (or, where desirable, attitude towards purchasing the brand); and
5. Purchase intention (PI) – i.e., recipients' assessments of the likelihood that they will purchase the brand in the future.

Imagine standing on the platform of a London Underground Station and opposite you see an advertisement for Jack Daniels whisky (see Figure 2.4). There are ad cognitions which recognise that you are on the platform and seeing the advertisement. You recognise that anything on the other side of the platform is an advertisement, but perhaps you were

Figure 2.4 Advertisement for Jack Daniels

Source: Jack Daniels.

more interested in your train arriving in a few minutes, and you haven't taken the time to process the advert. In addition, you recognise the brand is Jack Daniels which explains the brand cognitions. Based on this exposure to the advertisement and brand, there is a more profound process whereby the attitude towards the advertisement is further revealed upon closer engagement. Perhaps the train is delayed, and you have more time to look at the advertisement – you have the time and you make an effort to process the advertisement further. You like the black and white design, the image that has been used and the storyline. You have a positive attitude to the advertisement, *but* because you do not drink alcohol, you have a different attitude towards the brand. You might like the advertisement (because of its design) but may not like the brand (for personal reasons), and therefore there is no intention to purchase. The theory of attitude to advertisements, therefore, postulates that if there is a positive attitude to an advert and a brand, there is an increased intention to purchase (Kadić-Maglajlić et al., 2017; Mogaji, 2016).

Source credibility theory

This theory looks at how people react to information and give a positive reaction to an advert, information or suggestion based on the source of the information. This theory in advertising maintains that the receiver's acceptance or otherwise of a message depends fully on how credible the sender of the message is. Furthermore, source credibility theory (Berlo, et al., 1969; Hovland & Weiss, 1952) explains how the persuasiveness of a communication is determined in part by the perceived credibility of the source of the communication. The theory explains how the information provided by advertisers can be judged as more credible than others. This is an established theory that has been adopted in different fields as it implies the communicator's positive characteristics that affect the receiver's acceptance of a message. Fogg (2002) described surface credibility from "initial judgments based on surface traits such as a person's looks, his or her dress, or hairstyle" (p. 132). From an advertising perspective, source credibility would mean the design of your advertisement and how people would consider it credible. Is it designed professionally to appeal to people? This also recognises the model that is used for the advertisement. If you are advertising a dental health clinic for teenagers, would you use an influencer, or a dentist for the campaign? Who do you think is more credible to give advice regarding dental treatment? Advertisers must make sure that while trying to get the attention of their customers, their design (including choice of images and text) should convey a form of credibility. If consumers consider the information credible, they are more inclined to process it further and to act.

Congruency theory

Congruency theory is a theory proposed by Newcomb (1968). As far as advertising is concerned, it has to with a situation in which a person's experience and goals/objectives are consistent or very similar. The theory is helpful for examining the effects of exogenous variables on consumer responses to advertising (Cui & Yang, 2009). Congruency theory postulates that, to maintain harmony and symmetry, individuals tend to be more responsive to people and messages that are consistent with their own beliefs and attitudes (Hong & Zinkhan, 1995). For advertising in an international market, this view suggests that marketers need to localise their advertising strategies in other countries because messages originating in one culture may be ineffective or even offensive in another (Leach & Liu, 1998). Many advertising professionals advocate the practice of incorporating culturally relevant and congruent appeals by adapting advertising messages to reflect local values (Zhang & Gelb, 1996)

Congruency theory also recognises using images and other creative elements that can reflect diversity as the brand aims to reach out to consumers (Mogaji, 2015). This could be using a model from a different ethnic group, a different gender or different text to make sure the message is in congruence with the values and beliefs of the target audience.

Nando's has different advertisements for the different countries in which they operate; often they change the copy of their advertisement to reflect the situation of a particular country.

Likewise, there are different advertisements from Volvo operating in different countries. In one of their Facebook campaigns, they used same-sex couples in the United Kingdom where same-sex marriage is legally allowed and recognised. Volvo used the image of two males (as a couple) watching over their child in the car; but in Poland, Volvo adopted a different approach by using parents of different genders. Volvo ensured that their advertisement was in congruence with the values of their customers in the United Kingdom where same-sex marriage is recognised, which might not be applicable in other countries where same-sex marriage is not recognised and is frowned upon.

Schema theory

A schema is a hypothetical cognitive structure that guides perception, thought and action based on prior knowledge of stimuli gained through experience, media exposure, etc. (McDaniel, 1999). Schema theory recognises that we store information about things we have encountered in our brain. They are stored in schema units, and when we meet new information or stimuli we correlate it with what we already have. For example, if you have once had a dog while growing up, the positive experience with the dog is stored; thus, when you see a dog in an advertisement, you are more likely to react positively because it aligns with what is already in your schema unit. However, for someone who has been attacked by a dog, there is already a negative perception about dogs, so when a dog is seen in an advert, it arouses those negative experiences, and such customer may not engage well with the advertisement.

Schema theory can also be used to explore the concept of congruency, though often on a personal level (where congruency theory may be seen on a more general level). For example, everyone in India may like cows and have a positive attitude towards advertisements where cows are used to describe a concept or brand. That is in congruence with the universal values but there may be individuals with negative experiences of cows (the individual schema). This is mainly because the focus of schema theory is on the psychological processing within the mind of the individual, rather than on the characteristics of the stimulus that elicit schematic processing (Markus & Zajonc, 1985). Schmidt and Hitchon (1999) define schema congruency as "the extent to which information fits with category-based expectations about the descriptive characteristics of the stimulus. Descriptive characteristics include tangible and intangible features but exclude evaluative assessments. Lynch and Schuler (1994) also demonstrated the match-up effect of the spokesperson with the product congruency, recognising that individuals in advertisements can also influence the schema-based information processing paradigm where consumers possess schemas that influence their reactions to advertising based on creative elements that have been embedded within the advertisement.

Involvement theory

This theory suggests that the level of involvement will determine the attitude towards advertisements. In another light, involvement theory in advertising has to do with the amount of mental processing that is required of the audience to be able to understand and get the message in an advert. This mental process that is required by the audience is directly proportionate to the quality and quantity of audience involvement in the advert. This mostly affects reception or rejection of a brand or advertisement. It is then advised that advertisers carefully consider their audience demographics, especially their level of understanding and reasoning before creating an advert (Czarnecka & Mogaji, 2019).

This also has some implications for the design and development of the advertisements. Involvement recognises how much time and effort is needed to gather information about deciding to buy a product or service or, better still, to decide. For example, if you want to donate blood, you want to read more about it, talk to doctors, the organisation and even your family. You don't just decide in an instant. Also, if you want to attend a university for your postgraduate studies, you want to be involved in the information search process. These are high involving purchases. Compare this to when you want to buy a drink or candy, these things are often just picked up from the shelf. These are low involving products. This level of involvement also influences the way the advertisement is designed and developed. For high involving products, the advertisement will have contained a considerable amount of information to allow the customer to make a choice; whereas for the low involvement product, there is little information provided. This involvement feeds into the FCB grid which matches the involvement in four different quadrants.

FCB grid

Advertisers need to recognise that advertising schema can influence selective attention, perception of and response to advertising (Mogaji, 2016), as consumers process marketing communications by matching visual and contextual cues from an advertisement (and possibly the media vehicle where it appears) to their prior knowledge of similar stimuli stored in the appropriate schema (Goodstein, 1993). Advertisers may not be aware of the prior knowledge of their target audience, and this however necessitates the need for research into understanding human behaviour and perception about advertisement which can influence future designs.

As there are advancements in knowledge, more theories recognise a multiplicity of advertising situations; that is, they recognise that advertisement does not work in a direct line as suggested by linear communications theory. This leads to more theories that identify the level of involvement of the customers and the type of product to be purchased. These models address phenomena such as different levels of involvement and the sequence and significance of cognitive and affective processing. These models shape advertising practices and make significant contributions to the understanding of the advertising and communication processes and to the promotion of the need for advertising planners to develop marketing communication objectives and strategies on an explicit model of the communication process. One of these models is the FCB grid (Figure 2.5) which was developed by Richard Vaughn, the Senior Vice President of Foote, Cone and Belding way back in 1980 (Vaughn, 1980). The grid has four quadrants that help understand where a product stands in the mind of a consumer and the type of advertising strategy that may be suitable.

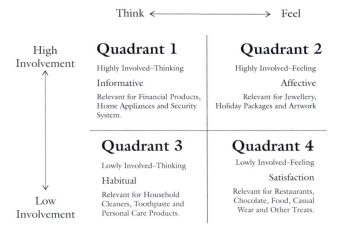

Figure 2.5 An illustration of FCB grid
Source: author.

The decision to buy lies somewhere on that graph, in one of its four quadrants:

1. At the upper left, **Quadrant 1 decisions are based on highly involved thinking**. Purchase requires information first, which leads to awareness and a considered buy. A Leica needs analysis. There is also emotion, which pushes the German camera closer to the right-most feeling side of the chart, but it is a thoughtful purchase. Health insurance is at the top of high involvement, above high-end optics. Ironically, it is just slightly more to the right-most feeling side of the chart because it's more important (or costs more) than the camera.
2. At the upper right, **Quadrant 2 decisions are based on highly involved feeling**. Purchase requires reflection first, as personal ego and self-esteem cajole us into buying. Skin-softening soap is just at the beginning of the feeling side of the grid. Perfume blows it away, ending up on the far right of feeling. The fragrance evokes a higher feeling than a Hallmark card, and also requires higher involvement.
3. At the lower left, **Quadrant 3 decisions are based on lowly involved thinking**. Purchase of practical goods is based on habit and routine behaviour. We learn about the product only after taking it home and not before. It is the detergent we assess after the first wash. It is also Yelp.
4. At the lower right, **Quadrant 4 decisions are based on lowly involved feeling**. It's the purchase of pleasure products driven by quick personal or peer-led satisfaction. Quadrant 4's motto is: "Just do it". Cookies are a low intellectual item. The less you think about them, the more you want them. Like Spotify.

There are also other grid models that explore the role of involvement and brand awareness, prominent among which is the Rossiter–Percy grid. This grid was developed in 1987 but a newer and improved alternative advertising planning grid was developed in 1991 (Percy & Donovan, 1991). The other grid model is the eclectic model of advertising.

Reed and Ewing (2004) also explain further how advertising works by providing alternative situational and attitudinal explanations. They developed seven models for a variety of purchase situations including different levels of involvement, situations where product trial is possible or not, and differences between first-time and sequential buying situations. The models distinguish between conceptual and experiential attitudes and, accordingly, emphasise the importance of conation (direct experience) in the process of attitude formation. They address many limitations of earlier work and, in particular, provide for a more extensive range of purchase situations than popular models developed by Vaughn (1980) and Rossiter et al. (1984) that are constrained by their use of 2×2 grid formats. Both of these models show a dichotomous relationship between cognition and affect; Vaughn with "thinking" and "feeling" on opposite ends of the continuum and, similarly, Rossiter et al. with "informational" (the equivalent to the "thinking" side of Vaughn's grid) and "transformational" (the equivalent of "feeling") motivations opposed to one another. The models proposed and provided varying levels of cognitive and affective processing, including situations where both can operate at optimum levels.

Case study 2.1

Citroën C4 Happy Day advertisement

Citroën is a French automobile manufacturer, part of the PSA Peugeot Citroën group. In September 2020, they launched an advertisement titled Happy Day for their Citroën C4, celebrating 100 years and the global celebration of the electrification of the compact sedan, which began in 1928. The advertisement was created by BETC, France, featuring the song "Happy Day" being sung as the onlookers watch the car travelling through key periods of the Citroën sedan.

Adopting three different theories, this case study deconstructs these advertisements to understand the key stakeholders, the creative decisions made in the development of the advertisement and the creative elements which were integrated to make the advertisement appealing and engaging. This should help you understand how theories work and how they can be used in explaining and developing an advertisement.

From communications theory, we can recognise Citroën as the brand sending the message; they have commissioned BETC, France to develop the advertisement. The agency has embedded different creative elements like the choice of images, music and location to make the advertisement appealing. The advertisement is also being transferred through the media, in this case, the advertisement is being broadcast through social networks. Importantly, consumers are decoding these advertisements once they receive them. Upon exposure to the advertisement, consumers provide feedback in the form of positive attitude towards the advertisements, the brand and an inclination to buy an electric Citroën C4. Any distractions while watching the advertisement, such as notifications on your phone, are noises, according to the model.

Likewise, we can use the AIDA model to deconstruct this advertisement. There are the attention-grabbing elements of the advertisement, which include the choice of song, the colour of the car, the actors' involvement with the song, singing along and the car being featured with backgrounds of different generations. Then there is the interest as indicated by everyone looking at the car as it emerges; everyone seems interested in the car and you too, the viewer. This is then followed by the desire to be a part of the experience – the feeling that you are the odd one out if you are not driving a Citroën C4. The action at the end of the advertisement concludes the model for this advert. Viewers are being nudged to act and consider buying the 100% electric, petrol or diesel model.

Another model that is applicable here is congruency theory which is a practice-based model suggesting the need for advertisers to make a conscious creative decision about the creative elements they use in their advertisements, as it is important to align with the expectations of the society. First and most importantly, the song "Happy Day", which may be deemed religious, has been slightly changed to fit a wider audience. Second, the song is presented as a form of sing-along; everyone seems involved and engaged and it brings back memories for many who may have grown up singing that song. Third, the cinematic expression with the car moving from different scenes builds an emotional connection with the audience; everyone can see a piece of themselves in the car, those enjoying the road trip, the bikers and even the office workers, showing a creative effort to bring everyone on board. Fourth, the static drink in the cup after the car has just passed over a speed bump highlights a rational appeal for prospective customers; and lastly, the different offers available meet the growing need of customers for more sustainable offers – the car is now available as an 100% electric vehicle. These little insights connect with everyone and make the advertisement congruent with the viewers' expectations.

Here we see three different theories being used to explain an advertisement. It is, however, important that all the theories in advertisement may not be applicable to an advertisement but, notwithstanding, some will be relevant and suitable for use in deconstructing an advertisement.

Reflective questions

1. Citroën opens a new chapter of road history with the launch of the new C4, how important would you consider the creative decision to allow the car to travel through key periods in the advertisement?
2. The colour of the Citroën C4 in the advertisement was red. Why do you think that was a critical creative decision?
3. Why do you think it was necessary to slightly change the lyrics of the song in the advertisement?

A summary of the theories

As indicated, the theories are evolving. New theories are being developed to explain the current situation of things. Likewise, there are still overlapping explanations in the theories as seen with the ELM, involvement theory and the FCB grid. This all recognises the variations in the level of engagement with a product and how advertisements should be developed.

While acknowledging these vast amounts of theories, I have made an effort to summarise the key features and offer a holistic summary of the relevant advertising theories and their implications for practice.

1. **A message with a value**. Advertisers must ensure a value in what they are communicating. This is not just for products but also for behavioural changes. Advertisers and brands should be able to answer what they are expecting the viewers and audience to do after seeing their advertisements.
2. **Recognise the differences**. This builds on the congruency and schema theories, whereby individuals are different, and engage with advertisements on different levels. Individuals filter advertisements through their personal experience and process information that they have stored in their brains. Advertisers often try to make sure their advertisements appeal to the differences in humans, and they use images that the majority can appreciate. An HSBC campaign – *Together we thrive* – featured a football team with copy that highlights Spanish, French, Belgian and Nigerian connections while Sky Sports includes supporters of different football teams in their advertisements.
3. **Emotional appeals**. This builds on the FCB grid that recognises the "feel" element and the peripheral route of ELM. Sometimes, it is about engaging with the consumer in a much less severe manner, and humour plays an important role here, whereby viewers are presented with emotionally appealing advertisements which can create interest and grab their attention. An advertisement from Lloyds Bank about their mortgage was presented in a very emotional manner; while a mortgage may be considered a high involving purchase, it was approached with an emotional appeal – a father laughing and playing with his daughters.
4. **Rational appeal**. This builds on the "think" element of the FCB grid and the central route of the ELM. Information for high involving products should be rationally presented. Consumers should be encouraged to make an informed choice; therefore, it is not surprising to see some advertisements including footnotes and disclaimers, to ensure that consumers are making a rational decision.
5. **Creativity**. This aligns with the construct of attention in the different theories. The creative element of the advertisement should attract viewers. This could be the model that has been used, the copy and the image, creating an advertisement that is appealing and visually engaging. This also builds on the credibility source, congruency theory and schema. The use of image should be from a credible source, and likewise the images and other creative elements should be congruent, as much as possible, with the audiences' values and beliefs. This will also link up with the attitude towards the advertisement construct. When the advertisement is creative, it attracts, and the brand is also seen.
6. **Media placement**. This addresses the construct of awareness in the theories. An advertisement must be seen in the right place before it can make people engage with it. This ensures that the creative advertisement is placed in a way to attract attention. This could be the number of times it is displayed in a newspaper, the position of the billboard or sponsored posts on social media. Here is an advert from the Samaritans, a charity organisation providing emotional support to anyone at risk of suicide throughout the United Kingdom and Ireland. This advertisement was placed at the end of the train platform; perhaps anyone at risk of suicide whilst on that platform would engage with the advert and seek help. Rather than placing this advertisement in a newspaper or on TV, the train platform makes it unique and more likely to be effective.

7. **Monitoring and engagement**. To understand how well consumers are engaging with the message, advertisers must understand the information processing of their customers. This also reveals their congruency and schema which can aid the development of future design. This aligns with the feedback from communication theory. Brands and advertisers need to understand how consumers are engaging with their advertisements so that they can make informed decisions. Figure 2.6 highlights the seven key points of the theoretical summary.

Figure 2.6 Summary of the theories
Source: author

Case study 2.2

KFC–FCK

The week commencing 19th February 2018 was not a great one for KFC. Delivery problems meant hundreds of their restaurants had to close. It was a huge national news story, and it demanded an equally noteworthy response from KFC. The advertisement was developed by Mother London (Mother London, n.d.). When the chain faced widespread store closures due to a severe and unexpected chicken shortage, it had all the makings of a PR disaster – the kind some brands never truly recover from. The marketing team and its agency, Mother London, knew they had to respond. But how? They came up with a unique apology letter, printed in the *Sun* and *Metro* newspapers.

   The summary of the theories as presented in Figure 2.6 is used to explore this campaign.

1. A message with a value: KFC knew they had made a mistake. "A chicken restaurant without any chicken. It's not ideal", was the first line of the advertisement. They knew they were not providing that top-quality service they promised their customers, therefore they had to do something – at least apologise. This indicates there is value in this message – an inherent meaning and motivation to communicate. There was a sense of remorsefulness and they needed to apologise.

2. Recognise the differences: People respond differently to swear words and foul language. While many may be fine with it, KFC recognised that it was not something publishable in their advertisement; however they gave an indication of how angry they were and how they wanted to verbally express themselves, but were cautious and used "FCK" as an alternative.

3. Emotional appeals: There was an emotional appeal in this advertisement – consumers seemed to recognise how remorseful KFC were, and accepted their apologies. The consumers recognised that that anyone can make a mistake and sometimes empathy is needed. Therefore, there was no need to complain unnecessarily but to understand that KFC had no chicken and everyone could laugh about the advertisements and move on.

4. Rational appeal: KFC did not try to hide their mistake or blame another brand or supplier, instead they took responsibility. No doubt chicken is still important for KFC. Even though they apologised, they made a promise to make amends and do something right moving on. Here we see the brand using honesty and humour (emotional appeal) to weather the storm.

5. Creativity: The choice of colour, copy and image placements were all a creative effort to make the advertisement stand out and be memorable and engaging. Spelling out "FCK" on an empty chicken bucket has been described as a "very fcking clever campaign" (Brownsell, 2018). Many conscious creative efforts were made in the advertisements to convey the apology.

6. Media placement: This campaign may not be suitable on TV as you need to pronounce it and possibly it would be censored; moreover, KFC had to deliver the message as soon as possible and there was no time to shoot and start editing a TV advertisement. This highlights some practical implications for newspapers as a suitable medium. Newsworks (2018), the marketing body for UK national newspapers, noted that "newspapers are THE channel for delivering a timely, topical, and powerful message, within an environment that is proven to gain the trust of our audience, to encourage conversation and generate positive sentiment". The advertisement was placed on a full page in the *Sun* and *Metro* newspapers, which have the highest readership in the United Kingdom.

7. Monitoring and engagement: According to Newsworks (2018), "733 articles have been dedicated to KFC FCK". This delivered 796,709,795 impressions globally. The commentary was positive, with KFC praised for acknowledging their error and the brand tone. In social media, KFC's FCK ad was shared extensively, totalling 219,138,216 impressions. Making the combined impression count of KFC's FCK ad by May 2018 a staggering 1,015,848,01! The reaction on social media was overwhelmingly positive. The campaign won many industry awards including a Yellow Pencil PR campaign at D&AD Awards 2018 and a Print and Publishing gold Cannes Lion in 2018. Mother London was the only UK agency to be awarded a gong in the category. This is evidence that the advertisement was very engaging.

Reflective Questions

1. Why do you think it was important for KFC to advertise their apology letter?
2. How emotional would you consider the advert?
3. What are the implications for printing this advertisement in the *Sun* and *Metro* newspapers?

Summary

This chapter is about theories in advertising. Fundamental insight into theories has been provided with specific focus on some selected theories of advertising. It is expected that advertising students appreciate these theories to acquire a better understanding of how advertising works. The chapter also indicated that some theories are for the advertisers (to shape their design) while others are for the customers (to explore and explain how viewers engage with advertisements). While advertisers may not be able to understand what consumers are thinking, efforts should be made to engage with the audience – to provide information encoded with congruent creative elements. It is also essential that the information/messages which a brand wants to communicate are shared through the appropriate media and to the right audience at the right time.

Revision questions

1. What is your understanding of theories in advertisement?
2. Why do you think theories are necessary from practitioners?
3. Can you identify 5 theories and explain each with an advertisement of your choice.
4. Why should advertisers be concerned about consumers' attitude towards advertisement?
5. Taking into consideration media engagement is changing, and theories should be evolving, which of the theories discussed in this chapter do you think is no longer relevant?

Student activity

Applying theories in advertisement

*   Visit www.adsoftheworld.com
*   Filter advertisements using these filters – medium (film), industry (automobile) and country (all countries)
*   Select the 9th advertisement on the list
*   Explore these advertisements with the seven-summary point of advertising theory

    1. A message with a value: What is the value presented in the advert?
    2. Recognise the differences: What makes the advertisement different?
    3. Emotional appeals: What makes the advertisement emotional?
    4. Rational appeal: Does the advert contain any facts and figures?
    5. Creativity: What are the creative efforts within the advert?

6. Media placement: Where have these advert being placed, long enough for YouTube, short enough for TV)?
7. Monitoring and engagement: Would you consider the advertisement engaging and why?

- Share your findings with your group members and compare the results of their advertisement.

References

Berlo, D., Lemert, J. & Mertz, R., 1969. Dimensions for evaluating the acceptability of message sources. *Public Opinion Quarterly*, 33(4), pp. 563–576.

Brownsell, A., 2018. *KFC: A very fcking clever campaign*. [Online] Available at: www.campaignlive.co.uk/article/kfc-fcking-clever-campaign/1498912 [Accessed 2.2.2020].

Cacioppo, J. & Petty, R., 1984. The elaboration likelihood model of persuasion. *Advances in Consumer Research*, 11(1), p. 673–675.

Cambridge Dictionary, n.d. [Online] Available at: https://dictionary.cambridge.org/dictionary/english/theory.

Cluley, R., 2017. *Essentials of Advertising*. London: Kogan Page.

Colley, R., 1961. *Defining advertising goals for measured advertising results*. New York: Association of National Advertisers.

Cui, G. & Yang, X., 2009. Responses of Chinese consumers to sex appeals in international advertising: A test of congruency theory. *Journal of Global Marketing*, 22(3), pp. 229–245.

Czarnecka, B. & Mogaji, E., 2019. How are we tempted into debt? Emotional appeals in loan advertisements in UK newspapers. *International Journal of Bank Marketing*, 38(3), pp. 756–776.

Dictionary.com, n.d. [Online] Available at: www.dictionary.com/browse/theory?s=t.

Fogg, B., 2002. Persuasive technology: using computers to change what we think and do. *Ubiquity*, 132–145(4), pp. 2–8.

Gong, Z. & Cummins, R., 2020. Redefining rational and emotional advertising appeals as available processing resources: Toward an information processing perspective. *Journal of Promotion Management*, 26(2), pp. 277–299.

Goodstein, R., 1993. Category-based applications and extensions in advertising: Motivating more extensive ad processing. *Journal of Consumer Research*, 20(1), pp. 87–99.

Hazarika, N. & Zhang, X., 2019. Evolving theories of eco-innovation: A systematic review. *Sustainable Production and Consumption*, 19, pp. 64–78.

Hazel, D. & Kang, J., 2018. The contributions of perceived CSR information substantiality towards consumers' cognitive, affective, and conative responses: The hierarchy of effects model approach. *Clothing and Textiles Research Journal*, 36(2), pp. 62–77.

Hong, J. & Zinkhan, G., 1995. Self-concept and advertising effectiveness: The influence of congruency, conspicuousness, and response mode. *Psychology & Marketing*, 12(1), pp. 53–77.

Hovland, C. & Weiss, W., 1952. Source credibility and effective communication. *Public Opinion Quarterly*, 16(1), pp. 635–650.

Kadić-Maglajlić, S. et al., 2017. Controversial advert perceptions in SNS advertising: The role of ethical judgement and religious commitment. *Journal of Business Ethics*, 141(2), pp. 249–265.

Kazakova, S., Cauberghe, V., Hudders, L. & Labyt, C., 2016. The impact of media multitasking on the cognitive and attitudinal responses to television commercials: The moderating role of type of advertising appeal. *Journal of Advertising*, 45(4), pp. 403–416.

Kim, K., Hayes, J., Avant, J. & Reid, L., 2014. Trends in advertising research: A longitudinal analysis of leading advertising, marketing, and communication journals. *Journal of Advertising*, 43(3), pp. 296–316.

Kujur, F. & Singh, S., 2018. Emotions as predictor for consumer engagement in YouTube advertisement. *Journal of Advances in Management Research*, 15(2), pp. 184–197.

Lavidge, R. & Steiner, G., 1961. A model for predictive measurements of advertising effectiveness. *Journal of Marketing*, 25(6), pp. 59–62.

Leach, M. & Liu, A., 1998. The use of culturally relevant stimuli in international advertising. *Psychology & Marketing*, 15(6), pp. 523–546.

Lee, S. & Hoffman, K., 2015. Learning the ShamWow: Creating infomercials to teach the AIDA model. *Marketing Education Review*, 25(1), pp. 9–14.

Lynch, J. & Schuler, D., 1994. The matchup effect of spokesperson and product congruency: A schema theory interpretation. *Psychology & Marketing*, 11(5), pp. 417–445.

Markus, H. & Zajonc, R., 1985. The cognitive perspective in social psychology. *Handbook of social psychology*, 1(1), pp. 137–230.

McDaniel, S., 1999. An investigation of match-up effects in sport sponsorship advertising: The implications of consumer advertising schemas. *Psychology & Marketing*, 16(2), pp. 163–184.

Melewar, T. & Nguyen, B., 2014. Five areas to advance branding theory and practice. *Journal of Brand Management*, 21(9), pp. 758–769.

Mogaji, E., 2015. Reflecting a diversified country: A content analysis of newspaper advertisements in Great Britain. *Marketing Intelligence & Planning*, 33(6), pp. 908–926.

Mogaji, E., 2016. This advert makes me cry: Disclosure of emotional response to advertisement on Facebook. *Cogent Business & Management*, 3(1), p. 1177906.

Mogaji, E., 2018. *Emotional appeals in advertising banking services*. London: Emerald.

Newsworks, 2018. *KFC – The Great Chicken Crisis*. [Online] Available at: www.newsworks.org.uk/resources/the-great-chicken-crisis [Accessed 6.6.2020].

Mother London, n.d. Available at: https://motherlondon.com/work/kfc-fck.

Newcomb, T. M., 1968. Interpersonal balance. In: R. P. Abelson, ed. *Theory of cognitive consistency: A sourcebook* (pp. 10–51). Chicago, IL: McNally.

Percy, L. & Donovan, R., 1991. A better advertising planning grid. *Journal of Advertising Research*, 31(5), pp. 11–21.

Reed, P. & Ewing, M., 2004. How advertising works: Alternative situational and attitudinal explanations. *Marketing Theory*, 41(1–2), pp. 91–112.

Rossiter, J. R., Percy, L. & Donovan, R. J., 1984. The advertising plan and advertising communication models. *Australian Marketing Researcher*, 8(2), pp. 7–44.

Schmidt, T. & Hitchon, J., 1999. When advertising and public relations converge: An application of schema theory to the persuasive impact of alignment ads. *Journalism & Mass Communication Quarterly*, 76(3), pp. 433–455.

Vaughn, R., 1980. How advertising works: A planning model. *Journal of Advertising Research*, 20(5), pp. 27–33.

Vaughn, R., 1986. How advertising works: A planning model revisited. *Journal of Advertising Research*, 26(1), pp. 57–66.

Von Nordenflycht, A., 2010. What is a professional service firm? Toward a theory and taxonomy of knowledge-intensive firms. *Academy of management Review*, 35(1), pp. 155–174.

Weilbacher, W., 2001. Point of view: Does advertising cause a "hierarchy of effects"?. *Journal of Advertising Research*, 41(6), pp. 19–26.

Xiao, L., Guo, Z. & D'Ambra, J., 2017. Analyzing consumer goal structure in online group buying: A means–end chain approach. *Information & Management*, 54(8), pp. 1097–1119.

Zhang, Y. & Gelb, B., 1996. Matching advertising appeals to culture: The influence of products' use conditions. *Journal of Advertising*, 25(3), pp. 29–46.

Zhou, X., Funk, D., Lu, L. & Kunkel, T., 2020. Solving the athleisure myth: A means–end chain analysis of female activewear consumption. *Journal of Sport Management*, 1(1), pp. 1–13.

3 Advertising agencies working on the message

Brands need to send a message to their target audience; however, they often do not have the manpower and resources to do so, so they contact an advertising agency to help them work on the message. This chapter presents the dynamics between the advertising agency and the brand and how agencies deal with pitching ads and re-pitching to keep their business running. The chapter also introduces the various roles and departments within the agencies (graphic designers, copywriters), the different agency groups (WPP, Omnicom, Publicis Groupe) and different types of agencies serving the brand (full service, boutique). The global nature of the advertising industry is also discussed in this chapter. This chapter gives you an early insight into the industry you may want to work in and the dynamics, roles and opportunities that exist. In addition, the demise/ alteration of the agency in favour of in-house agencies and small independent contractors are discussed.

Learning outcome

At the conclusion of this teaching, students will be able to:

- Describe an advertising agency;
- Recognise the different roles of an advertising agency;
- Give examples of working relationships of an advertising agency;
- Give examples of challenges of an advertising agency;
- Explain the diversity challenges in the advertising industry.

Introduction

With brands' desire to communicate their messages, they consult professionals to get this done. As there are legal practitioners to solve legal cases, there are advertising agencies to develop and disseminate the messages on behalf of the brand. It is important to note that the size of the brand and their capabilities will determine if and to what extent they will use an advertising agency. Business owners who may not be able to afford to use the service of an advertising agency may consult a freelancer to help develop an advertisement to be shared on Facebook. The intensiveness of the message to be communicated justifies the need to use an advertising agency.

This teaching will give an overview of the advertising industry, highlighting the roles of the agencies, the different types of agencies and the challenges they face. Students will be exposed to various opportunities within the advertising industry, an indication of opportunities for entrepreneurial individuals and awareness for future career plans and progression. Students understand the dynamics within the industry and are better positioned and informed with basic knowledge to explore career opportunities within the sector.

What is an advertising agency?

An advertising agency is a service business dedicated to designing, developing and disseminating advertisements on behalf of their clients. It is an organisation that bridges the communication gaps between brands and their target audience. They are responsible for designing the messages from the brand and conveying them to the target audience. The American Association of Advertising Agencies describes an advertising agency as an organisation that creates and places advertising or marketing communications (4As, 2020). A minimum of 50% of the applicant's gross income must result from payment for services usually performed by advertising or marketing communications organisations.

Case study 3.1

Brand name nomenclature of advertising agencies

Advertising agencies are often formed as a partnership between a minimum of two people. Choosing a business name may not be difficult as both partners may combine their last names to establish their business name, and often this arrangement has become a usual norm. However, with the growth within the profession, increased numbers of partners who may have to be included as named-partners, mergers and acquisition of firms, the role of technology (MarTech and AdTech) and consumer behaviour changing the demand for advertising services, there are considerable implications for the naming nomenclature of advertising agencies around the world.

Nomenclature is a system of choosing names for things. While its use is predominantly in the sciences, it is applicable in the case of service firms (Mogaji, 2020). There are examples in legal firms (Norton Rose Fulbright, a law firm formed from the merger of Norton Rose and Fulbright & Jaworski); accounting firms (PricewaterhouseCoopers for accounting firms with three people coming together) and architectural firms (Perkins and Will established by Lawrence Perkins and Philip Will).

This naming arrangement is also prevalent in advertising agencies. The BBDO advertising firm started as the George Batten Company, and in 1928, through a merger with Barton, Durstine & Osborn, the agency became Batten, Barton, Durstine & Osborn. Now we have Abbott Mead Vickers BBDO which is seen with seven different names with traces to the roots and foundations of the organisation. TBWA was founded in 1970 in Paris, France, by William G. Tragos, Claude Bonnange, Uli Wiesendanger and Paolo Ajroldi; Saatchi & Saatchi was founded in London by brothers Maurice and Charles in 1970; whilst Bartle Bogle Hegarty (or BBH) was founded John Bartle, Nigel Bogle and John Hegarty.

Mergers between agencies have also created different naming nomenclatures. Foote, Cone & Belding (FCB) merged with independent agency Inferno in 2013 to create FCB INFERNO. The White Agency and Grey Group Australia merged into whiteGREY to work under one brand and one financial structure in Australia – "white" is presented in lower case followed by "GREY" in capital letters. VML and Y&R were also merged globally to become VMLY&R. Look at these three mergers: FCB was more of an established brand and retained its name and position in the new brand identity. With the merger of VML (formed by John Valentine, Scott McCormick and Crag Ligibel) and Y&R (formed by John Orr Young and Raymond Rubicam), the merged agency used all their initials in the new agency.

The arrangement of these names can also be of concern, especially in deciding whose name comes first or last. In a case of initials and single name, initials and double name single name and initials, determining whose last name is retained or whose names are initialised is also an important consideration. In line with the usual mergers and acquisition arrangement, there are possibilities that the more substantial firm may have the right to retain their name.

The numbers of partners leaving their organisation to start another agency has also added to the growing numbers of this nomenclature. At the same time, some still go by the partner name nomenclature such as VCCP founded in 2002 by Charles Vallance, Rooney Carruthers, Adrian Coleman and Ian Priest, and many agencies are going for alternative names like Karmarama, Mother, Brothers&Sisters, Fold7, Lucky Generals and Anomaly.

Reflective questions

1. Why do you think advertising agencies like using the names of their founding partners for their agency name?
2. What are the advantages and disadvantages of using the name of the partners?
3. In case of a merger between two agencies with three different partners, how do you think the names should be arranged?
4. Why do you think some creative individuals will leave an advertising agency to create their agency?
5. If you were to start an advertising agency with three of your friends, what naming nomenclature would you adopt?

The task of an advertising agency

Advertising agencies are expected to:

Liaise with the brands

To have a good understanding of the message a brand want to send, this stage is paramount for the advertising agency that needs to understand the internet values of the brand (Mogaji, 2015). The advertising agency proposes how to strategically boost the message of the brand through innovation, research and creativity.

Audience research

Agencies are expected to do research into understanding the expectations of the target audiences and how best to engage with them. With success at the pitching, the agency needs to understand the demographics of the target audience, their behaviours, how they engage with media and other insights that can shape the design process (Rotfeld, 2003).

Design advertisement

The research findings should inform the design of the advertisement. Design advertisements that integrate the messages of the brand are expected to engage with the target audiences. This involves a creative decision with regard to the images to use, the copy to use and the media placement of the advertisements (Krouwer et al., 2017).

Develop advertisements

The advertisement needs to be developed to make it ready for dissemination. This stage involves the production of the advertisement, moving from an abstract form and story-boards in the design stage towards the actual production – recording the commercial in a specific location that best interprets the message that the brand intends to send the audience. This also includes post-production.

Disseminate advertisements

Advertisements must be disseminated on different media. The developed advertisements are shared on media spaces that have been planned and bought. This stage involves deciding the frequency of TV advertisements, the advertisement size, the location of the billboard and the promotions on social media. The created messaged must be put to the consumers in the most conducive way and in a manner that will not offend the sensibility of the consumers.

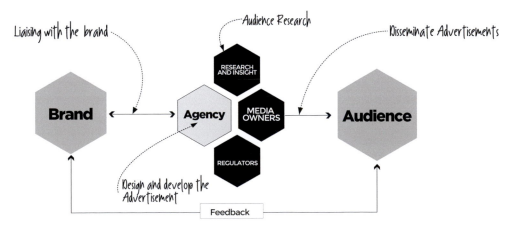

Figure 3.1 The task of an advertising agency
Source: author.

It is essential to identify that there are different advertising agencies, individuals and information technology that are required to address these tasks (Schultz & Kitchen, 1997). It is also possible to have an overlap – the person researching may end up being the one designing the advert. This depends on the size and capabilities of the agency. Figure 3.1 illustrates an overview of the task of an advertising agency.

Advertising agency's business domain

Services of an advertising agency include, among others, advertising, branding, content marketing, corporate social responsibility consulting, crisis communications, custom publishing, data analytics, database management, digital/direct marketing, digital transformation, entertainment marketing, experiential marketing, field marketing, financial/corporate business-to-business advertising, graphic arts/digital imaging, healthcare marketing and communications, in-store design, interactive marketing, investor relations, marketing research, media planning and buying, merchandising and point of sale, mobile marketing, multicultural marketing, non-profit marketing, organisational communications, package design, product placement, promotional marketing, public affairs, public relations, retail marketing, sales support, search engine marketing, shopper marketing, social media marketing and sports and event marketing.

R3, a global consulting firm with expertise in advertising agencies, classified advertising agencies into 15 groups in their yearly Agency Family Tree (R3, 2020):

1. Agency group
2. Integrated creative
3. Branding & identity
4. Customer relationship management (CRM)
5. Digital creative
6. Experiential marketing
7. Healthcare
8. Retail/Shopper/E-commerce
9. Integrated media
10. Digital Media
11. Public relations (PR)
12. Production services
13. Research
14. Social media
15. Other services.

It is important to note that advertising agencies are now specifically developing boutique agencies for sports, entertainment and health. WPP Health Practice is a leading global health marketing communications company, recognised for accelerating better health outcomes. Hill Holliday Health is a health marketing communication agency, and Mosaic Group is a full-service healthcare communications agency, both from IPG (Mosaic Group, n.d.). Langland is a global healthcare advertising agency under Publicis Groupe with a mission to improve people's health experiences through creativity (Langland, n.d.). FCBX is an experiential agency under IPG that amplifies commerce through culture

(FCBX, n.d.). The power of design and experiences is essentially used to bring brands to life across all five senses. FCBX specialises in multichannel sponsorship platforms, campaign and brand launch events, publisher and PR integrations, influencer immersions, pop-ups, social and digital content. Octagon is a sports marketing agency from IPG (Octagon, n.d.).

Types of advertising agencies: service provision

Advertising agencies vary in sizes and capabilities. While there are agencies employing thousands of people, there are also agencies employing tens of people. Technology has shaped the advertising industry, and it has opened opportunities for other creative sectors within the industry. As indicated earlier, there are various tasks for the advertising agencies, and some agencies can do all those tasks while others can only do a selected few. Advertising agencies vary in size and capabilities; the next section provides different types of advertising agencies based on their service provision.

Full-service agencies

These are advertising agencies that can provide most of the services within the business domain, as discussed above. These agencies have the human resources and size to pitch, carry out research, design and disseminate the advertisements. They are like a one-stop hub for everything that relates to advertisements and brand communications. They have size and number of employees to their advantage. Big brands likewise come to them because they know they have the resources to get all their messages to the right audiences. There could be smaller agencies who are full-service agencies, often working with small and medium enterprises. They can manage the small demands of their clients – they carry out research, develop the advertisement and share it across different media. Brands can benefit by working with full-service agencies as there is access to a huge pool of skills and resources. A full-service advertising agency can then be said to be an advertising agency that offers a comprehensive range of services. In a way these services address both the traditional and digital aspects of advertising. Most full-service advertising agencies comprise a team of professionals and experts in each niche. Examples of such agencies are BBH, BBDO.

Boutique agencies within networks

There are also possibilities to have boutique agencies within a networked agency. These may have been acquired or established as part of the group. Healix is global division within IPG Mediabrands focused on life science and healthcare brands. Launched in 2016, Landor is a global leader in brand consulting and design; it is part of the WPP network but focuses solely on brand development. Prodigious is a cross-media production agency, part of the Publicis Group. The Interpublic Group acquired Acxiom in 2018 (Adweek, 2018). Acxiom is a database marketing company that collects and distributes information drawn from an estimated 2.2 billion consumers around the world. It is anticipated that this will help the agency understand the target audience better, and they can effectively deliver their clients' messages to the right audience while relying less exclusively on tools provided by tech giants such as Facebook and Google.

Types of advertising agencies: affiliations

Networked agencies

This is a network of various advertising agencies across the world. They are connected and have a parent company. Many of these advertising agencies are significant on their own, but they have come together to form a network of more prominent agencies. In a networked agency, there is a level of interconnectivity and cooperation between different advertising agencies, helping them to develop and share ideas which facilitate the creation of unique advertisement for the brand. There are possibilities of agencies within the same network working with competing brands, and the profit goes to the network. Networks have come to dominate the advertising industry (Moeran, 2015). WPP (UK), Omnicom (USA), Publicis (France), Interpublic (USA) and Dentsu (Japan) are the world's five biggest networked agencies.

These networks are formed through mergers, acquisitions and starting a new venture to meet a growing need. Batten Company merged with BDO (Barton, Durstine & Osborn) to become Batten, Barton, Durstine & Osborn (BBDO) Worldwide. Likewise, Bill Bernbach and Ned Doyle both worked together at Grey Advertising in New York. In 1949, they teamed up with Mac Dane, who has a small advertising agency, and together they started Doyle Dane Bernbach. Driven by our clients' continuous demand for more effective and efficient marketing activities, advertising agencies strive to provide an extensive range of advertising, marketing and corporate communications services through various client-centric networks that are organised to meet specific client objectives. These require the agencies to expand their business operations and form a network. This is achieved by starting a new business arm, merging with other agencies or acquiring other agencies. These network agencies can also acquire other businesses, often based on various factors, including specialised know-how, reputation, geographic coverage, competitive position and service offerings of the target businesses, as well as their experience and judgement. For example, if an advertising agency wants to extend to an African country, they may decide to acquire an existing firm and change the name, instead of starting a new venture. Such acquisition is based on the geographical location.

WPP Group, London

WPP is the world's leading global agency network – across all communications, experience, commerce and technology disciplines (WPP Group, n.d.). It started as Wire and Plastic Products, a British wire shopping basket manufacturer. WPP acquired J. Walter Thompson, Ogilvy and Mather, Young & Rubicam and Grey. The company employs over 130,000 people across 112 countries. It is quoted on the London Stock Exchange and the New York Stock Exchange. Clients include 369 of the Fortune Global 500, all 30 of the Dow Jones 30 and 71 of the NASDAQ 100. The group has agencies for media, data and insight, public relations and public affairs, brand consulting, production and health and wellness.

Omnicom Group, New York City

Omnicom is an inter-connected global network of leading marketing communications companies. The organisation offers a diverse, comprehensive range of marketing solutions spanning brand advertising, customer relationship management (CRM), media planning and buying services, public relations and numerous speciality communications services to drive bottom-line results for their clients. The network employs over 70,000 staff serving over 5,000+ brands. It has over 1500 agencies in over 100 countries connected by Omnicom as the parent company dedicated to leveraging collective and individual offerings (Omnicom, n.d.).

Their portfolio includes three global advertising agency networks: BBDO, DDB and TBWA; three of the world's premier providers of media services: OMD, PHD and Hearts & Science as part of Omnicom Media Group. The network also manages a diversified global group of agencies, under the DAS Group of Companies. DAS includes over 200 brands across numerous marketing disciplines: public relations, medical and pharmaceutical marketing, customer relationship management, entertainment and events, shopper, branding and design, and research. Omnicom Group is therefore a perfect example of networks in advertising.

Publicis Groupe, Paris

Publicis Groupe was founded in 1926 by Marcel Bleustein-Blanchet. The company was named Publicis after the French word for advertising and "6" – his favourite number. It is the world's third-largest communications group. The group is organised into four solutions hubs for more effortless connectivity and integration: Publicis Communications, Publicis Sapient, Publicis Media and Publicis Health. In this model, all agency brands still exist but share an operational backbone, which gives them the power and expertise of all the solution hubs combined to deliver the scale required to compete and win in the new world markets.

Interpublic Group, New York City

Interpublic Group is a global provider of marketing solutions (Interpublic Group, n.d.). With 54,000 employees in all major world markets, Interpublic has three global networks which provide integrated, large-scale advertising and marketing solutions for clients: McCann Worldgroup is a leading global marketing solutions network united across more than 100 countries, FCB is a global marketing communications company, while MullenLowe Group is a creatively driven integrated marketing communications network. Besides, there are other organisations within their network such as IPG Mediabrands – global media and data. Public relations agencies such as Weber Shandwick, Jack Morton are global brand experience agencies, and FutureBrand is a leading brand consultancy. Octagon is a global sports, entertainment and lifestyle marketing agency. R/GA, Huge and MRM//McCann, are digital specialist agencies. Acxiom is a database marketing company.

Dentsu, Tokyo

Dentsu Group is the driving force in Japan's advertising industry. Their operations are led by Dentsu in Japan and Dentsu Aegis Network internationally. Dentsu has group companies in Japan, Global Network Brands including CARAT, IProspect and isobar and Specialist brands. Dentsu acquired UK media group Aegis to form Dentsu Aegis Network, creating a global marketing services giant and becoming the fifth largest advertising network in the whole world. Since then, the network has made 150 additional acquisitions and investments. In October 2018, Dentsu Aegis Network reached an agreement to acquire a 69% stake in Branded Ltd, a leading producer of live media events in the Asia Pacific, with an option of making it a wholly owned subsidiary in the future. In June 2019 Dentsu Aegis Network enhanced its creative offering with the acquisition of Newcastle-based commercial production company re:production, was founded in 2010, which delivers high-quality production solutions for TV commercials, animation and idents, and radio from its dedicated studios in Newcastle. In July 2019, Dentsu Aegis Network acquired New Zealand-based technology and business consultancy firm, Davanti Consulting, which then formed a part of their Isobar Group. Dentsu Aegis Network now operates in 145 countries and regions.

Affiliated agencies

These are agencies that were independently owned but are affiliated with another networked agency. The big agencies and networks need the affiliates to expand their market and strengthen their footprint in other markets. Affiliated agencies benefit from the global network in which they belong; commissions and fees will, however, be paid on the agreement. There are affiliated agencies that may decide to include or indicate their affiliations in their brand name. Examples are Gwaga which is affiliated to M&C Saatchi Africa, MUM Saatchi & Saatchi in Slovakia affiliated with Saatchi & Saatchi, TBWA Concept in Nigeria, affiliated with TBWA and Insight Publicis in Nigeria, affiliated to Publicis. Insight was previously affiliated with the Grey Group EMEA for several years. Some agencies may be affiliated but still retain their brand name and identity. Noah's Ark in Nigeria joined the Dentsu Aegis Network, and their brand identity has not changed.

Independent agencies

These agencies could be full service or boutique but, in terms of their affiliation, they are independent. They do not have a network to align with. While this gives them the liberty to explore the market and be very creative, there are limitations with sizes and how they may compete with others. For example, if an affiliated agency and an independent agency in Rwanda are competing for a global brand that wants to enter the Rwandan market, the affiliated agency will bring on board their international network and resources to connect the global brands to the Rwandan market. Figure 3.2 shows different types and structures of advertising network agency.

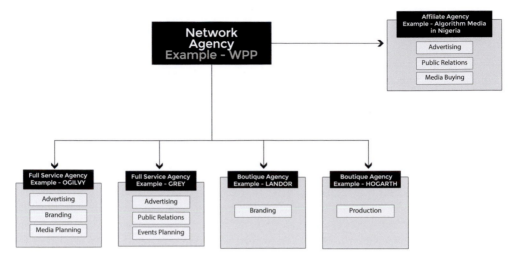

Figure 3.2 Different types and structures of advertising network agency
Source: author.

Case study 3.2

WPP acquisition to fame and world domination in the field of advertising

WPP Group is a British multinational company considered the world's largest advertising company. WPP's 2019 revenue totalled $16,899 billion. Though it started as Wire and Plastic Products plc in 1971, manufacturing wire shopping baskets, WPP has grown to become the largest agency holding company in the world. This growth has been supported through business expansion, mergers and acquisition and strategic partnerships.

INITIAL ACQUISITION

After Sir Martin Sorrell's acquisition on a 30% stake in WPP in 1985, he renamed the company WPP Group. Then began a series of acquisitions to change the course of the business from a manufacturing company to an advertising giant. This started with the acquisition of 11 agencies in 1986. Prominent acquisitions along the way to greatness were J. Walter Thompson Group for $566 million in 1987, Ogilvy Group in 1989 costing $864 million, Young & Rubicam Group (Y&R) in 2020 and Grey for an estimated $750 million in 2004.

ACQUISITION

WPP has expertise in healthcare advertising, sports marketing, digital marketing and data management, retail and corporate consultancy, and industries. This expertise has been strengthened through acquisitions of strategic companies. WPP acquired Thomas G. Ferguson Associates, a healthcare advertising firm in 1990. This was followed by sports marketing company Prism Group in 1999. In October 2008, WPP acquired market research firm Taylor Nelson Sofres, and in 2009, took a stake in Facebook marketing platform Buddy Media (though later acquired by Salesforce). In 2020, they acquired Sandtable, the data science company that specialises in behavioural analytics and advanced simulations.

MERGERS

With the growing number of agencies and possible duplications and pitching for same clients, WPP merged some of these agencies to streamline their business practises. In 2018, WPP merged Burson-Marsteller with Cohn & Wolfe to become BCW (Burson Cohn & Wolfe), Poster Publicity and Portland were merged to create global outdoor media company Kinetic. In 2017, WPP merged Landor and Designworks Australia, with the combined business operating under the Landor brand. The White Agency and Grey Group Australia were also merged into whiteGREY to work under one brand and one financial structure in Australia. VML and Y&R were also merged globally to become VMLY&R.

NEW BUSINESSES

WPP expanded their operations through creating new business divisions to meet the growing needs of their clients. In 2001, WPP announced the launch of Red Cell, a global communications network focusing on the needs of "challenger" brands. In 2010, WPP established the Midas Exchange, a media execution and asset trading firm that provides innovative, strategic marketing and financial solutions to brands and their corporate parent companies. In 2014, WPP launched a global Government & Public Sector Practice to drive excellence in government communications. Their main activities involve creating communication strategies for public policy and services, country branding and trade and investment marketing.

EXPANSION AND EXTENSION

WPP expanded through many acquisitions in different countries around the world. In Africa, WPP consolidated its presence through investments in Kenya-based Scangroup and stakes in Mindshare South Africa and Ogilvy South Africa. In February 2018, WPP acquired a majority stake in The Glitch, a digitally led creative agency in India. In May 2018, it established its mark in Southeast Asia, Taiwan and Japan by taking full ownership of Y&R and Wunderman joint venture agencies in these regions. WPP also has presence in Brazil through the acquisition of 70% of F.biz Ltda., the largest independent digital advertising agency in Brazil and another 70% stake in Gringo Publicidade Ltda, a leading digital agency. In July 2019, WPP extended its reach into Italy through the acquisition of a majority stake in Italian technology-driven creative agency, AQuest. And recently, WPP acquired Velvet Consulting, a leading French customer experience consultancy, in September 2020.

These acquisitions have no doubt positioned WPP as a dominating force in the Advertising industry, it highlights how different advertising agencies can be brought together to provide the transformative ideas promised by WPP and guarantee outcomes for its clients through an integrated offer of communications, experience, commerce and technology.

Reflective questions

1. Why do you think it was important for WPP to acquire many advertising agencies when Sir Martin Sorrell took over the company?
2. WPP has created new businesses over the years, why do you think it makes business sense to create a new business instead of acquiring an existing agency?
3. Considering WPP is known for acquiring advertising agencies, would you envisage any rebellion against WPP acquiring another advertising agency or do you think that agency would be willing to be acquired and join the group?
4. What are the benefits for WPP for expanding and extending their business operations into different countries?
5. What are the advantages and disadvantages of merging different agencies within the WPP group?

Roles within the advertising agencies

As highlighted earlier, there are different tasks within the advertising agencies, and likewise there are different teams to work on those tasks. There are five key roles within a typical full-service agency. It should be noted that for a boutique agency, this could be limited or overlapping. More so, in bigger agencies, many roles exist within these departments. Interpublic employed 54,000 people on 31 December 2018, and this highlights the vast amount of opportunities and roles within the industry. These roles are not set in stone, they may vary across different agencies depending on their size but are used in this context to illustrate various tasks within an agency.

Accounts manager: getting the job

These are individuals are responsible for building the relationship between the clients and the agencies. For each advertising pitch or contract won, there is an account manager responsible for building the relationship. Accounts, in this case, means if BT (brand) has a contract with Saatchi and Saatchi (advertising agency), that is an account – BT's account at Saatchi and Saatchi Advertising Agency – and there will be a team managing that account. It is possible to have many managers on one account, depending on the size of the agency and the size of the brands' account. Likewise, it is possible to have an individual managing many accounts. These account managers are the middle men, conveying what the brand wants to the agency and bringing back what the agency has designed to the brand. Therefore, when advertising agency is being discussed, an account manager is that individual whose primary job is simply to manage sales and the brand's relationships with particular customers. The account manager is expected to ensure that the company maintains a good relationship with the clients. To do that, an advertising agency account manager maintains the company's existing relationships with a client or group of clients, so that they will continue using the brand for their advert and other creative works through which they can send their intended messages to their target audience. The account managers are expected to have good interpersonal relationships with the brand's clients and understand the dynamics of the advertising industry. They will be able to understand the creative terminologies as they engage with the brands. It is important to note that brands will also have brand managers or marketing communications managers who will be communicating with the agency's staff.

Creative team: designing the job

This team works on the brief of the organisation as provided by the account's managers. The team may have a research person. The team is working on understanding the target audience. The team also hopes to shape the advertising campaign persuasively. To ensure that, the creative team will also have a graphic designer working on the graphics element and also the copywriter who is bringing the text and copy to the advertisements. There is also an art director who is responsible for the artistic direction of the advertisement. This team liaises with the account managers to ensure that the idea of the brand is well thought through and delivered as intended. Creative skills, innovativeness and imagination are needed in this team to be able to develop something creative and engaging, yet convincing enough to persuade.

Accounts planner: sharing the job

This team is responsible for the flow of work between the accounts manager, creative teams and the media planner, and they ensure that the work goes according to plan by preparing a budget for the job to be done and ensuring the job is delivered on the deadline. Project management skills are essential in this department, as the team must understand what the brand (client) is expecting (from the brief), understand how the creative team have developed it and how the media planners will disseminate it.

Media planners: disseminate the job

As previously indicated, advertisements are shared through the media for the consumers to see. There is a department that is responsible for putting the message in the right place at the right time. The media is not just limited to TV or billboards, it also includes social media and other non-traditional media. Members of this team are good with calculations and have high numeracy skills and can quickly identify how best to ensure the highest number of the target audience see the advertisement. They are also known to be using Programmatic which involves using software, machine learning, artificial intelligence and algorithms to purchase display space. Programmatic has not taken over the complete automation of the ad buying process as media buying on traditional media like TV, billboards and newspapers is still done through tenders, quotes and human negotiation. These teams are expected to be excellent negotiators in buying space for their developed advertisements at cheaper rates.

Management team: manage the agency

These teams are responsible for the day-to-day management of the agency. Depending on the size of the agency, their responsibilities may vary. Notwithstanding their size, they are expected to be involved in building the agency, bringing in more clients and making sure the organisation remains commercially viable. Often those in these teams move up through the rank. They may have been a graphics designer, then have job mobility to become an art director and eventually move to the management team.

Working relationships of an advertising agency

Irrespective of the size or affiliation of the agency, there are working relationships that exist within the advertising industry. These include relationships with competing agencies, government, regulators and brands. This section highlights eight critical relationships of an advertising agency.

In-house team

As different teams are working on different sections of the advertising campaign, it is crucial to nurture the relationships within the team. The account managers get the information and brief from a brand that wants to develop a campaign on social media. The creative team wants to make sure the advertisement is 59 seconds as the media planning team wants to promote it on Instagram. Such working relationship helps the agency in delivering the messages as anticipated by the brands.

Global network

As there are many agencies within the network, there are possibilities of working together to achieve an objective. This could be as an independent agency within a global network or an affiliate in another country. Agencies need to be aware of the strength of their colleagues and be able to contact them and reach out if need be.

Regulators

Advertising contents are often regulated around the work. It is, therefore, crucial for advertisers to recognise the role of the regulators. The advertising and marketing services that agencies provide are subject to governmental regulation and other actions in all the jurisdictions in which the Company operates. While agencies want to be creative, it is essential to recognise the custodians of values and cultural belief that are inherent and which advertisement must align with. The European Advertising Standards Alliance (EASA, n.d.) is the single authoritative voice on advertising self-regulation issues in Europe. The Advertising Standards Authority (ASA, n.d.) is the United Kingdom's regulator of advertising and ARPP (ARPP, n.d.) is the French advertising self-regulatory organisation. Goals of these regulators are to maintain high standards in terms of legal, honest and truthful advertising, which is in the interest of both the consumers and the advertisers. Any advertiser, advertising agency or media company can submit its non-finalised project to the legal experts of the regulators to provide guidance. The roles of the regulators will be covered in Chapter 8.

Brands

As I have maintained so far, brand is not just a name, design, term, symbol or any other feature that identifies one seller's good or service as distinct from those of other sellers, but what a consumer or brand user sees when he/she sees an entity that offers a value, service or product. Remember my advertisement for my students in Chapter 1: I could be considered as the brand sending out that message. When it comes to advertising, agencies are communicating the messages on behalf of the brand, and a good working relationship is expected for the company to remain commercially viable. The brands are the financiers of the industry; they pay advertising agencies to develop and disseminate their messages. While agencies are being changed more often, building a working relationship with a brand is a guarantee for continued success for the agency.

Manjur (2016) recognised that the best way to regularly connect to share best practice was by focusing on outcomes, not inputs, and taking digital media seriously – some of the things needed to make a long-standing relationship between an agency and a brand work. Unilever, Procter & Gamble and General Motors have relationships with major agencies dating back to 1922 or earlier. Trust, respect, adaptation are essential in these long-lasting relationships. In a rapidly changing marketplace, brands are interested in agencies that can maximise the value of data and give them competitive advantage.

Competitors

The advertising industry is changing and getting more fragmented. With the advent of technology, which is shaping the competition, there are opportunities for other creative inputs. There is competition with sizeable multinational advertising and marketing communications companies as well as numerous independent and niche agencies and new forms of market participants to win new clients and maintain existing client relationships. Those with skills in design and social media marketing can now describe themselves as advertising agencies providing services for small- and medium-scale enterprises. There are many freelancers online who can provide creative designs that would have necessarily been done before by an advertising agency. Advertising agencies need to be aware of this as they bid for accounts with full services agencies and the boutique ones. There are possibilities for sharing the job and outsourcing. A good relationship with competitors is essential and healthy for the industry. The Walt Disney Company awarded the most significant pieces of its massive $2.2 billion global media assignment to Omnicom Media Group (OMG) and Publicis Groupe. These are two competing agencies sharing an account from one of the biggest advertisers.

Media

Advertisements will be shared through the media. There is a working relationship between the custodian of the media platforms, especially traditional media like newspapers and television (Czarnecka & Mogaji, 2019; Gökerik, et al., 2018). The agency builds a working relationship with these media as they can negotiate and get good deals for their clients. Imagine two advertising agencies calling a newspaper about the cost and availability of a full-page advertisement space. A good working relationship could endure a good deal. The Dentsu Group has formed business ties with significant advertisers in Japan. It has also maintained stable and long-term relationships with many of its current clients. The Group has also established strong relationships with Japan's mass media companies, which enhances its ability to coordinate operations and sales activities between advertisers and media companies, and thereby facilitate transactions.

Intermediaries

These are firms that help brands select the advertising agency for them. These organisations were discussed in Chapter 1. They include the AAR Group, Creativebrief and Oystercatchers. Understanding how to work with these intermediaries is essential for the agency.

Trade associations

As advertising agencies are competing with themselves for business, it is important to recognise they also work together under various trade associations. These are groups of agencies, both in a local and global context, coming together to create a voice for the players within the industry.

Since 1938, the International Advertising Association (IAA, n.d.) has been a one-of-a-kind strategic partnership which champions the common interests of all the disciplines across the full spectrum of marketing communications – from advertisers to media companies to agencies to direct marketing firms – as well as individual practitioners.

Advertising Agencies Association of India (AAAI, n.d.) is the official, national organisation of advertising agencies, formed in 1945, to promote their interests. The Association promotes professionalism, through its founding principles, which uphold sound business practices between advertisers and advertising agencies and the various media. AAAI today is truly representative, with a considerable number of small-, medium- and large-sized agencies as its members, who together account for almost 80% of the advertising business placed in the country. It is thus recognised as the apex body of and the spokesperson for the advertising industry at all forums – advertisers and media owners, their associations and government.

In 1917, the American Association of Advertising Agencies (4As, n.d.) (was established to promote, advance and defend the interests of member agencies, employees and the industry at large. The association provides community, leadership, advocacy, guidance and best-in-class training that enable agencies to innovate, evolve and grow. The organisation serves 600+ member agencies across 1,200 offices, which control more than 85% of total US advertising spend.

The Advertising Association represents UK advertisers, agencies, media and research services in the advertising industry (Advertising Association, n.d.). Founded in 1924, the organisation promotes the rights, roles and responsibilities of advertising domestically and internationally, acting as the link between practitioners and the politicians and policymakers whose decisions impact the sector. In concert with the advertising industry's think tank Credos, the organisation produces and disseminates research and reports that enable their members to make informed decisions. Their work is focused around some policy areas, including gambling and HFSS (high in fat, salt or sugar) advertising, industrial strategy, data and e-privacy, trust and more.

The Institute of Practitioners in Advertising (IPA) is one of the world's pre-eminent trade bodies for marketing communications agencies (IPA, n.d.). The IPA has over 270 of the United Kingdom's brightest and best agencies in its membership, from a broad range of disciplines, who between them handle an estimated 85% of all UK advertising spend. The IPA has a dual role within the agency business. Firstly, it acts as spokesman for its members, representing them on issues of common concern and speaking on their behalf in negotiations with media bodies, government departments and unions. Secondly, it contributes to the effective operation of member companies through its advisory, training and information services.

The European Association of Communications Agencies (EACA), formerly the European Association of Advertising Agencies (EAAA) and founded in 1959, is the sole central service organisation for the European advertising agency industry (EACA, n.d.). The EACA, located in Brussels, combines the knowledge and input of the membership groups, i.e., the National Advertising Agency Associations, the International Advertising Agencies and the pan-European Media Agencies. EACA is the voice of Europe's communications agencies and associations, promoting the economic and social contribution of commercial communications to society. Our members comprise advertising, media, digital, branding and PR agencies as well as their national associations – together they represent more than 2,500 organisations from nearly 30 European countries that directly employ over 120,000 people.

The Interactive Advertising Bureau (IAB) empowers the media and marketing industries to thrive in the digital economy (IAB, n.d.). Its membership comprises more than 650 leading media companies, brands and the technology firms responsible for selling, delivering and optimising digital ad marketing campaigns.

While those listed above are trade organisations for the agencies, there are organisations as well for the brands. World Federation of Advertisers is a trade association that represents the common interests of marketers (World Federation of Advertisers, n.d.). It brings together the biggest markets and marketers worldwide, representing roughly 90% of all the global marketing communications expenses and revenues, almost US$ 900 billion annually. WFA champions responsible and effective marketing communications. It champions and defends marketers' interests, helps set standards for responsible marketing communications worldwide and encourages leadership initiatives, which go beyond compliance with existing industry standards. The Association of National Advertisers (ANA) is another trade organisation for the advertisers (ANA, n.d.). It was founded in 1910. Their members represent some of the most powerful and influential brands in the world.

Sources of revenue

Advertising agencies revenues are primarily derived from the planning and execution of multi-channel advertising, marketing and communications programmes around the world. Their revenues are directly dependent upon the advertising, marketing and corporate communications requirements of our existing clients and our ability to win new clients. Most of their client contracts are individually negotiated, and, accordingly, the terms of client engagements and the bases on which they earn commissions and fees vary significantly. As it is customary in the industry, their contracts generally provide for termination by either party on relatively short notice, usually 90 days or less.

Revenues for the creation and production of advertising or the planning and placement of media are determined primarily on a negotiated fee basis and, to a lesser extent, on a commission basis. Fees are usually calculated to reflect hourly rates plus proportional overhead and a mark-up. Many clients include an incentive compensation component in their total compensation package. This provides added revenue based on achieving mutually agreed-upon qualitative or quantitative metrics within specified periods. Commissions are earned based on services provided. Advertising agencies can also generate revenue in negotiated fees from their public relations, sales promotion, event marketing, sports and entertainment marketing, and corporate and brand identity services.

Challenges

The industry is highly susceptible to changes, and some challenges can affect agencies as they attempt to deliver their services to their clients. This is not limited to small agencies losing their talented staff or losing an account but also global agencies operating in different countries with different currencies, government policies and economic instabilities. This section highlights critical challenges of advertising agencies and how they can be mitigated.

Reduction in client spending

Advertising agencies make their money through brands that are willing to spend money to communicate their messages. There are possibilities for these clients to reduce their budget for advertising and marketing communications. This could be due to global or regional economic conditions. If a client is expressing financial distress, it could necessitate the need to reduce, postpone or cancel spending on advertising, marketing and corporate communications projects (Graham, 2020). This reduction in spending would reduce the demand for services from advertising agencies and could result in decline in revenue. A reduction in working capital for the agencies would negatively impact their operating cash flow.

Clients review and change

While clients may not be reducing their spending, there are situations whereby they want to get more value for their money. For that reason, they might decide to review the advertising agencies they are working with. Many companies put their advertising and marketing communications business up for competitive review from time to time (Vizard, 2017). Clients may terminate or reduce their relationships with agencies at short notice. If an agency is unable to remain competitive or retain critical clients by providing and demonstrating evidence of value for the clients, their financial position may be adversely affected. There could be a substantial decline in income if an agency loses the advertising and marketing accounts of a large client, and even the loss of a significant part of its business could have a materially adverse effect upon their business. In such situation, a lost client is not replaced by new clients nor is there is there any significant increase in business from existing clients; thus, such situations could adversely affect the agency's revenue.

Agencies, therefore, are competing to attract new clients and to retain existing clients, developing solutions that meet client needs in a rapidly changing environment. Therefore, the quality and effectiveness of their services and ability to serve their clients efficiently, especially large multinational clients, on a broad geographic basis are essential for business success.

Highly competitive industry

The advertising industry is highly competitive. The advertising and marketing communications business is highly competitive and continually changing. There is competition to retain existing clients, competition to win pitches and acquire new clients. There are mergers among domestic advertising companies, further entry into the market by sizeable global advertising companies and smaller agencies that specialise in one or more countries or local markets. This is altering the advertising landscape, increasing competition to secure clients. Competitive challenges also arise from rapidly evolving and new technologies in the marketing and advertising space, creating opportunities for an increasing number of companies in adjacent industries, including general trading and consulting companies. Fields related to Internet advertising and social networking services are also seeing a sharp increase in the number of new market entrants. While there are many long-standing client relationships with agencies, there are still possibilities for losing accounts as clients from time to time put their advertising, marketing and corporate communications business up for competitive review. Agencies try to retain and recruit the best talents to make their work stand out; they invest and acquire businesses to give them competitive advantages. They also merge with or join an international network to gain access to broad geographic markets, range of services and technologies, and to boost efficiency and reduce costs to remain commercially viable. Failure to adapt to the evolving and competitive market could harm the competitive position of the agency.

Human resources

There is competition for human resources in the industry. Considering the agency's principal asset is its people – their skills and relationships with clients – there is competition for the best talents. Individuals with the required skills can be easily poached to work in another agency. The industry is characterised by a high degree of employee mobility. Acquiring new clients and retaining existing clients depends on human resources to work on these accounts. The growth and expansion of the agency are highly dependent upon attracting, retaining and developing excellent human resources. Dentsu recruits necessary talent by hiring a stable number of new graduates and by recruiting mid-career professionals with expertise and experience that will make an immediate contribution. Agencies offer training opportunities, benefits and commissions. Identifying and developing the appropriate talent and attracting and retaining key employees and management personnel is paramount for an agency. If an agency cannot attract and retain key personnel, their ability to provide their services in the manner clients expect may be adversely affected, which could harm their reputation and result in a loss of clients and revenue. On the grand scheme of things, this could have an adverse effect on their business, results of operations and financial position. Immigration rules to allow for free movement of people may also present adverse effects as agencies tried to expand their workforce.

Global operations

Due to the fact that advertising agencies operate across many countries, there are some challenges they may face as they deliver their services. Local legislation, currency variation, exchange control restrictions, local labour and employment laws may affect their productivity. Government agencies and consumer groups directly or indirectly affect or attempt to affect the scope, content and manner of presentation of advertising, marketing and corporate communications services, through regulation or other governmental action, currency exchange rate fluctuations (across different countries) which could impact their business. BREXIT could also have an impact on global advertising agencies operating in London. This could cause increased regulatory and legal complexities and negative economic impacts. Operating in developing countries also has its challenges, such as slower receipt of payments, nationalisation, social and economic instability, currency repatriation restrictions and undeveloped or inconsistently enforced commercial laws. These limitations might hinder some advertising agencies entering into those markets.

Regulations

Advertising agencies are subject to regulations. In each of the countries they operate, they need to be aware of the regulations and code of practice that affect their services. The variation in regulations hinders the standardisation of advertisements. For example, an advertisement (featuring gay couples) may be accepted in the United Kingdom but cannot be used for the same brand in Nigeria, where same-sex couples are not recognised. These regulations could resist the activities and hinder the performance of the agencies. There are consumer groups that may also want to challenge advertising practices through legislation, regulation, judicial action or otherwise, for example because the advertising is false and deceptive or injurious to public welfare. Also, there are challenges for agencies advertising cigarettes, foods high in fat, salt or sugar (HFSS) as there are brands tackling childhood obesity, health complications etc., and they would not want to see anything that could put their work and the health of children in jeopardy. The UK Institute of Practitioners in Advertising (IPA) rejects tougher rules on HFSS advertising, stating that such action would be ineffective and disproportionate (IPA, 2019b). Existing and proposed laws and regulations in the European Union and the United States concerning user privacy, use of personal information and online tracking technologies could affect the efficacy and profitability of internet-based, digital and targeted marketing. This includes the General Data Protection Regulation (GDPR) in Europe and California Consumer Privacy Act (CCPA).

Information technology

Information technology is shaping the advertising industry. Internet advertising expenditures have continued to grow and have reached a level surpassing the amounts allocated to newspaper, magazine or radio advertising, which are three of the four traditional mass media (newspapers, magazines, radio and television). Any agency not fully on board with information technology will lose its competitive edge (Behboudi et al., 2012). Advertising agencies are acquiring companies/startups that complement their offering with information technology, data analytics and digital marketing. An M1 member of the Dentsu Aegis Network creates competitive advantage for brands by turning consumer data into addressable insight, powered by dynamic content that delivers consumer engagement, where data scientists and the best technology talent are driving innovation in machine learning, artificial intelligence and cognitive algorithms to augment the agency's expertise in data analytics, media and marketing (Dwivedi et al., 2019, M1, n.d.). Agencies rely on information technology systems and infrastructure to process, store and transmit data, summarise results, manage our business and maintain client advertising and marketing information. The reliance on technology also opens agencies to various risks concerning malicious technology-related events, such as cyber attacks, computer hacking, computer viruses, worms or other destructive or disruptive software. Furthermore, phishing attacks and other attempts to gain unauthorised access to confidential or personal data, denial of service attacks or other malicious activities is on the rise worldwide and these problems highlight the need for continual and effective cyber security awareness and education.

Diversity in the industry

Brands are demanding agencies working on their accounts to be more diverse. Verizon's EVP/CMO Diego Scotti sent a related letter to advertising agencies working on their brands asking them to "make an important commitment to drastically improve the percentage of women and people of colour in leadership roles and continue to support our diverse supplier community by awarding more subcontracting work to diverse businesses" (Coffee, 2016). HP and General Mills have also joined the call for agencies to act. Diageo has also asked to see its ad agencies' diversity plans (Faull, 2018). There are two current diversity issues within the industry, and they are subsequently discussed.

Racial diversity

There are growing demands for equal opportunities for talented individuals in the industry, irrespective of their race. There have been various backlashes towards brands for using sensitive racial features in their advertisements. Dove had to apologise for an ad showing a black woman turning into a white one, a Pepsi advert with Kendall Jenner was pulled after a colossal backlash, and H&M apologised over a "racist" image of a black boy in a hoodie; these has raised questions about the place of ethnic minorities within the advertising agency. According to the 2019 IPA diversity survey (IPA, 2019a), ethnic diversity among ad agencies is at its highest recorded level, with 13.8% of individuals from a BAME background, up from 12.9% in 2017. At creative agencies, 12.4% of employees are from BAME backgrounds compared with 10.7% last year, while within media agencies, this figure is 15.2%, up from 15.0% in 2017. The number of BAME individuals at Executive/Leadership level (known as C-suite level) has increased from 4.7% in 2017 to 5.5%. To address this lack of representation, Trade organisations are putting initiatives in place. In the United Kingdom, Creative Pioneers connects apprentice and advertising agencies (Creative Pioneers, n.d.). Likewise, Saatchi & Saatchi launched a suite of programmes aimed at inspiring, enabling and progressing more diverse talent from across the United Kingdom – Saatchi Ignite for students in Year 7 to Year 13; Saatchi Open, an entry level programme for six people every year with provision for mentoring, business planning support, commercial backing and access to clients and their briefs; and Saatchi Home, providing tiered affordable accommodation for interns, Saatchi Open candidates and junior agency talent below a set salary threshold. In the United States, 4As has the Multicultural Advertising Intern Program (MAIP, n.d.) which allows students to work at prestigious advertising agencies on various accounts, interact with advertising professionals on a day-to-day basis, and gain valuable professional credentials to get their first job in the advertising industry. This allows the fostering of the growing community of diverse, talented, and committed individuals throughout the advertising industry. To be eligible to apply for MAIP, a student must be identified as a person of colour or multicultural.

Gender diversity

In 2016, Kevin Roberts who was the Chairman of Saatchi & Saatchi (an advertising agency) resigned following his controversial gender diversity comments where he said debate about bias was "all over" and denied that the lack of women in leadership roles was a problem (Kollewe, 2016). This actually is not the case as there are still challenges for women within the industry. According to the 2019 IPA diversity survey, there has been a marginal increase in the number of women at the C-suite level from 31.2% in 2017 to 32.7% this year (IPA, 2019a). At creative agencies, women now occupy 32.8% of C-suite roles, up from 30.5% last year. At media agencies, there has been a slight increase in female representation at board level, from 32.2% to 32.7% this year. Agencies need to increase the number, seniority and influence of women in their leadership roles. Inclusion and diversity lead to business success, so female leaders do not have to conform to stereotypes. We need to change the narrative and show that there are as many stories of leadership as there are women. Omnicom UK plays a vital role in increasing opportunities and support for women through Omniwomen UK + Allies (Omiwomen UK, n.d.), 4As offers Executive Leadership forums and Mothers@Agencies supports mothers in the advertising industry (Mothers@Agencies, n.d.). IPA provides support through the Women of Tomorrow Awards which is about giving women the recognition they deserve (IPA, n.d.).

Summary

This teaching has provided a holistic view of the advertising industry. It explains different types of agencies based on their business domain, service provision and affiliations. The roles within the agencies and various working relationships were subsequently discussed. Besides, the challenges and diversity within the industry were discussed. The advertising industry is changing and evolving. Agencies are acquiring businesses that can complement their business, while some are merging to remain economic variables, and start-up and new companies are using social media and digital marketing to meet brands' needs.

You may be asking yourself, why is this information relevant or necessary, all I want to know is how to advertise. I will highlight a few reasons that will show you why this information is relevant as I bring this chapter to an end.

1. It is essential for you to understand how the industry works, especially for your career progression. With the understanding of the vastness of the industry, you can begin to explore various opportunities with regard to the business domain you may want

to work in – your understanding of the agency's working dynamics and a degree in advertising open opportunities for you. You know there are opportunities, what must you do to grab those opportunities? For those who are entrepreneurial, there are opportunities to explore as well. There are boutique agencies that can meet the needs that the big agencies want. You find a gap in the industry, develop your skills set and aspire to meet that need. Social media and digital marketing are business domains that are worth considering.

2. Be open to opportunities for mergers and acquisitions. While you may be thinking you want to run your agency yourself, be aware that your offering may be enticing to more prominent agencies who may want to acquire your agency, and also there are possibilities merging with others for the greater good of yourself and the industry.

Revision questions

1. What is your understanding of an advertising agency?
2. What are the different tasks of an advertising agency?
3. What is the difference between full services and boutique agencies?
4. Can you list five advertising agencies under each of the five network groups?
5. What are the sources of revenue for advertising agencies?
6. What is the role of intermediaries like AAR Group, Creativebrief and The Oystercatchers in the advertising industry?
7. What would you consider if you want to start your own advertising agency?
8. While recognising the naming nomenclature of advertising agencies, what name would you give to your advertising agency

Student activity

Identifying advertising agencies and credit for Happy Moving Day advertisement

1st July is the unofficial Moving Day in Quebec. Canada. Most residential leases come to an end on the very same day. Every year thousands of people pack their belongings on this specific day and move into their new homes around the province. Quebecers refer to it as "Moving Day" and many brands have tapped into this day, creating a series of visuals to celebrate this unique tradition.

Find "Happy Moving Day" Advert online (you can check www.adsoftheworld.com, Behance, YouTube and Facebook).

Identify the advertising agency that created the advertisement.

Identify the credit line (you may find these roles relevant and applicable. You can check www.adsoftheworld.com or the agency's website for the credit line of the advert).

- Creative Director:
- Art Director:
- Copywriter:
- Production Company: Merman
- Producer:
- Senior Producer:

- Executive Producer:
- Music Production Company:
- Music Composer:
- Sound Design:
- Sound Designer:
- Visual Effects (VFX):
- Lead Flame Artist:

References

Advertising Agencies Association of India (AAAI), n.d. [Online] Available at: www.aaai.org/.

Association of National Advertisers (ANA), n.d. [Online] Available at: www.ana.net/about/.

Advertising Association, n.d. [Online] Available at: www.adassoc.org.uk/about-us/#our-network/.

Advertising Standards Authority (ASA), n.d. [Online] Available at: https://www.asa.org.uk/.

Adweek, 2018. Interpublic Goup acquired Acxiom. [Online] Available at: www.adweek.com/agencies/ipg-confirms-2-3-billion-deal-to-acquire-date-marketing-company-acxiom.

American Association of Advertising Agencies (4As), 2020. *Membership*. [Online] Available at: www.aaaa.org/home-page/membership/ [Accessed 7.7.2020].

American Association of Advertising Agencies (4As), n.d. [Online] Available at: www.aaaa.org/our-mission/.

ARPP, n.d. [Online] Available at: www.arpp.org/the-arpp/.

Behboudi, M. et al., 2012. A review of the activities of advertising agencies in online world. *International Journal of Marketing Studies*, 4(1), pp. 138–148.

Coffee, P., 2016. *Verizon is the latest client to demand more diversity from its agencies*. [Online] Available at: www.adweek.com/agencyspy/verizon-is-the-latest-client-to-demand-more-diversity-from-its-agencies/117921/ [Accessed 2.2.2020].

Creative Pioneers, n.d. [Online] Available at: www.creativepioneers2.co.uk.

Czarnecka, B. & Mogaji, E., 2019. How are we tempted into debt? Emotional appeals in loan advertisements in UK newspapers. *International Journal of Bank Marketing*, 38(3), pp. 756–776.

Dwivedi, Y. K. et al., 2019. Artificial Intelligence (AI): Multidisciplinary perspectives on emerging challenges, opportunities, and agenda for research, practice and policy. *International Journal of Information Management*.

European Advertising Standards Alliance (EASA), n.d. [Online] Available at: www.easa-alliance.org/.

European Association of Communictions Agencies (EACA), n.d. [Online] Available at: https://eaca.eu/about-us.

Faull, J., 2018. *Diageo is asking to see its ad agencies' diversity plans but it has been met with 'some blank faces'*. [Online] Available at: www.thedrum.com/news/2018/07/02/diageo-asking-see-its-ad-agencies-diversity-plans-it-has-been-met-with-some-blank [Accessed 9.9.2020].

FCBX, n.d. [Online] Available at: www.interpublic.com/our-companies/fcbx/.

Gökerik, M. Gürbüz, A., Erkan, I., Mogaji, E., & Sap, S., 2018. Surprise me with your ads! The impacts of guerrilla marketing in social media on brand image. *Asia Pacific Journal of Marketing and Logistics*, 30(5), pp. 1222–1238.

Graham, M., 2020. *Advertising companies brace for downturn as coronavirus rattles ad spending*. [Online] Available at: www.cnbc.com/2020/04/14/advertising-companies-brace-for-downturn-as-coronavirus-rattles-ad-spending.html [Accessed 9.9.2020].

International Advertising Association (IAA), n.d. [Online] Available at: https://iaaglobal.org/about.

International Advertising Bureau (IAB), n.d. [Online] Available at: https://iab.com/our-story/.

Interpublic Group, n.d. [Online] Available at: https://interpublic.com/about.

Institute of Practitioners in Advertising (IPA), n.d. [Online] Available at: https://ipa.co.uk/about/about-the-ipa

Institute of Practitioners in Advertising (IPA), 2019a. *Diversity figures improve for Adland.* [Online] Available at: https://ipa.co.uk/news/diversity-figures-improve-for-adland [Accessed 8.8.2020].

Institute of Practitioners in Advertising (IPA), 2019b. *IPA against further HFSS ad restrictions.* [Online] Available at: https://ipa.co.uk/news/ipa-against-further-hfss-ad-restrictions/ [Accessed 8.8.2020].

Institute of Practitioners in Advertising (IPA), n.d. Women of Tomorrow Awards, [Online] Available at: https://ipa.co.uk/awards-events/women-of-tomorrow-awards.

Kollewe, J., 2016. *Saatchi executive chairman put on leave over gender comments.* [Online] Available at: www.theguardian.com/media/2016/jul/31/saatchi-executive-chairman-kevin-roberts-put-on-leave-over-gender-comments.

Krouwer, S., Poels, K. & Paulussen, S., 2017. To disguise or to disclose? The influence of disclosure recognition and brand presence on readers' responses toward native advertisements in online news media. *Journal of Interactive Advertising*, 17(2), pp. 124–137.

Langland, n.d. [Online] Available at: www.langland.co.uk.

M1 (n.d.), [Online] Available at: www. dentsuaegisnetwork.com/who-we-are/our-agencies/m1#top.

Manjur, R., 2016. *Top 40 client-agency relationships that have stood the test of time.* [Online] Available at: www.marketing-interactive.com/top-40-client-agency-relationships-that-have-stood-the-test-of-time [Accessed 9.9.2020].

Moeran, B., 2015. Advertising agencies. In: James D. Wright, ed. *International encyclopedia of the social & behavioral sciences.* Amsterdam: Elsevier, pp. 189–193.

Mogaji, E., 2015. Reflecting a diversified country: A content analysis of newspaper advertisements in Great Britain. *Marketing Intelligence & Planning*, 33(6), pp. 908–926.

Mogaji, E., 2020. Brand name nomenclature of UK law firms. *SSRN Electronic Journal*, [Online] Available at SSRN: https://ssrn.com/abstract=3644042.

R3, 2020. *R3 Global family tree 2020.* [Online] Available at: https://rthree.com/insights/r3-global-family-tree-2020/ [Accessed 9.9.2020].

Mosaic Group, n.d. [Online] Available at: http://mosaic-magency.com/.

Octagon, n.d. [Online] Available at: https://octagon.com/about.

Mothers@Agencies, n.d. [Online] Available at: https://.enroll.aaaa.org/virtual-programs/mothersatagencies.html.

Multicultural Advertising Intern Program (MAIP), n.d. [Online] Available at: https://maip.aaaa.org/.

Omnicom, n.d. [Online] Available at: www.omnicomgroup.com/our-agencies/.

Publicis Groupe, n.d. [Online] Available at: www.publicisgroupe.com/en/the-groupe/about-publicis-groupe.

Omniwomen UK + Allies, n.d. [Online] Available at: www.omniwomenuk.com/.

Rotfeld, H., 2003. Misplaced marketing: Who do you hire when the advertising audience isn't you?. *Journal of Consumer Marketing*, 20(2), pp. 87–89.

Schultz, D. & Kitchen, P., 1997. Integrated marketing communications in US advertising agencies: An exploratory study. *Journal of Advertising Research*, 37(5), pp. 7–19.

Vizard, s., 2017. *How marketing is changing and why agencies are not keeping pace.* [Online] Available at: www.marketingweek.com/marketing-changing-agencies-pace/ [Accessed 9.9.2020].

WPP Group (London), n.d. [Online] Available at: www.wppgroup.com/contacts.

World Federation of Advertisers, n.d. [Online] Available at: www.wfanet.org/.

4 The creative elements of advertisements

The advertising agency has the team to ensure advertisements are well presented, using the right creative elements to convey the message as intended by the brand. This chapter looks at the creative elements in advertisements across various media. International cases and examples of creative elements with cultural and religious embedded meanings are included in this chapter. The theory behind the design and concept of an advertisement, the choice of colour and layout are also discussed. It discusses basic design principles such as typography, colour, selecting the right visuals/images, the layout of the design, copywriting and art direction. Building on the creative elements used in advertisements, the chapter presents rational and emotional appeal, positive and negative emotional appeal, the theory of emotional appeal and how advertising appeal varies according to the message, the media and the brand.

Learning outcome

At the conclusion of this teaching, students will be able to:

- Describe the creative elements of advertisement;
- Recognise the different visual, audio and touch elements that can be used in advertisement;
- Describe advertising appeals;
- Give examples of emotional appeals in advertisements;
- Explain the creative element selection process.

Introduction

As previously explained, advertising is about creatively communicating a message from a brand to an audience. No doubt messages can be communicated in different formats. The creative approach adopted in a message has been found to make a difference in the way the receiver engages with it. The chapter of theories (Chapter 2) recognises the need to arouse attention in an advertisement, making the advertisement irresistible and engaging. This process aligns with the encoding stage of the communication theory before sending it through the media.

This chapter focuses on the creative elements of advertisements. These are more of the tools in a tool kit that can be used to address a task. These creative elements are integrated to effectively communicate a message. Their use varies according to media and the messages that are to be communicated to the audience. Understanding the various elements is essential for advertising practitioners. This understanding is enough to recognise when, how and where to use the creative elements.

The chapter presents different creative elements and highlights their unique features and benefits for the communications strategy. Design principles for integrating the selected ideas are also discussed. The chapter also illustrates the combination of the various creative elements to develop an advertisement that appeals. Rational and emotional appeals are presented as the two types of advertising appeals. Creatively deciding on which elements to use in order to develop the advertising appeals strategy is also discussed.

Creative elements in advertising

These are features that are embedded within advertisements to communicate the message for the brand. These elements involve creative choice in the sense that decisions are made about them; designers must choose between different options and variations. They are also referred to as execution cues. The elements can be changed and replaced to convey a different meaning. The creativity presents the difference between the message and the way receivers will engage with it. Something creative can beat the media clusters and make the brand message stand out from others. The creative elements have been grouped under three different headings, which highlight how viewers engage with advertisement.

Visuals

These are what can be seen in advertisements. Viewers engage with these elements to appreciate and comprehend the messages being sent by the brands. As visual is a represented idea, such as an image, picture, diagram or piece of film that shows or explains something clearly and lucidly, as an advertiser, you must always remember to use your visuals to reinforce your core message or advertisement. That must be done in a way that your visuals will not detract your target audience from what you intend to communicate.

Images

Images can be said to be the most important of the creative elements in advertisements. It is often said that pictures tell a thousand words. Images alone can be used to convey a message with text or no text at all. The choice of images is essential in advertisement, and it has a significant effect on its effectiveness. Unlike language/text, images break the language barriers. Likewise, they break the age barrier which means that, irrespective of your language or your age, you can understand what an image is conveying. The image is not limited to still photographs as seen in print media like billboards or newspapers but also as seen on TV and social media for video. The inherent meanings viewers have about images cannot be ignored (this aligns with theories as discussed in Chapter 2 – schema and congruency theories where a person has a different meaning for dog because of their experience); this suggests reasons why brands and agency need to be mindful of the images they are selecting for their campaign, as in some cases, this might be negatively received – the Dove advert is a good example.

Various types of images can be used in advertisements. It is a creative choice that must be made which reflects the values and message of the brand. The list is inexhaustible but here are some examples:

CARTOONS

This type of image includes illustrations, hand-drawn images and animated characters. They can be attractive, creatively adopted and offer a unique approach. They are flexible and can convey any form of story without having a real human character. Lloyds TSB and TSB Bank have used this. The Halifax has previously adopted Top Cat, The Flintstones, Scooby-Doo and, lately, the Thunderbirds in their campaigns.

To grab the attention of the audience for Nivea Sun cream, FCB Inferno created a droll new character, "Mr Sun". Mr Sun's character in Figure 4.1 was created by award-winning

Figure 4.1 Mr Sun's character
Source: Publicis One Touch/NIVEA.

Figure 4.2 Advertisement from Network Rail
Source: Network Rail.

VFX company Framestore. Some brands may not have the right to use the image of foot-ballers in their campaign, but they can afford to have a caricature to illustrate their message. Flat illustrations and cartoons can also be used to bring a different design to an advert. As seen with the advertisement from Network Rail in Figure 4.2 asking participants to use the hand sanitiser, they could have used a photograph of a person's hand but adopting such illustration was a creative decision to liven up the design. Likewise cartoons and illustration also have the possibilities of having many characters in a single image, as they can be easily drawn together. Figure 4.3 also shows an advertisement for Paga, a payment company in Nigeria using cartoons and illustrated images.

ANIMALS

Cadbury used Gorilla in their advertisement which won the Campaign of the Year and was named by *Marketing* magazine as the nation's all-time favourite (Caird, 2016). *Campaign* magazine noted that the advert was so effective that "it touches a nation, reshapes a brand and leaves advertising purist scrambling for the rulebook" (Staff, 2007). Lloyds Bank has the black horse of Lloyds bank as part of their logo, adopted in the bank's

Figure 4.3 Advertisement for Paga money transfer

Source: Noah's Ark Communications, creative director: Abolaji Alausa, copywriter: Abolaji Alausa/Seyi Owolawi, art director: Olalekan Akinyele and illustrator: Kimson Osaghae.

advertisement (Mogaji, 2016). Guinness's "Surfer" ad also featured horses. To illustrate the ideas of "Simple Investment, Return Beyond Expectation", Kiatnakin Bank in Thailand used a dog for advertising their KK Smart Investment product. Doritos' Pug Attack ad also featured a dog. The choice of the dog breed is a creative decision to convey a message. You ask, why didn't they use a Mastiff or Rottweiler that is considerably bigger and capable of breaking a door. The Government Employees Insurance Company (GEICO), an American auto insurance company with headquarters in Maryland, has used various animals for their campaign, including Gecko, Pony, Lobster, Dogs and Walrus. Examples of animals used in adverts include:

1. The Taco Bell chihuahua, aka Gidget, took a big bite out of advertising with the catchphrase "Yo Quiero Taco Bell" in 1997. The advertising impact of it is that Gidget was so wildly successful that Taco Bell used him in their advertising for three years. Aside from the commercials, you could also get your hands on a slew of promotional merchandise, most notably cute plush toys and bobbleheads (Mertes, 2020).
2. Coca-Cola is an advertising powerhouse. One of their beloved and iconic ads came out in 1993 and featured a family of polar bears sharing the fizzy drink in their arctic home. The advertising impact of this is that the "Northern Lights" campaign was a

huge success. The polar bears went on to star in commercials, holiday ads, Olympic sports, on billboards, and countless branded items like coolers, posters and t-shirts (Quality Logo Products Blog, 2020).

3. Cadbury Dairy Milk chocolate released an advert in 2007 featuring a drummer in an animatronic gorilla costume, playing the drums to Phil Collins's 1981 hit "In the Air Tonight". Featuring the gorilla made the advertisement unique and the advertisement was named by *Marketing* magazine as the nation's all-time favourite.

4. As illustrated in Figure 4.4, Fidelity International, an investment management services provider has also used a dog in their print advertisement.

5. Figure 4.5 shows another advert featuring a dog. An advertisement for AA designed by adam&eveDDB and photographed by James Day.

CELEBRITIES

This is very common in advertisements. There are celebrities+ that are endorsing a brand and their images are being used in the advertisements. These are often considered as

Figure 4.4 Fidelity International print advertisement

Source: used with permission from Fidelity International. Photograph by Jack Terry.

Figure 4.5 Advert for AA featuring a dog

Source: AA and adam&eveDDB. Photograph by James Day.

spokespersons, but it can also include influencers being used for advertisements and promotions on social media. In most cases, the name of the celebrity will be included in the advertisement. These celebrities are also considered brand ambassadors, and they can be used on any marketing communications from the brand. Santander Bank agreed a deal with Ant and Dec – presenters of Ant & Dec's Saturday Night Takeaway, Britain's Got Talent, and I'm a Celebrity . . . Get Me Out of Here! – to act as brand ambassadors for the bank. While the brands can ride on the positive vibes of these brand ambassadors, influencers and celebrities, there are some disadvantages, especially when there are scandals with the celebrity. When US Olympic swimmer Ryan Lochte lied about being robbed at gunpoint, several brands, including Speedo and Ralph Lauren, disassociated themselves from Lochte. This also affected tennis star Maria Sharapova when she failed a drug test. Likewise, brands (like Gatorade, AT&T and Accenture) cut ties with Tiger Woods after his marital infidelity scandals. Chanel and Burberry dropped British model Kate Moss as a brand ambassador as soon as the police started an inquiry into alleged cocaine use.

CHILDREN AND PARENTS

Often you can feel the love and bonds in a family when these campaigns are presented. Banks and retailers often use families as they appeal to consumers' emotions. Mogaji (2018) found that UK banks use children to convey emotional appeal in their advertisements. Nationwide had an advertisement where they used the metaphor of a scarf passed down through generations to show how supportive they have been to their customers. This is used to indicate a sense of care, support and security and assurance of being in the safe company of the brand.

STAFF MEMBERS

In 2016, Natwest Bank accepted that they had made a mistake and had to take responsibility for their actions; so, they created an advert – "We are what we do" – predominantly black and white, which was fronted by Sherene Richards, a Senior Personal Banker at the Bank (YouTube, n.d.). Currys PC World also uses images of their staff on their advertisements to demonstrate their products. Adopting staff members as images in advertisements can be considered an effort towards making the service provision tangible (Mittal, 1999; Mogaji & Erkan, 2019. Prospective customers can associate the service with people: you want a haircut (barber services), so you associate it with an image of a barber. You want to use a financial service provided by a bank; you associate it with the bank cashier. Stafford (1996) noted that effectiveness of the symbolic representation of a service brand, instead of a generalised feature of the services, works well. The use of images to either represent a physical object related to the service or customers and staff using the service as a documentation strategy led Mittal (1999) to describe it as "transformational advertising", which is the key to making the intangible tangible in service advertisements.

CEOS

While acknowledging that the strategy of "CEO as frontman" has been adopted by numerous brands in the past 30 years, Peter Daboll, CEO of Ace Metrix noted that it has never been entirely clear whether this strategy is effective because one of the biggest concerns is the failure of the CEO to come across as authentic (Daboll, 2012). Frank Perdue, the owner of Perdue chicken, has featured in many of the company's advertisements with his tagline – "It takes a tough man to grow a tender chicken". Papa John's CEO John Schnatter has featured in many of the company's adverts. The study by Ace Metrix found that Schnatter was perceived to be "authentic" and "genuine", two hallmarks of CEO ad success (Daboll, 2012). As Facebook kicked off a major national ad campaign to win back trust, there were advertisements in the newspaper with a letter bearing the signature of co-founder and CEO of Facebook, Mark Zuckerberg. Nick Grey, GTech founder, is also known to feature on company advertisements, demonstrating the unique features of their vacuum cleaner.

CUSTOMERS

A significant number of advertisement brands and advertising agencies use images of customers for advertising their products and services. The use of customers is often with the aim of giving the impression about those who use the product regularly, perhaps to convey a message that anybody can use it. The Co-operative Bank featured Richard Reynolds, one of their customers in their "It Is Good to Be Different" campaign, highlighting their ethical positioning and impact in the community in anticipation that consumers will find that appealing. Lloyds Bank has also used their business customers to highlight how they are contributing to the growth of businesses in the United Kingdom. LinkedIn likewise illustrates how users are engaging and making use of the social media network. Getting a customer to front the campaign is essential as it can build trust and connection – people see names, and there is a sense of attachment. It is not surprising to see an agency use a model and describe the model as a customer by just putting a name on him/her. That is why it is better to use a proper location, like the business location of the customer, so it can build that trust, assurance and authenticity that a customer is making those comments in the advertisements and not a model that has been paid.

MODELS

It is essential to highlight that the choice of models is a creative decision by the advertising agency. Models are considered different from celebrities or brand ambassadors, different from CEOs or customers. A model is a person with a role either to promote, display or advertise a brand or to serve as a visual aid for advertisers who are creating an advertisement for a brand (Napoli et al., 2003). Models may work professionally or casually, depending on the seriousness of the advertisement and the target audience. Models are mostly professionals, paid to model (and illustrate) how to use a product that, unlike the CEO or customers, they may not be using. Likewise, you can have the same model on different products. Notwithstanding these models can be very popular and well known to the extent that they become celebrities (like Naomi Campbell), often the models are unknown, and they are used solely for advertising the products. Agencies are scouting for models of all ages, genders and races for advertisements. Unlike celebrities or brand ambassadors, you may not have the name of the model in the advertisement (Mogaji et al., 2020). There are also a growing number of computer-generated imagery (CGI) models and influencers. CGI influencers like Miquela, Bermuda, and Shudu are now on Instagram, modelling for different brands and engaging with their followers (Dodgson, 2019).

PRODUCT

The images of the product being advertised can also be shown in the advertisement, as the product is the entity that is being offered for sale by a brand. To reach the target audience, the advertising agency can include the actual image of the product in the advertisement or use an illustrative or computer-generated image. This can be considered the most straightforward form of advertisement. If you are selling a mobile phone, put an image of a mobile phone in the advertisement. The art direction of the photograph makes a difference as the image is made to convey a meaning and interest the viewer. This highlights the benefits of creativity in conveying a message. The photographs of the image are taken from a unique angle, showing different views and features of the product. This image could feature a small part of the product and leave the viewers in suspense. It is a creative decision. For McDonald's, Costa Coffee and other restaurants, images of their food and drinks are commissioned and taken explicitly for the brand and products as they may not be available on stock photos.

Websites like Shutterstock Custom and Tribe are now working with photographers, videographers and visual artists who create authentic custom content to work with brands to plan and produce authentic content quickly and easily that fits their brand guidelines at a reasonable price. The brand gives a brief, the content creator shares the content with the brand, and the brand gets to choose the one they like. The brand can either buy the content and licence it for their advertising channels (Content Campaign) or approve the content that has been created, and the content creator will share it on their profile with their followers (Influencer Campaign).

LICENSED IMAGES

Some images may have to be licensed before being used by a brand for the marketing communication campaign. This often happens when brands decide to use an image to which they do not have the copyright or permission. This could be BT using images from the *Big Friendly Giant* movie, Sky Broadband using images from *Toy Story* and Direct Line using the *Ninja Turtles*. These film characters arouse some feelings and an attitude towards the advertisement; they are unique, and the brands can ride on the goodwill of these images, but there are financial commitments which may make this approach unsuitable for smaller brands.

MULTIPLE USAGES

Creativity suggests that the same image can be used in different contexts to convey different meanings. For example, M&S and Shelter used the picture of a sandwich to illustrate their corporate social responsibility in donating to help the homeless; Yorkshire Building Society used it for advertising their mortgage, imploring prospective customers to get their mortgage and buy lunch. Likewise, there are possibilities of having a celebrity fronting different campaigns for different brands. Understanding how and when to use the images is essential. The list of images is inexhaustible, but this section offers a general overview of the types of images that can be used in an advertisement.

Colour

Colours play an important role in advertisements. Colour is the characteristic of visual perception that is used to reinforce or project an idea in advertisements (Aslam, 2006). Advertisement agencies use colour subtly. However, this perception of colour is wholly derived from the stimulation of photoreceptor cells by electromagnetic radiation. Colour helps target audiences associate a particular brand's product, service or item with an ideal that is similar to theirs. It is essential to consider the use of colours in advertisements, as they often have attached meanings (Lichtlé, 2007). For example, blue symbolises calmness, coolness, relaxation and harmony. Grey is considered a non-emotional colour, which signifies boredom. White is regarded as a more neutral colour, which suggests cleanliness and innocence. Red stands for warmth, eroticism and anger, but also power and strength.

Brand identity

Brand identity is the collection of every element that a particular brand has developed to portray the right yet positive image to its consumer. While recognising that the brand is sending the message, the identity of the brand can also be reflected in the advertisements. This is illustrated with the blue colour of 02, the green colour of Asda and the purple colour of NatWest. These are identity elements of the brands that the advertising agency must recognise and try to adopt. They would have been discussed during the engagement with the brand (Liaising stage in Chapter 3). No doubt there are opportunities to deviate from the primary colours, but generally they are used. So, a Coca-Cola advert is most likely to have a touch of red (but probably not blue like Pepsi).

Advertisements were previously in one or two colours because of the cost of printing in colour, but these days there are opportunities for printing coloured advertisements in newspapers and having coloured advertisements on TV. However, there are instances whereby advertisements are still presented in black and white or monochrome. A good example is from First Direct Bank in the United Kingdom where most of the advertisements are in white text printed on black background. This aligns with their brand identity which has black as their primary colour.

Creative identity

The choice of colour could also be a creative decision towards aligning with an identity. This is seen with many advertisements on Black Friday where the advertisements are predominantly presented in black to correlate with the idea of Black Friday. This is also the same as the red used over Christmas and for Valentine's Day. Some brands may want to align with the Black Friday themes and have their advertisements in black but will still have a shade of their own brand identity. Besides, charity advertisements, often presented in black and white, also deserve mention; the choice of colour could be to arouse a sense of guilt or sorrow, persuading people to donate towards their appeal.

Text

This may be more applicable in print advertisements (and in images/advertisements shared on social media).

LAYOUT

Layout is an aspect of text design that deals with the arrangement of elements in advertisements. It generally involves organisational principles of composition to achieve specific communication objectives. The layout of the text can indicate the hierarchy of importance. Texts in print advertisements are copy (they are spoken words or voice-overs on broadcast media). The copy includes the headline and then the body of the text. It is arranged intentionally to stir engagement with the reader, who is more likely to read the words in the bigger fonts before reading those in the smaller fonts. Figure 4.6 illustrates the headline and the body.

The headlines are:

• Often in a bigger font, bolder and more imposing.
• They can complement, contradict or may not be relevant to the image.
• Often printed in the top part of the advert.
• They present the key messages but are also further buttressed by the body.

Figure 4.6 Illustrating headline and body in an advertisement
Source: author.

The body:

- Complements the headline and gives much more detail about the message.
- Can also complement or contradict the image in the advert.
- Often presented in lower font size and in lower case.
- Often presented at the bottom of the advertisement to better engage the reader.
- Depending on the nature of the media, newspaper or billboard, the body may contain considerably more words than the header.
- Can also include a call to action for the reader. This could be a website to visit or a number to call for more information.

As seen with the Oatly advertisement in Figure 4.7, the headline is on the left, presented in a bigger, bolder and different font while the image is in between and the body on the right has a smaller font size and length. This advertisement presents a different arrangement but the whole concept around layout is demonstrated here as well. It is important to note that on a billboard (Figure 4.8), the copy is removed as passers-by or those driving by may not be able to read all the body, so they focus more on the headline.

So what is this oat drink anyway? Milk? No, it's not milk. Milk comes from a cow. It was designed for baby cows. Oats grow. You plant them in the soil of the earth and allow the sun to shine on them and they grow. Tall and strong and full of purpose.

A couple of decades ago, we looked into the nutritional characteristics of oats and thought: what if we forgot the cow altogether and turned these oats into a drink that was designed for humans? So we did. And here it is. Please do enjoy!

Figure 4.7 Oatly advertisement
Source: Oatly.

Figure 4.8 Oatly advertisement
Source: photography by author.

TYPOGRAPH

The text in advertisements can be explored in two contexts – the typography which is the *arrangement* of the letters, as seen with the Fuel advert, the typeface is the *feature* of the letters. In essence, typography has to do with the arrangement of texts and letters in a way that makes the copy clear, legible and visually appealing to the target audience. Typography involves appearance, font style and structure, which aims to elicit certain emotions and convey specific messages to the readers of a print advertisement. Typography is used in presenting words in a creative manner to convey a message of importance and emphasis. The presentation encourages and engages with the readers and makes the message stand out (McCarthy & Mothersbaugh, 2002). An example to illustrate the creative possibilities of letters in advertisements is the advert for Oatly in Figure 4.8 where the text is arranged to create emphasis and attention. As seen with the illustration in Figure 4.9, the message is to appreciate patronage, but the focus is on the "THANK YOU" which was presented in the middle and bolder. This highlights a creative desire to arrange the works in a way to indicate hierarchy and power behind each word. Even though the same words were used yet they were arranged differently.

Figure 4.10 is an advertisement for Plus Four Market Research Ltd designed by NOAH Advertising Agency. The creative decision to turn the copy around and make it appear in reverse form makes the advertisement stand out and grabs the attention of the reader. Seeing this advertisement, you will want to engage your brain to understand the message. Likewise, Figure 4.11, which features an advertisement from Avanti West Coast, created by adam&eveDDB, highlighting the possibilities of creating a unique advertisement with text. The advertisement illustrates typography and the arrangement of words to create an engaging message. The "hello" in the advert is boldly presented to attract the readers.

TYPEFACE

The typeface is the unique feature of each of the letters. The choice of typeface to use is also an essential creative element (Wang et al., 2020). Some fonts are selected to make a bold statement while some are presented to make a friendly statement. The font size and boldness are also creative decisions to make a statement and a form of identification. So,

Figure 4.9 Typographic arrangement of same text
Source: author.

GET
TO KNOW
YOUR
CUSTOMERS
INSIDE OUT

LISTENING TO YOUR CUSTOMERS IS MORE IMPORTANT THAN EVER

What your customers want is changing and will affect the products and services they buy, how they buy them and which brands they trust. We use customer insights to help you stay one step ahead of your competition and plan more effectively for the future. As a boutique agency with 50 years' experience, we provide cost effective bespoke research solutions that could ultimately save you money. Get in touch today to discuss how we can help you move your business forward through these challenging times.

Tel: 020 8254 4444   plus4.co.uk

**plusfour
market research**

Figure 4.10 Advertisement from Plus Four Market Research Ltd

Source: brand: Plus Four Market Research Ltd, www.plus4.co.uk; client: Cara Allan, associate director; agency: NOAH, www.noahlondon.com; creative directors: Simon Mackness (copy) and Graeme Thompson (art direction).

we can say typeface is a set of characters of the same design. Typeface includes letters, punctuation marks, numbers and symbols. This is necessary for the advertiser to understand to be able to reach the target audience with a compelling message.

SERIF AND SANS-SERIF

Serif typeface contains a little decorative stroke at the end of the characters while sans-serif does not contain such decorative strokes (see Figure 4.12). It is about readability. When you are combining different typefaces, usually you will have one typeface for the heading and a different one for the body (Wayne et al., 2020). Moreover, this is to create a slight contrast and interest in your designs. Sans-serif has slightly increased readability compared to serif, which is why sans-serif is an excellent typeface for the body of

Figure 4.11 Advertisement from Avanti West Coast

Source: Avanti West Coast, adam&eveDDB and King Henry.

text. As a matter of rule, it is advised to use only two fonts in design (perhaps one from the serif family and the other from sans-serif). Too many fonts in one design is not a good thing.

WEIGHT

The typeface is presented in different weights (see Figure 4.13). There are several ranges of weight such as light, medium, bold, extra bold and so on. With creativity, you can use

THANK YOU

THANK YOU

Figure 4.12 Serif (with decorative strokes) and sans-serif (with none)
Source: author.

GOTHAM LIGHT
GOTHAM XLIGHT
GOTHAM LIGHT
GOTHAM BOOK
GOTHAM BLACK
GOTHAM ULTRA

Figure 4.13 Gotham font in different weights
Source: author.

different weights and contrast them to create exciting designs. Bold can be used for the headlines while medium is used for the rest of the copy.

SIZE

The font size is also essential to indicate emphasis and show legibility. The advertisement should have a legible font for viewers to read in newspapers (close up) or billboards (possible while walking or driving). This is not just limited to print advertisement but also applies to the font on TV advertisements or social media advertisements. As illustrated in Figure 4.14, the creative decision to vary the size of the fonts may also enhance the readability and emphasis in an advertisement. Often you want to have a balance between being too small, making it unreadable, and too big, appearing that you are "shouting".

LETTER CASE

There are opportunities to change the letter case of the letters. Some advertisement copy may have upper case while some may just have the first letter in upper case. The copy may also appear in lower case. Combining these letter case options gives a creative approach to the advertisement. Adopting the same message as in Figure 4.14, Figure 4.15 presents the messages in different cases, these are creative decisions that have been made. Now reflect on these three slides and identify which one you prefer. Some may not like all uppercase as the advert may appear "intrusive and disturbing" while some may find it more emphatic as it is needed for such public health campaign.

JUSTIFICATION

This describes how the type is arranged on a line. In most cases, the copy is aligned towards the left as there is the direction in which we read in English, but in Arabic it is justified to the right. There are also possibilities for centre justified. As illustrated in **Figure 4.16**, the first copy is left justified, the middle one is centre justified while the third one is right-justified. There is also a possibility for fully justified, which means the copy is stretched evenly across the advert.

Figure 4.14 Varying size of copy in an advert
Source: author.

Figure 4.15 Varying letter case of copy in an advert

Source: author.

Figure 4.16 Varying justification of copy in an advert

Source: author.

Shape

The shapes used in advertisements are essential tools that help advertisers create an aesthetically pleasing message. This also helps the advertisers to get their message across to their target audience in a way that the message is not offensive but appealing. The shape of an advertisement is also a graphical element that is observed. This can likewise convey a unique message about the brand – deciding on the shape to adopt is a creative decision that needs to be made and supported by the brands. This shape includes the size of the advertisement in the newspaper or billboard, the location and likewise the site and shape of the advertisement. Figure 4.17 shows an advertisement for a DeLonghi Coffee Machine on two different sides of the newspaper. This was a creative decision to buy different spaces in the newspaper and create advertisements that specifically fit those spaces. In addition, having an advertisement in London's Piccadilly Circus or New York Times Square are creative decisions that need to be made as this will influence the design (and layout) of the advertisement (Pilelienė & Grigaliūnaitė, 2016).

This shape is not limited to newspapers or billboards, but also includes the duration of an advertisement on social media, TV or even radio. These are visual elements (excluding radio) that consumers will engage with. How long or short should the advertisement be? Should it be a 5-second advertisement on YouTube or a 30-second advertisement on TV? It becomes a creative decision because the art director needs to recognise the key messages that need to be included in the 30-seconds- advertisement even though they might have two hours of raw footage from the recording. Deciding on the essential elements to include in the 30-second slot is crucial.

The financial implications of these creative elements cannot be ignored. It can be expensive to make a good advertisement. It starts from the cost of finding models, shooting the advertisement, post-production, promoting it on social media, buying media spaces like billboards and full-page adverts. These costs inadvertently have an impact on the creativity of the advertisement and how unique it might be. This has always been a challenge for advertisers, to see how best to create a unique and engaging advertisement on a budget.

Figure 4.17 Advertisement for DeLonghi coffee machine
Source: DeLonghi/GOLIN.

Audio

Audio in advertisement has to do with the music and auditory message embedded in the advert. Music in advertising is influential and can be emotionally appealing (Mogaji, 2018). It has become a standard element and a crucial feature in advertisements (Alpert et al., 2008), whether as foreground or background music. Advertisers use it in various ways to appeal to consumer emotions: making consumers smile, laugh, cry or feel nostalgic (Allan, 2006). The choice of which type of music used is a conscious and creative decision that needs to be strategic. Music for advertisements could be popular songs (including original versions), stock songs that are pre-recorded (like with stock images) or customised jingles (specifically written and produced for a specific advertisement) (Taylor, 2015). Popular songs can be expensive to use, but consumers can associate with them.

Conversely, stock songs may not be easily adapted and customised – their use can be limited even though quite affordable. Additionally, while customised music provides freedom and creates an association with the brand, it may not prove to be very popular with consumers. However, it is authentic, unique and can be more affordable, depending on the producer or the singer.

Consumers are known to favour products that elicit some degree of recognition or familiarity, and music can be used to reinforce this memorability. Craton and Lantos (2011) introduced the attitude to advertisement music (A_{am}) construct, which describes how consumers respond to advertisement music. This is a predisposition that can be considered favourable or unfavourable when consumers are exposed to music in advertisements. This is what the consumer perceives, thinks and feels when they listen to music in an advertisement – that is, how the consumer consciously experiences the music (Craton et al., 2017). Using popular song has often being used to enhance the A_{am}; it increases the memorability of a product or the product's name (Alpert et al., 2008) as the effects of such popular songs linger on in the consumers' minds. Popular music is considered the most used. This is "well-liked and well-favoured" music (Middleton, 1990), listened to by "ordinary people" (Shuker, 1994) and has broad exposure and appeal, but usually only for a fixed period (Allan, 2006). It has been used extensively to get the attention of the young demographic (Chou & Singhal, 2017) as it is involving, engaging and can persuade the potential consumer to purchase the advertised product or service (Allan, 2006). Chou and Lien (2014) noted that it could be used to evoke consumer nostalgia in response to TV commercials. Content analysis of music in Super Bowl commercials revealed that popular music was used in more than a quarter of the commercials analysed (Allan & Tryce, 2016).

Most research on music in advertising shows that popular music is most often considered. Allan (2006) highlighted three typologies based on popular music: advertising using original popular music vocals; altered popular music vocals; and original popular music instrumentals. However, it is essential to note that there are many other forms of music relevant to advertisements, which highlights further gaps in knowledge that need to be explored. Roehm (2001) identified the prospects of using unfamiliar song and instrumentals, suggesting that vocal versions of a different song can be very useful. Furthermore, instrumentals can be more effective in evoking the advertising message recall if the song is already familiar. Likewise, some jingles are "catchy songs about a product or service that usually carry the advertising theme and a simple message" (Belch & Belch, 2015, p. 325). These are not popular songs but customised songs specifically for the advertisement. Though its use has declined over the last few decades, some advertisers still consider the relevance for their campaign (Taylor, 2015).

FOREGROUND MUSIC

Foreground music is playing when the artist is not talking. This music conveys the message of the advertisement without the voice-over. Often the foreground music contains lyrics/copy about the product or services. This is often used in radio advertisements whereby the advertisement is the songs that are being played. These are also called jingles, especially written and produced songs for a specific advertisement (Taylor, 2015). They are "catchy songs about a product or service that usually carry the advertising theme and a simple message" (Belch & Belch, 2015, p. 325).

BACKGROUND MUSIC

This is the music being played when the artist is talking in the advertisement. These songs go in the background and complement the voice-over or the artist involved in the advertisement. This could be an instrumental, a popular song or a customised song. In addition, background music used in advertisements refers to a deliberate mode of musical performance that accompanies the presentation of an advert. It is worthy of note that this background music is not intended by advertisers to be the main focus of the target audience; however, its character, content and volume level are intentionally preselected to affect the behavioural and emotional responses of the target audience. Most of the time these responses could be relaxation, concentration, distraction, joy, happiness, excitement or sympathy. Advertisers use background music to drive home their points and inadvertently force the target audience into listening to the message being presented. It also happens that adverts with background music create a certain connection between the advert and the target audience to the extent that the target audience can immediately recognise the advert whenever he/she hears that unique background music.

VOICE-OVER

This is the voice of the person reading/saying the copy of the advert. These are spoken words on advertisements on broadcast media such as radio and TV, and videos on social media. Most times, advertising agencies hire a popular actor/actress to this effect. The voice-over is read from a script and may be spoken by a specialist voice talent. The voice-over is a critical component of advertising, conveying brand messages and connecting with an audience emotionally. Like the typography is the text for advertisements, the voice-over brings a different level of engagement to the text of an advertisement. This is not just about reading a text but recognising the impact of the tempo and tune on how the advertisement is being delivered. Voice-over varies in gender, accents and pace. There are calls for having more women star in audio creative roles as voice-over artists, as men predominately dominate it.

Typology of music in advertisement

Mogaji (2019) developed a typology of music in advertising, focusing on the originality of the music and the level of interaction.

High involving popular music

The audience knows these songs already as they have received massive airplay. This type of song has a very wide appeal and is typically known and loved by large audiences. The audience for this type of song cuts across age, religion, tribe, income and other forms of disparity. This could also be a remixed version sung by another musician or one which Allan (2006) describes as "original popular music instrumentals". These are all still derivatives of popular music. Also, characters sing, dance or engage in activities that align with the song being played. An example from the Super Bowl is the NFL advertisement where players (Manning and Beckham Jr.) were practising passing routes and recreated the iconic dance scene from the 1987 hit movie *Dirty Dancing* to the theme song (I have had) "The Time of My Life" sung by Bill Medley and Jennifer Warnes. This is an incredibly popular song but was not just used as a background song as the main characters were involved in the advertisement.

Low involving popular music

These are popular songs – people know the tune and are familiar with the lyrics. However, the difference is that there is less engagement with the song. There is not much congruency and infusion between the songs or the characters in the advert. Budweiser's 2018 Super Bowl commercial used a very popular song, "Stand by You", but it was used as background music and actors were not involved. Considering it is a popular song, it can arouse a positive emotion towards the advert, but because it is less involving, it can also discourage the audience. However, this can also be seen as suitable for some types of product whereby the message of the advertisements needs to be more emphatic, and the background music complements the message. Brands were using popular songs but not in congruency with the character's involvement. Often, this type of music is used without a voice-over.

High involving customised music

These are customised songs, created explicitly for the advertisements. The lyrics are used to communicate messages which offer advertisers the opportunity for both logical, factual and emotionally appealing advertisements (Huron, 1989). Even though they are customised, they are still engaging. Characters in the advertisements engage with the song, as they dance and sing along. Sainsbury's 2017 Christmas advert in the United Kingdom was centred around an upbeat, festive song written by lyricist Ben "Doc Brown" Smith and was composed by Mikis Michaelides. The song was specially commissioned for the campaign which features members of the public and Sainsbury's colleagues singing about the things that help them to live well at Christmas time. This type of music for advertisements can be expensive as the songs are customised, especially if professional songwriters, producers or artists are involved.

Low involving customised music

These appear to be the most common and easy option for using music in advertisements. They are customised songs but may not be as engaging or involving as others. This is because they are often used as background music. This can often be from two sources. Firstly, music is commissioned for the advertisement. Secondly, the music could also be a form of stock music. This is "pre-recorded music that can be rented or bought" (Russell & Lane, 1999, p. 549). The Jeep Jurassic advertisement used the theme song from *Jurassic Park*, composed by John Williams. Bud Light's Bud Knight ad used a commercial song from *The Sound Lounge*. This song was produced especially for the commercial, and it has not been made available to purchase or download.

Case study 4.1

Subway (w)rap battle

When Subway was launching their new wraps product, the Signature Loaded Wraps, they invited rappers Tommy B, Lady Sanity and MysDiggi to create short tracks for the advertisements. These lyrical geniuses were asked to go head-to-head in a (W)rap battle with the honorary Sandwich Artist, TrueMendous as they order their wraps and she ends each order by saying, "You can rap, it's just that Subway can wrap better." This campaign featured three head-to-head (W)rap battle videos.

The campaign was able to use the music to address two key features of an advertisement. First, the rap became the spoken works, which is the copy of the advertisement; the rap artists were rapping about the features of the different wraps they were ordering. Second, the wrap became the background music of the advertisement; it was well integrated into the advertisement and not distracting.

These advertisements contain high involving customised music where the characters are fully involved in the advertisement. The song was specifically created and customised for the product. The music can be played on its own (perhaps on radio) while still retaining a link with Subway. Importantly as well, Subway has gone with upcoming artists who are more likely to have a cheaper commissioning fee and the artists are given the opportunity to showcase their skills. This alliance is beneficial for both parties.

You can watch the adverts here -

- www.youtube.com/watch?v=aeUEItUgATI (Tommy B)
- www.youtube.com/watch?v=YZ582CEiYzE (Lady Sanity)
- www.youtube.com/watch?v=iJDTdC8wJ2M (MysDiggi)

Selecting the music in advertisements

Choosing a popular song and getting the artist involved in the advert could be very good as seen with Tom Jones' "Things go better with Coca- Cola", Michael Jackson's "New Generation" and David Bowie and Tina Turner's "Creation" for Pepsi which highlight the possibilities for involving characters in advertisements. Also, familiarity is considered an essential element in advertising (Krishna et al., 2016), justifying the use of popular music or the possible commission of a famous artist to sing about the product. However, the cost implication of using a popular song should be acknowledged, suggesting why customised or stock music may be advisable.

However, a better option could be using the music from an upcoming artist. Moreover, there are considerable benefits to using music from an upcoming artist: (1) it can be seen as customised and unique because it has not received much publicity or airplay; (2) this lack of awareness allows the advertisements to break through the media clusters as this is something that was not previously very popular and not everyone has heard it before; (3) it can be considerably more affordable than using a more popular song from an established artist or customising a song, and also, the upcoming artist feels appreciated and supported in their career; (4) this could lead to a co-creation and increase the equity of the brand as the artist will be willing to be associated with the advert and share among their contacts. With customised music, there is a sense of uniqueness to the advertisements and with the possibilities of breaking through media clusters. Copies of the song can also be sold or given away as a download, leading to more engagement and co-creation of values. It can be considered worthwhile because it is unique and can be specifically customised to meet the style of the advertisements, and the art director has the liberty to direct the song as seen fit. Likewise, this type of music can be used to break clusters in a global market. Global brand owners can commission local artists to develop songs they can use in their advertisements, and local audiences can perform different dance steps to the music.

Customised music can be a worthwhile investment in production. With the right music producer and art director, music can be made to align with the main idea of the advertisement. Often the brand owner will have full rights to the music and can control how it is shared. It can become the brand's identity and sensory marketing (Craton et al., 2017). However, the cost implications of this arrangement should not be ignored as it may be seen as more expensive. Stock music, on the other hand, is considered a cheaper alternative when in need of customised music for an advertisement. It is, however, relatively less involving and it may not offer the creative liberty to align with the message of the advertisement. It could also be bought by many other people who may be interested in using it for their advertisements; thereby, the music may no longer be unique for an advert. Legal issues with royalties and rights may also be an issue to consider when using stock music.

Touch

This highlights another physical element for creating an advertisement. This recognises the texture of print advertisements and importantly braille as an effort towards diversity and inclusion. Hertenstein et al. (2009) also highlighted the importance of touch. Considered as the first language we learn, touching, right from the womb, remains our richest means of emotional expression throughout life.

Printed material

This recognises the quality of paper in which the advertisements have been printed. This is, however, limited to just print media. There are situations in which the front cover of newspapers is printed on glossy paper which are different from the usual and other pages of the newspaper. For the release of the iPhone 8, O2 offered an additional incentive for contract deals; cover of the first screen replacement. To convey their message, the cover of *Metro* newspaper contained the headline of the campaign – "Oops" – which included a media-first: a translucent double cover wrap on *Metro*. The first layer of the wrap created the effect of broken glass, while the second layer was branded with "Oops"; an execution which conveyed O2's simple quick fix to broken screens. Overall, 2.7 million people were exposed to the cover wrap. There are also possibilities of having inserts in a newspaper printed on thick paper. This also includes handbills and leaflets printed on thick paper to convey prestige, value and authenticity.

Braille

In 2017, Mars brand, Maltesers used model chocolates to create a braille poster to champion diversity in advertising. The advert, which appeared on a London bus shelter, spells out the words: "Caught a really fast bus once, turns out it was a fire engine." Agency AMV BBDO designed the poster. This perhaps seems to be the only type of strategy, but it conveys a creative idea to engage with audiences who may not be able to see advertisements because they are visually impaired.

Advertising appeals

Advertising appeals are used to influence consumers' attention towards the advertisement and attitude towards the brand. Mishra (2009) argued that advertising appeal provides a reason to buy a product, through the central message of the advertising, presenting something that attracts consumers and develops their interest in the product. Johar and Sirgy (1991) noted that the choice of a proper appeal is one of advertisers' most crucial creative strategy decisions; some advertisements are designed to be rationally appealing while others are designed to be emotionally appealing (Srivastava & Sharma, 2008).

Arousing emotions has been found to mediate the way an advertisement is processed (Percy & Rosenbaum-Elliott, 2016) as advertisers must encode messages in such a way that consumers can understand and decode them, in addition to creating a positive attitude to the brand (Duncan & Moriarty, 1998). Advertisements are professionally conceived and developed communication messages which are persuasive by intent and design (Pollay & Gallagher, 1990). Appeals are incorporated into advertisements in the form of text, images, background music and voice-over to attract viewers' attention and provide information about the brand. Advertising appeals offer reasons and motivation for getting the attention of the viewers, thereby leading to a positive attitude towards the advertised product or service (Mogaji, 2018).

Advertisement appeals are commonly classified as emotional or rational; however, they are sometimes referred to as transformational, evaluative or feeling for emotionally appealing advertisements, and informational, factual or thinking for rationally appealing advertisements. Bagozzi et al. (1999) noted that advertisements can be classified according to their content – thinking and feeling advertisements. Information and product attributes are presented in thinking ads, which could be representing rational appeals while feeling ads are value-expressive, concentrating on creating a sense of belonging through using the product, appealing to consumers' emotions.

To understand this better, advertising appeals are the conscious creative decision made regarding the development, content, layout and distribution of a marketing campaign, either to appeal to your brain – rational appeal – or appeal to your heart – emotional appeal. Mishra (2009) concluded that the appeals incorporated into the advertisement form the core of the message, providing the motivation to consider the product, and therefore need to be unique and present something that fascinates the consumers and develops their interest in the product.

Rational appeals in advertisements

Practical and functional features of a product or service are often presented as rational appeals (Bovée & Arens, 2000). Kotler and Armstrong (2013) submit that rational appeal highlights the features and benefits of a product; it showcases how it differs from others, thus allowing customers to make an informed decision based on logic. Rational appeals emphasise the essential attributes and associated benefits of the product or service. They are informative, based on the logic and reasons for buying the product, and focus on the product's suitability (Baines et al., 2013; Mishra, 2009).

A rational appeal in advertising places more emphasis on the factual information and specific details of a product and its benefits. It gives users/consumers of a product more details on how to use the product or why the product is best among the rest. Furthermore, rational appeals motivate through information; they are presented in the form of testimonies from previous uses, boldly written prices, reviews and star ratings, awards and recognitions, staff competencies and other factual details to convince prospective consumers that they are making the right choice. For example, a laser surgery clinic will want to showcase the level of their doctor's competency, their number of years of experience, industry awards and recognition. This information is provided for consumers to make an informed decision. Such clinics are often loaded with information, often used for advertising a high involving product (Involvement and FCB Grid Theory).

Emotional appeals in advertisements

Emotional appeal is described as "any communication that is intended to elicit an emotional response from some or all who receive it" (Brader, 2006, p. 68), it focuses on the psychological parts of consumers' desires and the feelings associated with the product (Mishra, 2009; Bovée & Arens, 2000). Baines et al. (2013) suggested that they are based upon consumers' feelings and emotions.

Advertisements embedded with emotional appeals are meant to appeal to consumers' hearts, making them feel special, and a part of the brand. Luxury brands often use this strategy to appeal to consumers; for example, a perfume is advertised on a full page of *Elle* which has been endorsed by a celebrity and surprisingly the price is not indicated (unlike in rational appeals). This is presented to appeal to your heart – you want to start imagining how the perfume will look good on you when you wear it and you feel special by wearing what your adored celebrity is wearing; with your heart loving it already, you are more likely to convince your brain to justify the price when you later find out.

Johar and Sirgy (1991, p. 27) describe it as the image strategy – "a value-expressive advertising appeal, (which) holds a creative objective to create an image of the generalised use of the advertised brand". Aaker and Stayman (1992) describe emotional advertisements as those serving mainly to elicit effective responses. Emotionally appealing advertisements have been found to increase loyalty and make brands distinct (Panda et al., 2013). It is essential to know that emotional appeals are creative strategies to present an advertising message in a manner that the prospective customers can relate to and appreciate. Therefore, emotional appeals in advertisements deal with advertising messages that are generally based on imagery, rather than details or factual information, which attempts to achieve the advertisers objectives by evoking strong emotional feelings (anger, fear, passion, etc.) rather than by a rational appeal.

Types of emotional appeals

Emotional appeals are classified as positive and negative emotional appeals. Negative emotional appeals inspire feelings of fear, guilt and shame – for instance, they are often used in public health campaigns against, for example, smoking or driving under the influence of drugs or alcohol (Gagnon et al., 2010). On the other hand, positive emotions reduce irritation and allow better judgement of the message, which leads to a higher intention to buy the product or service when used in advertisements (Morris et al., 2002). Positive appeals include love, joy and excitement.

Regarding the various lists of advertising appeals, there has never been a consensus as it depends on how the appeals can be interpreted and presented in text or images. This is considered a challenge for both practitioners and academia in identifying a unified list of emotional appeals. Cho and Cheon (2005) suggest that appeals are often interchanged with values because appeals are used to attract the values a consumer holds; they concluded that values are the underlying source of appeals. Mogaji (2016) developed an applicable set of appeals by combining Pollay's (1983) emotional advertising appeals, Moriarty's (1991) emotional appeal list, precisely because it contained negative emotional appeals, Fowles's (1998) 15 advertising appeals and Hetsroni's (2000) list, leading to an applicable typology of 15 emotional appeals. These appeals are – adventure (escape, freedom), affiliation, beauty (aesthetics/ornamental), excitement (humour, happiness, joy), family (nurture), fear (danger, personal embarrassment), guilt, popular, relief (relaxation), secure, sex, sorrow (grief, suffering, poignancy), status – pride/achievement, tradition (nostalgia) and youth.

How are they presented: conduits and channels of emotional appeal

Advertising appeals in advertisements are presented through a combination of the various creative elements. These include the choice of colour to arouse particular emotions, the use of images and the number of words that are provided in the advertisement.

COLOURS

Colours are considered critical graphic elements in arousing emotions and generating attention towards the advertisement across various media. They create an emotional tone and can also be a dominant feature within the advertisement (Salander, 2010). The difference in attention to advertisements based on the colours that are used has been substantial. Percy and Elliott (2016) noted the reduction in attention paid to advertisements in black and white compared to coloured, suggesting that coloured advertisements are useful in transmitting emotion and viewers can engage with them better.

Coloured advertisements have also been found to enhance the positive perception of a brand and increase the trust in the advertised product (Meyers-Levy & Peracchio, 1995). In addition to attracting attention, Lester (2006) noted a link between the eyes and the brain; the colours are acknowledged and interpreted accordingly which enhances the arousal of emotions by the advertisement. As emotions are considered responses to stimuli which vary from individual to individual, various cultural meanings attached to colours are also acknowledged. Lester (2006) also found that broader cultural meanings can be connected to colours. Individuals react differently to colours and the emotional responses elicited play an essential role in determining whether the advertisement will be accepted or rejected by consumers (Ang & Low, 2000).

There are considerable differences in colour perception across gender, age, culture and even religion and this affects how creative decisions are made. Meanings associated with different colours are valuable to marketers because, if consumers associate specific meanings with individual colours and colour combinations, this will also affect their emotional reaction towards any colourful advertisement. Understanding the effects of colours in advertising is critical in international marketing (De Bortoli & Maroto, 2011).

IMAGES

Images are considered very important as visual cues for emotional appeals. Notably, a significant amount of research has been carried out on the use and importance of images in advertisements, which includes the use of eye-tracking devices to explore how viewers engage with images, highlighting the importance of an appropriate image in creating positive attitudes towards both the advertisements and the brand. Advertising images are sophisticated forms of visual rhetoric and representations that are used to encourage consumers into buying a certain product or using a certain service.

An emotionally appealing image can be considered as the primary channel of communication, replacing copy and headlines as the most crucial element in advertisements (Brader, 2006; Mezo, 1997; Salander, 2010). It can be considered as an essential feature of a print advertisement, often the body presented on the page; it is of considerable significance as well that these images, when embedded with emotional appeals, can convey emotions and arouse viewers' emotions more strongly than headlines and copy (Salander, 2010).

Unnava and Burnkrant (1991) described images as nonverbal stimuli commonly used in advertisements to buttress product attributes discussed in the verbal copy of the advertisement. They concluded that images in advertisements increase the recall of verbal information and the advertisement. Clow et al. (2005) noted that choosing an image that is memorable and that matches the written copy of the advertisement can enhance a positive inclination towards the brand and advertisement, which in turn directs attention to the brand and increases intention to purchase.

While examining emotional cues in advertisements targeting parents, Stanton and Guion (2013) found the use of images an interesting point of comparison among their respondents; images of babies and mothers were found appealing and led to the respondent's attention to the rest of the advertisement. Fowles (1998) noted that the images of two women drinking coffee together and of two men walking through the woods smoking cigarettes served as image strategies to arouse an appeal to friendship. Even without seeing the picture, the description can evoke feelings of love and happiness.

Researchers have indicated that consumers can recall information presented in a visual format better than verbal copy, suggesting that visual elements make them more firmly identify with the brand. Unnava and Burnkrant (1991) reported in their study that pictures in advertisements enhance consumer ability to remember the product features. Scott (1994) suggested that images do not just provide the usual meaning to advertisements, they are symbolic artefacts, deeply rooted in conventions of various cultures. Consumers may decode different messages from visual elements based on personal and cultural differences. However, textual elements in advertisements could be different; the understanding of written words in an advertisement may not be relative.

In understanding the appropriateness of an image to be used in advertisements, Scott (1994) identified three ideas: first, the cultural background of the viewers; second, the individuals' interpretation of the image as part of a past experience; and last, a sophisticated mental process that allows the individuals to think deeply in order to understand the abstract and conceptual images. The choice of image requires imagination and judgement. If the advertisers decide to use an abstract image, it will be essential to know whether the viewers can relate to it. Visuals – images, photographs and illustrations used in print advertisements can be interpreted differently based on individual and cultural differences which have been developed since childhood and reinforced throughout life.

The link between visual elements used in advertisements and the emotional appeals experienced by viewers has been established; it is agreed that emotional content from an advertisement generates an affective response that impacts attitudinal responses and determines the advertisement's effectiveness. Chowdhury et al. (2011) concluded, however, that more images in an advertisement do not necessarily make a difference in making the advertisement more efficient, as a single emotionally appealing image can have the same effect. What Chowdhury is saying here is that you do not need to put too many images in your advertisement to communicate your intentions, to sell your products or services to the customers or to make the message appealing to the consumers. A one-image advertisement can do the magic and spread the message for you.

SIZE

An empirical study of advertising techniques by Pollay (1985) found that advertisement sizes increased in the first 80 years of the twentieth century and that this growth in size was accompanied by a reduction in the amount of text in advertisements and an increase in the use of images. Advertisements presented in large sizes have been empirically found to attract more attention and produce a more favourable attitude (Rossiter & Percy, 1997). The role of advertisement size in getting the attention of the consumers cannot be ignored, as Elliott (1995) reported that an increase in the size of an advertisement increases the amount of attention it receives.

Brands can communicate implicit messages through their advertisement position and sizes. There are expensive print advert sizes such as cover wrap, double spread and full pages which attract attention and have a unique presentation, perhaps a sense of prestige and exclusivity, saying "*we are not cheap*" and, coupled with excellent images and text, they enhance the possibilities of arousing more positive emotions.

Advertisement size includes not only print options, but also various outdoor campaigns, e.g., billboards, posters and bus shelters. Similar to size in print advertisements, brands can use these outdoor spaces to make ground-breaking statements about their products and services. In 2014, LG created a massive billboard in Saudi Arabia that was awarded the "the largest outdoor advertising structure" by Guinness World Records. This approach enabled the company to differentiate itself from its competitors.

As something that we see, it is essential to note that advertisement size not only conveys emotional appeal, but also combines various other creative elements such as images and text – and even the location where the advertisement is placed also contributes to the effectiveness of the advertisement. High street billboard advertisements will have little text, enabling passers-by to read what is being communicated, compared to a newspaper advertisement, which may include more copy, as people can read it at their own pace. The latter may also be the case for advertisements in bus shelters or at the airport, where people have more time to observe them.

Advertisements on TV are often between 15 and 30 seconds long, depending on cost. Social media, however, offers the opportunity to better engage with consumers and additional opportunities for conduits to transfer emotional appeals. There are roughly two-to-three-minute advertisements on Facebook and YouTube, delivering a more in-depth message than on TV. Background music can last longer, and additional images and words can be included. As such, in addition to how emotional appeals are presented, the duration of an advertisement is considered critical.

TEXT

The text used in advertisements is considered as a verbal component; it includes all of the headlines, taglines and copy used to narrate the marketing communications. It must be clear, uncomplicated, direct, appropriately expressed and relevant to the target audience, and must be connected with the other components of the advertisement, including the visuals (Wilmshurst & Mackay, 2010; Decrop, 2007). Bovée and Arens (2000) concluded that the verbal components of an advertisement close the deal. Decrop (2007) found that textual elements of an advertisement must provide the customers with information regarding the advertised product or brand, emphasising its benefits and creating an intention to buy.

Just like a photograph is considered the most prominent visual component of an advertisement, the headline in a print advertisement is regarded as the most prominent textual element. Verbal cues, presented in the form of headlines and copy used in advertisements, can also evoke positive emotional appeals like excitement and joy, or negative feelings like fear and shame, as observed by Stanton and Guion (2013). The text presented in advertisements can evoke a range of emotional appeals, including happiness ("Best family vacation ever!"), confidence ("Recommended by doctors", "Quality you can trust") and negative emotions like shame ("Do not be fooled – not all formulas are alike"). This means advertisements with a conspicuous image and fewer textual elements can help advertisers and brands spread their message when the right words are used for the headline or caption. That way, the consumers or audience will be able to link the words said with the image and get the point of the advertisement being placed by the brand.

MUSIC

Emotional appeals can also be presented through what consumers hear in advertisements; this varies from background music, a voice-over and even the dialogue in the advertisement.

It is important to note that music, like images and text, is not an emotional appeal, but a channel for conveying the appeal; music is an external stimulus in advertisements that triggers emotions. Music contributes to the effectiveness of advertisements, particularly if it aligns with the storyline and voice-over of the advertisement. Popular songs are the most effective at invoking an emotional response, with pop songs delivering emotive power, while other genres are better suited to advertisements that appeal to rationality, in which advertisers attempt to get information across to audiences (Schiffer, 2015).

Huron (1989) presents six primary ways in which music can contribute to an effective broadcast advertisement: (1) entertainment; (2) structure/continuity; (3) memorability; (4) lyrical language; (5) targeting; (6) authority establishment. In addition to the entertainment purpose of music in advertisements, some songs are incredibly memorable. If consumers have an attachment to a particular genre or artist, these attachments can be transferred to brands. Advertisers often use familiar and popular sounds to engage with customers, giving rise to a sense of excitement, happiness and love – even a sense of uniqueness and exclusivity if they can retain an artist to sing a cover song for their advertisement.

In addition to what we hear in an advertisement that can trigger emotional responses, a voice-over can add to the complexity, ambiguity and hybridity of audio elements in terms of arousing emotional responses (Li, 2017). Voice-overs are commonly used in advertisements across the world (Brown, 2012); the choice of gender of the individual speaking the voice-over is often strategically considered (Strach, et al., 2015), and variation in terms of tone, accent or pace can all affect how the advertisement will be perceived and the emotions it arouses.

TEXTURE

In reaching out to a diversified marketplace in a diverse country such as the United Kingdom (Mogaji, 2015), appealing to consumers' emotions concerns not just what they can see or hear. Some individuals may not be able to experience emotions from the above sources, and as such, not surprisingly, brands are reaching out to their less-abled customers. It is essential to point out the creative approach taken by Mars chocolate in London as discussed above. This was an effort to engage with a different audience and arouse emotions as well as a positive attitude towards the brand.

The quality of the printed paper can also be considered a channel for emotional appeal, particularly for advertisements in newspapers, magazines or handbills and leaflets. Emotional appeals aim to arouse an emotional response towards an advertisement and, thereby, towards the brand. Glossy paper is applicable when using explicit photographs; silk is known for providing a luxurious and quality feel, while uncoated paper, slightly more expensive, is often used to induce an association with the environment, and where the focus is the message, not the medium (Premier Print Group, 2017). The choice of paper aims to convey a message of class, luxury and prestige. Texture refers to the surface qualities of an object. They can be smooth, suggesting refined tastes, or rough, suggesting toughness. This might be the distinction, for example, between an ad for Lexus and one for Chevy trucks. The surface features suggest the different associations attached to those different vehicles (Walter Johnson 2019).

In understanding the integration of all these elements to achieve an appealing advertisement, AMV BBDO's Walter Campbell, responsible for the Guinness "Surfer" ad, estimates he listened to about 2,000 tracks, searching for "the sound of the blood in the surfer's head when he is on the waves, and he knows he could die". It was pure chance he came across Leftfield's "Phat Planet"; it had not been released yet but was recommended by someone he knew who had worked on the film *Breaking the Waves.* "The one thing you do not need to tell people about Guinness is that it is Irish" (Vizard, 2018). This highlights how tactical and demanding it can be to select creative elements for a unique advertisement. Figure 4.18 presents the flow from the decision on the right visual elements to creating an advertising appeal, which is then shared on a suitable advertising media which the consumer can engage with.

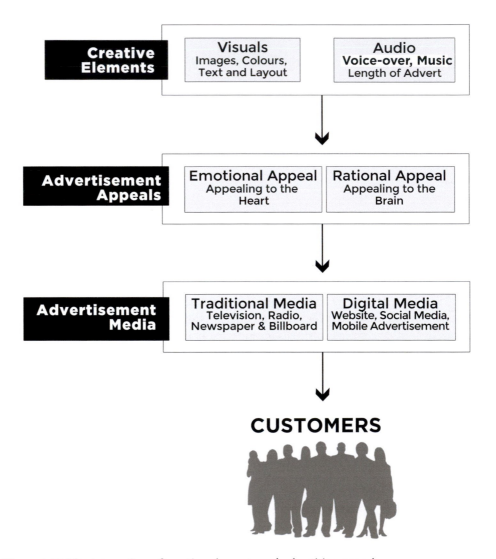

Figure 4.18 The integration of creative elements and advertising appeal
Source: author.

Limitations of emotional appeals

Advertisers must use the right appeals for the right products, and there are many creative options to combine to arouse emotions through advertisements. However, there are some limitations to emotional appeals in advertising, suggesting that one cap does not necessarily fit all; individuals engage with advertisements on different levels, and so also different emotions are aroused.

PRODUCT DIFFERENCES

There are conflicting suggestions regarding which appeals are most suitable for different kinds of products. However, it is essential to know that emotional appeals are not ideal for all products or services. For example, a laser eye surgery clinic might not want to use an emotional appeal to present a delicate service they are providing – doing laser eye surgery is not a joke. They might want to adopt a rationally appealing strategy where they highlight their success rate, experiences of their doctors and testimonies from other customers. Also, a funeral home will have to incorporate an emotional appeal in their advertisements that is different from a care home because they are offering various services and targeting different customers, indicating the need to differentiate the product or services with regard to an emotional appeal strategy to adopt if needed.

CULTURAL DIFFERENCES

It has been argued that advertisements which contain emotional appeals may be interpreted differently across various cultures and the cultural setting can influence this; associated means to the images and text and the advertising regulations, as well as emotional advertising is prone to differences in interpretation across cultures (Chang & Li, 2010; Scollon et al., 2004). This suggests that an emotional appeal for a product in one country may not necessarily work in another country, where they might not find it appealing. Huang (1997) thought that basic emotions could be suitable for global advertising campaigns to be featured in any culture because of their homogeneous characteristics. These primary/basic emotions are understood and universally accepted, but secondary emotions are socially constructed and may not be suitable for advertisements across different cultures (for example, humour is not necessarily universal). Differences in use of words to express emotions across different cultures is also a limitation for advertisers (Ortony & Turner, 1990).

INDIVIDUAL DIFFERENCES

It has also been found that individual variables, like gender and age, can affect advertisements' appeal. For instance, the presence of a baby in an image could be appealing to everyone, but for a woman trying to have a baby the picture might not create the desired appeal, as her present needs may cause an undesirable predisposition to the advertisement and brand. Variation in the intensity of the responses and attitude may limit the effectiveness of an emotionally appealing advertisement. This supports the claim that two people can be exposed to the same episode but have different emotional responses (Bagozzi et al., 1999).

However, regardless of these limitations, it is an accepted idea that emotional appeals in advertisements, when appropriately used, may enhance the audience's attitude to the advertisement and the brand, and increase purchasing intentions. It is, however, crucial to note that a particular advertisement might not be suitable for all products or services, cultures, and audience demographics. These factors need to be considered when deciding on which appeals to use to make the advertisement as efficient as possible. Figure 4.19 illustrates a summary of the creative elements and the advertising appeals derived from the integration of creative elements into an advertisement.

Selecting the creative elements

Now that all the creative elements have been discussed, they are available in the tool kits. These creative elements are rather like different colours on an artist's palette and

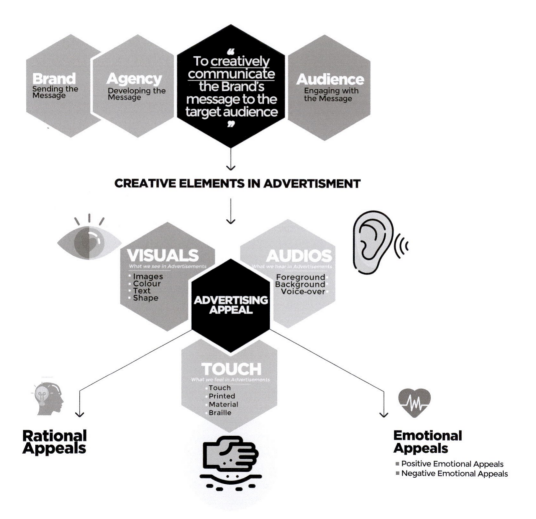

Figure 4.19 Summary of creative elements and advertising appeal
Source: author.

it is essential they are properly mixed to make a good painting. Advertisers are expected to select various creative elements and come up with how best to mix everything to deliver the message. The ability to hold together these seemingly inconsistent components of an advertisement is considered to be creativity (O'Guinn et al., 2006). Yu (2007) also described creativity in an advertisement as a combination of visuals and textual headings in a well laid-out manner which affects how the target audience will perceive it.

Case study 4.2

Same image and same copy

Images and copy (text) are creative elements in advertisements, often selected to complement each other. These creative elements are consciously selected and created to convey the right meaning. This case study highlights two different campaigns and how they have used images and text.

The first campaign is for Beefie Sausage Rolls. The copy says "the new bigger, fill you faster" and the advertisement shows different images of equipment filling up things like an industrial air pump being used to blow a balloon and a fire hydrant filling a drinking cup. (Figures 4.20, 4.21 and 4.22). These images show how the sausage roll can perform and deliver satisfaction at an exponential rate. The campaign maintained the same copy but used different images. On the other hand, the second campaign, for Skye Bank, has the same image – the skyline of the marina in Lagos Nigeria – but instead used different copy for the series (Figures 4.23, 4.24 and 4.25). The copy no doubt makes an effort to reiterate the idea of the sky and the services provided by the Bank.

Here you see different creative elements that have been adopted for these campaigns – different images with the same copy and different copy with the same image. This recognises the different roles within the advertising process – the designer and art director selecting an image that can convey the key message, albeit in an abstract manner, and the copywriter working on the right words to use on the advert, while aligning with the core idea of the campaign.

Reflective questions

1. What are the benefits of using an image that aligns with the copy in the advertisement?
2. What are the advantages and disadvantages of using different images for an advertisement campaign?
3. What are the advantages and disadvantages of using different copy for an advertisement campaign?

Figures 4.20–4.22 Advertisement for Beefie Sausage Roll: balloon (left), pan (center), cup (right).

Source: agency: Fuel; creative director: Tunde Makinwa; associate creative director/art director: Olalekan Akinyele; copywriter: Ayo Moore.

Figures 4.23–4.25 Skye Bank advertisement

Source: agency: Fuel; creative director/copywriter: Korede Zakariya; associate creative director/art director: Olalekan Akinyele.

Recognising your role

With the understanding of various creative elements, it is now time to add various elements of advertising together to deliver the campaign. However, before proceeding on this section, it is essential to understand your role. Four options are possible here.

Freelancer

A freelance advertiser is a self-employed advertiser who offers advertising services for multiple clients at one time. This type of advertiser is not, most times, directly responsible to any brand or agency. You could be a freelancer or an upcoming creative designer working for a brand, and this role is most likely to be for a small and medium enterprise which includes startups. You will be responsible for the conceptualisation, design, development and dissemination of the advertisements. Your client has given you full control, and you are responsible for effective delivery of a creative advertisement to convey the message. You can take pride in your work, build your portfolio and expand your business into a boutique agency.

Designer in an agency

You could be working in an advertising agency, possibly as a junior or middleweight designer. You are working on a project, and you may have been tasked to come up with an idea which you will show to the rest of the creative team. You will be creative, able to think on your feet and demonstrate your understanding of the psychology of selling and consumer behaviour, and able to convince and engage through design.

Copywriter in an agency

You could also be working in an advertising agency as a copywriter, researching to know more about the brands and how to craft their messages engagingly. You will have great communication and verbal skills. Working with the creative team, creating headlines, long and short copy texts for advertisements, an ability to develop storyboards and create content for web, press and social media will likely be parts of your job description as a copywriter for an advertising agency.

In-house designer

There are also opportunities for you to work in-house within a company. You could be responsible for the communication process or engage with the team from the advertising agency. This is seen as the client-side of the advertising business. There are possibilities as well for switching roles between the client's side and the agency side.

Recognising your challenges

While you have recognised your role, other challenges need to be considered as you embark on selecting and integrating the creative elements. Recognising the challenge is essential in the advertising industry. This is because you cannot defeat an enemy that you do not really understand or cannot identify – it is important you know your challenges, shortcomings and obstacles before you proceed with your advertising job. In life generally, some challenges can be easy to identify and accept. Others are more difficult to identify and accept. This is the same with advertising. Now, let us discuss these advertising challenges.

The brand

As discussed in Chapter 2, the brand is sending the message with the assistance of an advertising agency (which you work for); it is therefore essential to understand the values and features of the brand. What do they stand for? How would you want to communicate their message? How was their last advertisement? Can you build on it or do you want to deviate? Which agency was working with them before you got the pitch? Why did they change? Are you their first agency? Understanding these working principles will help you in shaping your design strategy. You may also want to understand their budget and target consumers.

The message

Many brands may want to send the same message out, but creativity differentiates it. An example is at the launch of a new phone, mobile carriers will want to create an advertisement (selling the same phone) but on a different network. Understanding the message is essential in developing campaigns that will align with the brand's values and identities. Though the same message is communicated, brands will want to make sure their advertisement stands out from the clusters. This understanding will inform your choice of creative elements such as the copy or the advertisement size to use to convey the message.

The appeal

Understanding the suitable appeals for the message is essential. With the understanding of the message, you have a better indication of the right advertising appeals to adopt. Perhaps, if it is a fashion product that is low evolving, you might want to go for a model and just a few words, making it emotionally appealing, but perhaps if it is a health product or financial services, you might want to go for a rational approach which highlights facts and figures, testimonies and credible sources endorsement. This could be an effort to convey trust in the product or services that are being advertised. You will not use humour to advertise a health product, and you want people to take the messages seriously and seek advice if they need further information. So, you must understand the product or service that a brand sells for you to determine the right advertising tools to use. This is a challenge that an advertiser faces and must be sure to overcome if he or she wishes to create an effective advertisement.

The overall picture

You need to understand if this is a standalone campaign or is part of an integrated campaign. This will also allow you to have a better understanding of the creative elements that will fit across the different channels and media. You may want to ascertain whether this will be a local or global design/campaign as some elements might be applicable in another market. You may also want to check whether you are working with other teams or your agency is the only agency responsible for the campaign. Understanding the overall picture and inherent working principles helps you to be better prepared on how best to address the task and eventually make you deliver an effective campaign.

The limitations

You know the message; you know the brands but that may not be all. It is essential to recognise your limitations as a designer and how best you can address them. Perhaps if you are a freelancer and the brands want a video produced for their social media profile – is that something you can do, or do you have a contact who can do that? Likewise, the financial capabilities and budget of the brands need to be recognised. Understanding their budget and how far you want to think with your creativity is necessary in creating an effective advertising campaign for a brand. For instance, it will not be worthwhile to use every dime of a brand's budget to sign up a Hollywood star for an advert when there are other aspects of the campaign to be sorted. Your creativity should be appropriate, but this should not, however, deter you from thinking outside the box; the human resources around you are also essential. Perhaps you may have a senior colleague within the team to share an idea with, but if you are a freelancer, you might look at developing and expanding your support network, getting inspiration from different websites, reading books and attending events.

Recognising your support network

Now the integration can start. You know the elements, and you know the message. You can now build on your support network to come up with creative ideas.

Brainstorming

This could be on your own or with your colleagues, brainstorming in ideas that reflect the brand's message. This could be having post-it notes on a whiteboard, writing different keywords, sharing different stories, preparing storyboards and coming up with different ideas. This may take days or even months, but it is vital to make sure that ideas are coming through. Your pen and paper are important – scribble things down and let your thoughts flow. Everything may not work well on the computer. If you are stuck, you can check inspirations from different websites, especially websites that have received awards. To free yourself from a mental block, you can also read creative blogs and get inspiration, speak about it with the team, free your mind by taking a break and coming back refreshed.

Develop and test

After the brainstorming, you should have a few ideas that you can test. This is often prepared in a manner that can tell a story; though still crude, it contains the basic concept of the campaign. You check whether it has conveyed the message as intended. Check if it is doable after considering your limitation and you believe it will appeal to the consumers. This is your decision. Your creative output is needed here. To test it, Tom Altstiel and Jean Grow advise the "business card test" whereby you put your idea on the back of a business card and check if it can still convey one thing about the brand. You can also do customer interplay to understand whether they will like the advertisement and how appealing it will be.

Check with colleagues

Provided you are working with a team, and you can share your design with the team, ask for feedback and especially their professional input. They can ask you questions to probe you and make you explore the ideas better. They can check whether it aligns with the usual output of their agency and if they can win awards with this. You must get your team to sign off this developed advertisement before presenting it to the client. Sometimes, there might be a disagreement, but if you are working under an art director, he/she is responsible for making the final call. The diversity of the team is vital at this stage; if the agency is diverse, they may identify issues that need to be readjusted because of stereotypical portrayals.

Check with client

Here it has passed through your quality control and the check of your colleagues, and now it is time to present it to the brand. If you are working in-house, this could be a presentation to the marketing director. You showcase the idea so far and get their input. Perhaps it is something they like, that can go into production, or they may want some changes to go with it. He who pays the piper dictates the tune, the client is the final judge, and they make the final decisions. If the client does not like it, you may need to go back to your drawing board and conceptualise a better idea.

Check with customers

You may also want to check with the customers, perhaps through a focus group to understand their perception of the campaign and how they are engaging with it – importantly, to check whether the message is being communicated as intended. There is no guarantee that the customers will like the advertisement but there could some insights provided by the customers who may highlight some areas to be changed.

Check with regulators

You may also want to share your advertisements with the regulators to ensure the advertisement is not breaking any advertising codes. The regulators (as discussed in Chapter 3 under the relationship of agency) can provide advice and guidance on the advertising concept. These regulators include the ASA and Clearcast, a non-governmental organisation which pre-approves most British television advertising. Clearcast refused to clear Iceland's 2018 advertisement for TV in the United Kingdom.

Value of creativity

There are many values in creative advertisements. The message stands out from the rest; it is memorable and adds value to the business. Creative advertisement achieves the objective of the brief to effectively communicate a message. There are possibilities for the campaign to win awards and get recognition. This is evidence of the peers' recognition of its creativity. These awards and recognition bring more business to the advertising agency. The agency can take pride in the fact that they developed the advertisement. Prospective clients and other colleagues in the industry get to know the agency and accord them the respect they deserve. Likewise, it can propel the career of anyone involved in the advertisement.

Revision questions

1. What are creative elements in an advertisement?
2. What other forms of creative elements do you think exist that have not been listed?
3. What other types of images do you think are being used in advertisements?
4. How do the creative elements vary across different media?
5. How would you describe advertising appeal?
6. What are the differences between emotional and rational advertising appeal?
7. What are the benefits of creativity in advertising?
8. How can creativity enhance the effectiveness of an advertisement?
9. How can you select creative elements for an advertisement?
10. What are the implications of companies like Shutterstock Custom and Tribe on creativity, content for advertisement and advertising industry?

Student activity

Identifying creative elements in an advertisement

Two different advertisements winning different awards from different competitions but for the same brand

* Burger King's Whopper Detour (created by FCB New York) picked up three Grand Prix prizes (Titanium, Direct and Mobile Grand Prix) at the 2019 Cannes Lions Festival.
* Burger King's Moldy Whopper (created by INGO Stockholm with DAVID Miami and Publicis Bucharest) won Best of Show at The One Show 2020.

Your task is to

1. Identify the creative elements in these advertisements.
2. Which of these advertisements would you consider emotionally appealing and why?
3. Explore the effectiveness of the creative elements in the advertisement.

References

Aaker, D. A. & Stayman, D. M., 1992. Implementing the concept of transformational advertising. *Psychology & Marketing*, 9(3), pp. 237–253.
Allan, D., 2006. Effects of popular music in advertising on attention and memory. *Journal of Advertising Research*, 46(4), pp. 434–444.

Allan, D. & Tryce, S., 2016. Popular music in Super Bowl commercials 2005–2014. *International Journal of Sports Marketing and Sponsorship*, 17(4), pp. 333–348.

Alpert, G. et al., 2008. Temporal characteristics of audiovisual information processing. *Journal of Neuroscience*, 28(20), pp. 5344–5349.

Ang, S. H. & Low, S. Y., 2000. Exploring the dimensions of ad creativity. 17(10), pp. 835–854.

Aslam, M., 2006. Are you selling the right colour? A cross-cultural review of colour as a marketing cue. *Journal of Marketing Communications*, 12(1), pp. 15–30.

Bagozzi, R. P., Gopinath, M. & Nyer, P. U., 1999. The role of emotions in marketing. *Journal of the Academy of Marketing Science*, 27(2), pp. 184–206.

Baines, P., Fill, C. & Page, K., 2013. *Essentials of marketing*. New York: Oxford University Press.

Belch, G. & Belch, M., 2015. *Introduction to advertising and promotion*. 10th ed. New York: McGraw Hill.

Bovée, C. & Arens, W. F., 2000. *Contemporary advertising*. 4th ed. Homewood, IL: Irwin.

Brader, T., 2006. *Campaigning for hearts and minds: How emotional appeals in political ads work*. Chicago, IL: University of Chicago Press.

Brown, M., 2012. *How should voiceovers be used in ads?*. [Online] Available at: www.wpp.com/wpp/marketing/advertising/how-should-voiceovers-be-used-in-ads/ [Accessed 9 10 2017].

Caird, J., 2016. *"I was basically told: you are never showing this" – how we made Cadbury's gorilla ad*. [Online] Available at: www.theguardian.com/media-network/2016/jan/07/how-we-made-cadburys-gorilla-ad [Accessed 2 2 2020].

Chang, C. & Li, H., 2010. Why are childlike portrayals appealing in East Asia? A cross-cultural comparison between Taiwan and the US. *International Journal of Advertising*, 3, pp. 451–472.

Cho, C. & Cheon, H. J., 2005. Cross-cultural comparisons of interactivity on corporate web sites: The United States, the United Kingdom, Japan, and South Korea. *Journal of Advertising*, 34(2), pp. 99–115.

Chou, H. & Lien, N., 2014. Old songs never die: Advertising effects of evoking nostalgia with popular songs. *Journal of Current Issues & Research in Advertising*, 35(1), pp. 29–49.

Chou, H. & Singhal, D., 2017. Nostalgia advertising and young Indian consumers: The power of old songs. *Asia Pacific Management Review*, 22(3), pp. 136–145.

Chowdhury, R. M., Olsen, G. D. & Pracejus, J. W., 2011. How many pictures should your print ad have?. *Journal of Business Research*, 64(1), pp. 3–6.

Clow, K. E., Berry, C. T., Kranenburg, K. E. & James, K. E., 2005. An Examination of the Visual Element of Service Advertisements. *Marketing Management Journal*, 15(1), pp. 33–45.

Craton, L. & Lantos, G., 2011. Attitude toward the advertising music: An overlooked potential pitfall in commercials. *Journal of Consumer Marketing*, 28(6), pp. 396–411.

Craton, L., Lantos, G. & Leventhal, R., 2017. Results may vary: Overcoming variability in consumer response to advertising music. *Psychology & Marketing*, 34(1), pp. 19–39.

Daboll, P., 2012. *Should CEOs be in TV ads?*. [Online] Available at: www.forbes.com/sites/onmarketing/2012/03/13/should-ceos-be-in-tv-ads/#3da366932138 [Accessed 8.8.2020].

De Bortoli, M. & Maroto, J., 2011. *Colours across cultures: Translating colours in interactive marketing communications*. Granada, Spain: Global Propaganda.

Decrop, A., 2007. The influence of message format on the effectiveness of print advertisements for tourism destinations. *International Journal of Advertising*, 26(4), pp. 505–525.

Dodgson, L., 2019. *13 computer-generated influencers you should be following on Instagram*. [Online] Available at: www.insider.com/cgi-influencers-you-should-be-following-instagram-2019-9 [Accessed 9.9.2020].

Duncan, T., & Moriarty, S. E., 1998. A communication-based marketing model for managing relationships. *Journal of Marketing*, 62(2), pp. 1–13.

Elliott, M. T., 1995. Differences in the portrayal of blacks: A content analysis of general media versus culturally-targeted commercials. *Journal of Current Issues & Research in Advertising*, 17(1), pp. 75–86.

Fowles, J., 1998. Advertising's fifteen basic appeals. In: M. Petracca & M. Sorapure, eds. *Common culture: Reading and writing about American popular culture*. Upper Saddle River, NJ: Prentice Hall, pp. 73–76.

Gagnon, M., Jacob, J. D. & Holmes, D., 2010. Governing through (in)security: a critical analysis of a fear-based public health campaign. *Critical Public Health*, 20(2), pp. 245–256.

Hertenstein, M., Holmes, R. & McCullough, M., 2009. The communication of emotion via touch. *Emotion*, 9(4), pp. 566–578.

Hetsroni, A., 2000. The relationship between values and appeals in Israeli advertising: a smallest space analysis. *Journal of Advertising*, 29(3), pp. 55–68.

Huang, M., 1997. Exploring a new typology of emotional appeals: Basic, versus social, emotional advertising. *Journal of Current Issues & Research in Advertising*, 19(2), pp. 23–37.

Huron, D., 1989. Music in advertising: An analytic paradigm. *Musical Quarterly*, 73(4), pp. 557–574.

Johar, J. S. & Sirgy, M. J., 1991. Value-expressive versus utilitarian advertising appeals: When and why to use which appeal. *Journal of Advertising*, 20(3), pp. 23–33.

Johnson, W., 2019. 7 visual elements of art used in advertisement. [Online] Available at: https://smallbusiness.chron.com/7-visual-elements-art-used-advertisement-25752.html.

Kotler, P., & Armstrong, G., 2013. *Principles of marketing*. 16th ed. London: Pearson.

Krishna, A., Cian, L. & Sokolova, T., 2016. The power of sensory marketing in advertising. *Current Opinion in Psychology*, 10(2), pp. 142–147.

Lester, P. M., 2006. *Visual communication: Images with messages*. 4th ed. Belmont, CA: Thomson Wadsworth.

Lichtlé, M., 2007. The effect of an advertisement's colour on emotions evoked by attitude towards the ad: The moderating role of the optimal stimulation level. *International Journal of Advertising*, 26(1), pp. 37–62.

Li, Z., 2017. The "Celeb" series: A close analysis of audio-visual elements in 2008 US presidential campaign ads. *Undergraduate Journal of Humanistic Studies*, 4(1), pp. 1–16.

McCarthy, M. & Mothersbaugh, D., 2002. Effects of typographic factors in advertising-based persuasion: A general model and initial empirical tests. *Psychology & Marketing*, 19(7–8), pp. 663–691.

Mertes, A., 2020. 10 of the greatest animals ever used in advertising. [Online] Available at www.qualitylogoproducts.com/blog/top-10-advertising-animals/.

Meyers-Levy, J. & Peracchio, L. A., 1995. Understanding the effects of color: How the correspondence between available and required resources affects attitudes. *Journal of Consumer Research*, 22(2), pp. 121–138.

Mezo, R. E., 1997. An adaptation of Aristotle: A note on the types of oratory. *Rhetoric Review*, 16(1), pp. 164–165.

Middleton, R., 1990. *Studying popular music*. London: McGraw-Hill Education.

Mishra, A., 2009. Indian perspective about advertising appeal. *International Journal of Marketing Studies*, 1(2), pp. 23–34.

Mittal, B. (1999). The advertising of services: Meeting the challenge of intangibility. *Journal of Service Research*, 2(1), pp. 98–116.

Mogaji, E., 2015. Reflecting a diversified country: A content analysis of newspaper advertisements in Great Britain. *Marketing Intelligence & Planning*, 33(6), pp. 908–926.

Mogaji, E., 2016. This advert makes me cry: Disclosure of emotional response to advertisement on Facebook. *Cogent Business & Management*, 3(1), p. 1177906.

Mogaji, E., 2018. *Emotional appeals in advertising banking services*. London: Emerald.

Mogaji, E., 2019. *Typology of music in advertising*. Krems, Austria, Published by The European Advertising Academy. Available at https://ssrn.com/abstract=3413436.

Mogaji, E., Badejo, F., Charles, S. & Millisits, J., 2020. To build my career or build my brand? Exploring the prospects, challenges and opportunities for sportswomen as human brand. *European Sport Management Quarterly*, https://doi.org/10.1080/16184742.2020.1791209, pp. 1–19.

Mogaji, E., & Erkan, I. (2019). Insight into consumer experience on UK train transportation services. *Travel Behaviour and Society*, 14, pp. 21–33.

Moriarty, S. E., 1991. *Creative Advertising Theory and Practice*. 2nd ed. Englewood Cliffs, NJ: Prentice-Hall.

Morris, J. D., Woo, C., Geason, J. A. & Kim, J., 2002. The power of affect: Predicting intention. *Journal of Advertising Research*, 42(3), pp. 7–17.

Napoli, J., Murgolo-Poore, M. & Boudville, I., 2003. Female gender images in adolescent magazine advertising. *Australasian Marketing Journal*, 11(1), pp. 60–69.

O'Guinn, T., Allen, C. & Semenik, R., 2006. *Advertising and integrated brand promotion*. 4th ed. Mason, OH: Thomson South-Western.

Ortony, A. & Turner, T. J., 1990. What's basic about basic emotions?. *Psychological review*, 97(3), pp. 315–331.

Panda, T. K., Panda, T. K. & Mishra, K., 2013. Does emotional appeal work in advertising? The rationality behind using emotional appeal to create favorable brand attitude. *IUP Journal of Brand Management*, 10(2), pp. 7–23.

Percy, L. & Rosenbaum-Elliott, R., 2016. *Strategic advertising management*. 5th ed. Oxford: Oxford University Press.

Pileliené, L. & Grigaliūnaité, V., 2016. Influence of print advertising layout complexity on visual attention. *Eurasian Business Review*, 6(2), pp. 237–251.

Pollay, R. W., 1983. Measuring the cultural values manifest in advertising. *Current Issues and Research in Advertising*, 6(1), pp. 71–92.

Pollay, P. W., 1985. The subsiding sizzle: A descriptive history of print advertising, 1900–1980. *The Journal of Marketing*, 49(3), pp. 24–37.

Pollay, R. W., & Gallagher, K., 1990. Advertising and cultural values: Reflections in the distorted mirror. *International Journal of Advertising*, 9(4), pp. 359–372.

Premier Print Group, 2017. *Paper Types*. [Online] Available at: www.premierprintgroup.com/resources/paper-types.

Roehm, M., 2001. Instrumental vs. vocal versions of popular music in advertising. *Journal of Advertising Research*, 41(3), pp. 49–58.

Rossiter, J. R. & Percy, L., 1997. *Advertising communications & promotion management*. New York: McGraw-Hill.

Russell, J. & Lane, W., 1999. *Kleppner's Advertising Procedure*. Upper Saddle River, NJ: Prentice Hall.

Salander, B., 2010. *Emotionality in business-to-business marketing communications*. Newcastle: University of Northumbria at Newcastle, unpublished PhD thesis.

Schiffer, J., 2015. *I second that emotion: The emotive power of music in advertising media*. [Online] Available at: www.nielsen.com/us/en/insights/news/2015/i-second-that-emotion-the-emotive-power-of-music-in-advertising.html [Accessed 15.12.2016].

Scollon, C. N., Diener, E., Oishi, S. & Biswas-Diener, R., 2004. Emotions across cultures and methods. *Journal of Cross-Cultural Psychology*, 35(3), pp. 304–326.

Scott, L. M., 1994. Images in advertising: The need for a theory of visual rhetoric. *Journal of Consumer Research*, 21(2), pp. 252–273.

Srivastava, M., & Sharma, M., 2008. The role of emotional appeals in Internet advertising: A study of the contributing factors involved. *ICFAI Journal of Management Research*, 7(9), pp. 27–36.

Shuker, R., 1994. *Understanding Popular Music*. New York: Routledge.

Staff, 2007. *Cadbury "gorilla" wins Campaign of the Year*. [Online] Available at: www.campaignlive.co.uk/article/cadbury-gorilla-wins-campaign-year/773064 [Accessed 2.2.2020].

Stafford, M., 1996. Demographic discriminators of service quality in the banking industry. *Journal of Services Marketing*, 10(4), pp. 6–22.

Stanton, J. V. & Guion, D. T., 2013. Taking advantage of a vulnerable group? Emotional cues in ads targeting parents. *Journal of Consumer Affairs*, 47(3), pp. 485–517.

Strach, P., Zuber, K., Fowler, E. F. & Ridout, T. N., 2015. In a different voice? Explaining the use of men and women as voice-over announcers in political advertising. *Political Communication*, 32(2), pp. 183–205.

Taylor, C., 2015. The imminent return of the advertising jingle. *International Journal of Advertising*, 34(5), pp. 717–719.

Unnava, H. R. & Burnkrant, R. E., 1991. An imagery-processing view of the role of pictures in print advertisements. *Journal of Marketing Research*, 28(2), pp. 226–231.

Vizard, S., 2018. *Guinness's "Surfer" ad didn't do that well in research "but we ignored it"*. [Online] Available at: www.marketingweek.com/guinness-surfer/ [Accessed 9.9.2020].

Wang, L., Yu, Y. & Li, O., 2020. The typeface curvature effect: The role of typeface curvature in increasing preference toward hedonic products. *Psychology & Marketing*, 37(8), pp. 1118–1137.

Wayne, T., Farinloye, F. & Mogaji, E., 2020. Analysis of African universities' corporate visual identities. In: E. Mogaji, F. Maringe & R. E. Hinson, eds. *Strategic Marketing of Higher Education in Africa*. London: Routledge.

Wilmshurst, J. & Mackay, A., 2010. *Fundamentals of advertising*. 2nd ed. London and New York: Routledge.

YouTube, n.d. [Online] Available at: https://youtu.be/ehttcb_zxsm.

Yu, L., 2007. Relating the visual and the headline in Chinese print advertisements. *Visible Language*, 41(2), pp. 163–189.

Theme 2
Sharing the message

5 Advertisements shared through traditional media

The newspaper is not dead, although it is dying. Radio and billboards still play an essential role in disseminating a brand's message. This chapter looks at the advantages and disadvantages of these traditional forms of media and how they can be used to distribute a message. You may want to always rely on new media; however, these traditional types of media cannot be ignored. The chapter explores the creative elements specific to these forms of media and how they can be used to reach out to the audience effectively. Social media networks have been known to advertise in traditional media. It is about using different media to complement each other when sending the message. The chapter also discusses how traditional advertisements fit with technological advancements and millennials.

Learning outcome

At the conclusion of this teaching, students will be able to:

- Recognise that traditional media is not dying but still relevant for an integrated campaign;
- Recognise that traditional media is evolving;
- Give examples of different traditional media;
- Describe the features of different traditional media;
- Describe the creative elements compatible with traditional media.

Introduction

The advertisement has been conceptualised and designed, and the message has been embedded with creative elements so the viewers can find it emotionally appealing. It is now time for viewers to see what the advertising agency has been preparing for the brand. The design is now leaving the computers for the consumers to engage with it. Advertisements need to be distributed and disseminated through the media.

As you can imagine, there are many media out there. This media is not just limited to social media but other avenues where we get informed and entertained. Kotler (2003) identified four of broadcasting channels for distributing marketing communications which are print (newspaper, brochures), broadcast (television, radio), electronic (emails, website pages) and display (posters and billboards). Each of these channels has unique features to enhance a positive attitude towards the advertisement for the brand. The focus of this chapter will be print, broadcast and display, which are considered traditional/old media. Electronic media (better described as digital/new media) will be discussed later in this book.

Traditional media is often for mass communications, and lacks personal features, unlike digital or social media (Gökerik et al., 2018). Often through digital media and marketing, you can find an advertisement that is specifically targeted towards you, but you would hardly find a TV advertisement specifically targeted towards you, nor would a newspaper advertisement have your full name on it. This inability to personalise and make advertisements direct to each consumer or prospect has been considered one of the most significant limitations of traditional media, as digital media can do that. No doubt the media landscape is changing. The way consumers are engaging with the media is changing. Media houses recognise this, brands are aware of it and they are changing their strategies and spending; likewise, advertising agencies are becoming more strategic in meeting the need of the brands who want to send their message in a sleek, cost-effective and modern way.

There is an argument that traditional media is dying, and everything should be digital; that traditional media should no longer be taught under advertising as everything is going digital. This is, however, not the case; while it is acknowledged that consumer engagement with these media is changing, the media is not dying but evolving, and that is why it is still being covered in this chapter. You see social media and tech giants advertising on

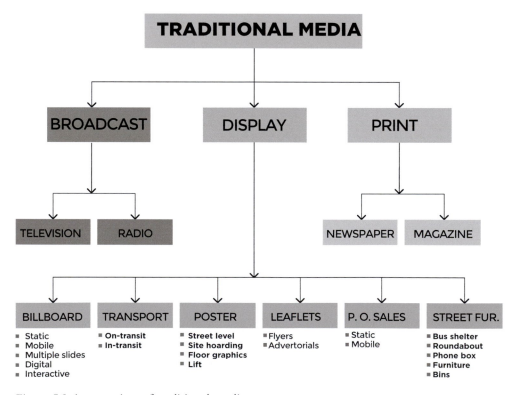

Figure 5.1 An overview of traditional media
Source: author.

newspapers. This shows there is something still relevant about traditional media that needs to be explored. Also, advertising agencies and media planners are responsible for effectively disseminating the message, and they know who and what can influence the decision of the media, and traditional media is still included in the mix.

This aspect of the book will explore three types of traditional media – broadcast, display and print. The features of these media will be discussed, including the applicable creative elements and how the media is evolving. The advantages and disadvantages of these media will be discussed as well. Figure 5.1 presents an overview of traditional media.

Broadcast media

Television

Television (TV), sometimes shortened to tele or telly, is a telecommunication medium used for transmitting moving images in monochrome (black and white), or colour, and in two or three dimensions with sound. Television is still one of the most popular media for disseminating advertisements. It reaches an enormous number of people. Advertisement is the primary revenue generator for commercial televisions. The first-ever television advert in the United Kingdom was broadcast on 22 September 1955. The advert was for Gibbs SR toothpaste. All it featured was a block of ice, a tube of toothpaste and commentary about its "tingling fresh" qualities. On 15 November 1969, the UK's first TV colour ad made its debut. It was for Birds Eye to promote peas. Unilever – who at the time owned Birds Eye – was reported to have bought the slot for £23.

A television advertisement can be used to launch a campaign which will then be supported by other media. It is the anchor for a brand's creative message. Having a TV advertisement is an achievement worth celebrating. As UK-based Starling Bank launched its first TV advertising campaign, there was huge publicity and a press release announcing the advertisement. Brands and agencies select TV spots to launch their campaigns. Many campaigns have been launched during *X factor*, and *Britain's Got Talent*. There is a series of idents – a short visual image employed by television programmes that works as a logo to locate the viewer to the channel – bookmarking popular programmes. Trainline rebranded itself from thetrainline.com and launched a new brand with a TV spot called "I am train" that was featured during *X Factor*. There is also the annual unveiling of Christmas adverts that could almost be described as a cultural event.

Buying this spot for the campaigns is often left to the media planners; this depends on the size of the agency. Some agencies might use the media planning team to negotiate. TV spots vary in length, some being just 5–10 seconds, others lasting as long as 2 minutes, especially the newly launched advertisements. However, most spots are either 30 or 60 seconds on television. The TV station (and the number of viewers), the time of day, length of adverts are some of the factors that can affect the prices paid for the spot. A spot airing in the commercial break of a prime-time show will be costly.

Television advertisements can be very engaging, emotionally appealing and informative as well. Television advertisement has most of the creative elements of an advertisement. There are the visuals to see the moving images and appreciate the cinematography, and there is colour, featured throughout the advertisement; there is audio which includes the background music and the voice-over. Creative integration of these elements can convey an emotionally appealing advertisement for the viewers. An example is Cadbury's famous

'Gorilla' spot made by agency Fallon which brings together a gorilla drumming to a Phil Collins song and Dairy Milk chocolate.

Despite its positive attribute, there are some disadvantages which deter brands from using TV, especially smaller brands. Television advertisements can be expensive to produce. The cost of spots is also considerably high. More prominent brands are often well-positioned financially to feature their advertisements on TV. Not surprising to see brands celebrate their first advertisement on TV. It is not an easy feat. Besides, there is a limitation with the personalisation strategy. Television is a mass media, and therefore it may not be specific for individuals.

The increasing use of tablets, smartphones and social media during "linear" viewing of TV programmes poses a limitation to television and how effective it can be. The availability of so many types of media and screens today means people are not watching as much television as they did before. There are second screens which are competing for viewers' attention. For example, if there is an advert on the TV, an individual can use that time to check the phone. People are channel surfing, quickly scanning through different television channels to find something interesting to watch. People are now watching movies and using subscription and streaming services like Netflix and Amazon Prime. The tolerance for watching advertisements is reducing. So, there are reduced chances of seeing an advertisement on TV.

Advertisers are aware of this, and they need quantitative data to plan their marketing campaigns – they want media that gives them value for money. Television advertising relies on third party audience tracking companies, like Nielsen and ComScore, to determine audience demographics and ad targets. Sky also has Ad Smart, which can target advertisements, and different advertisements can be shown to different households watching the same program. This allows for smaller brands to come on TV and pay for targeting their smaller market instead of the usual broadcasting to everyone in the country. This ensures that advertisers are providing added experiences, making advertisements useful, personal and immediate.

Integrating the social media campaign with a TV advertisement could be a way of dealing with the second screen dilemma. Brands need to recognise that consumer behaviours are changing – the brands cannot stop viewers from having a second screen, but they can be strategically integrated into the campaign, which allows hashtags for social media. Viewers can watch the advertisement on TV and engage with the brand on social media using the hashtags. This allows for a better evaluation and understanding of consumers' attitude towards the advertisement.

Advertisers need to understand that the second screen is changing its advertisement development strategy as well. TV content should, therefore, be developed to be shared across different media and channels. The design of the creative element becomes essential here. A 30-second advertisement for TV could be made into a 3-minute advert for YouTube and a 1-minute one for Instagram. Same message but developed in a different way to suit the media. Though television advertising is above-the-line advertising, many campaigns are released online at the same time, via a site such as YouTube, to increase awareness and defeat the ad-skipping technology in living rooms.

The difficulty in changing the message is another limitation of TV as a medium for advertising. If a company is doing sales, or promotions, they have to create new advertisements each time and buy new advertising spots. This could be financially draining and time-consuming. Unlike other digital advertisements or in a newspaper, where advertisements can be changed for the next day publications because the design can be easily changed, TV advertisements will have to go through another production and post-production session. This calls for a lot of resources and time, making it more rigid than other forms of advertising.

Evidence suggests that putting TV at the heart of an integrated campaign will make every other medium work better (ThinkBox, 2019). Television is an essential medium for advertisement if a brand can afford it. It is however essential as well to check whether the value is being received for the money spent. Advertisers may want to evaluate their campaign and:

- Try different lengths of commercial
- Try different TV stations
- Try different times of day
- Try different genres of programs
- Try different creative approaches
- Try different days of the week
- Try weekends instead of weekdays.

Radio

Radio is the technology of communicating using radio waves. Just like television, this media is used to send messages to a large group of audiences. However, it is impossible to send a visual message on radio and it is a traditional medium for advertising. Though limited with creative elements, it can construct a unique picture in the mind of the listeners (Cantor & Venus, 1980). This also has to do with using the right voice-over, background music and other sonic inputs to convey a message. Radio is essential for information, and people turn on the radio when they get in their cars. They play it in the office and at home – it therefore offers brands an avenue to reach their target audience with their message.

It is easier to produce with not much technical equipment, unlike shooting a TV commercial. This also ensures that it takes a short time to develop an advertisement for radio and send it to the station. Likewise, radio station scheduling is quite flexible, allowing advertisers to share their message without waiting for an extended period. There are local radio stations that can address the demographics of a particular region, allowing brands to deliver their message to a particular demographic. It gives the brand an ability to reach a segmented audience through a radio format or part of the day. A radio advertisement is considerably cheaper than a television one.

Specifically, radio presents three forms of targeting relevant for brands that want to advertise. Firstly, it offers *contextual targeting*, and this involves targeting customers who listen to a radio station. Most individuals have one or two favourite stations they listen to, and they become loyal audiences that brands can target. Secondly, radio offers *geographical targeting* as there are local stations which are being listened to by the local people; this allows the brand to send the message to customers within that geographical area where the radio is being transmitted. Radio advertisement can run on local stations and programming only but can also be distributed nationally. Thirdly, radio offers a *demographic targeting*. Demographics such as race, gender or age may be listening to a radio station which allows the brand to target the listeners effectively. For example, there is a radio station that is specifically for Africans in the United Kingdom; money transfer brands like Western Union or MoneyGram may want to use that media to reach out to individuals who may want to send money back to their families. The brand recognises that those listening to that particular radio station are their target audience.

Despite these positives, radio as a media channel has its limitations with regard to advertisements. The lack of visual appeals is a great limitation for radio. It has one of the three creative elements (audio, visual and touch) – unlike television which can be very entertaining and has the multi-sensory appeal, radio can only impact your audience through sound. A good advertisement on the radio should create a visual in the minds of the listener. This could necessitate the need to have expected sound engineers to create the sounds which create the imaginary picture for the listeners.

Besides, people listening to radio are often doing something else, engaged in other activities like driving or working and may not be very attentive to the advertisement. There is poor attentiveness and listeners are fragmented and disinterested in the message. The lack of durability is also a limitation of radio. Unlike a TV advertisement, you can watch it over on YouTube. For newspaper or magazine, you can cut out the advertisement and keep it for future reference; for a billboard advertisement, you can take a photograph; advertisements on radio, however, are not durable. Once you miss it, it is gone, unless it is played again at another time. Once you have heard what you have heard, you have no option but to remember it or hope to hear it again some time and that some time can be any time.

Radio, as a medium, has had its digital challengers as well. Podcasts and internet radio are disrupting the media. Therefore, it is imperative for stations to be more engaged and creative in reaching out and making themselves a viable option for advertising. The terrestrial station now has an online version, there is digital audio broadcasting (DAB), and they also create content, recording themselves in the radio station. Smart speakers like Google Home and Amazon Echo are also changing how consumers engage with radio content (Merritt, 2017). All these are affecting how viable radio stations remain as a platform for advertising. With a proper understanding of what radio as a medium has to offer, advertisers can make the best decisions about their marketing mix and how to get the best results.

Radio is always likely to be a support (not lead) medium as it has been found to work very well with other media, increasing the response to media such as direct mail. Radio adverts should be stimulating, to get the attention of the listeners, and contain a simple, short message that is easy to internalise. Repetition is cheap, and it is essential to get the advert noticed. Creatives should be varied to give several different adverts. When buying airtime/spot, think first about your audience as different stations appeal to different audiences. Time of day and day of the week are worth testing. Peak radio listening is in the mornings. Weekends often attract higher percentage responses than weekdays, but from lower audiences.

Display media

These display media are also called out-of-home (OOH) advertising media. This broadly refers to any media outside the home (TV and radio are predominantly confined to a home setting). Consumers engage with these advertisements whenever they are outside their home. Most of these displays are also going digital. Therefore, there is more digital out-of-home (DOOH) advertising media, allowing for graphic and moving images and real live data updates, which can be more interactive. Famous examples are the screen at Piccadilly Circus in London and New York Times Square in New York. These screens are outside the buildings in very populated areas with huge footfall, so many people see them. People do not have to pay to see an advertisement on a billboard (unlike newspaper or cinema). Display media are visible to people on foot, public transport or from their car. It is usually quick as it is readily available, on the go and impactful. Display media are evolving as media owners are working closely with agencies and brands to incorporate digital social media and interactive strategies to increase consumer engagement.

Billboards

This is a media space that is dedicated to posting bills. "Bill" is a nineteenth-century word for advertising poster. Billboards are often large surface advertising media that are strategically located in key locations, popular places with high footfall. They are often visibly located along key arterial routes so that people can easily see them, and they are also used to capture the attention of motorists and pedestrians. Billboards require planning permission as they are physical structures and there are height and width restrictions. Like TV stations, these media spaces are owned by companies who install and maintain them. JCDecaux is the world's largest outdoor advertising company, spearheading OOH digital transformation. They operate in 900 London bus shelters and are airport advertising market leaders. Clear Channel UK is one of the world's leading OOH media owners with more than 40,000 sites nationwide.

There are different types of billboard, depending on the design of the poster and the frequency at which they are being changed.

Static billboard

These are the basic billboards which are typically on the roadside. These static billboards allow large format print that can be pasted or attached. As illustrated in Figure 5.2, these static billboards can also be lit to allow illumination at night. These billboards are static because their content cannot be changed until the campaign is over. These billboards are often rented for 12 weeks, and the poster may not be changed during that period. This suggests that the message must be relevant for that period. The downside is that viewers may be tired of seeing the same advertisement for a long time in the same place.

Mobile billboards

These mobile billboards are also known as the "digital billboard trucks". They are communication, or advertising devices that are used to communicate a brand's intentions to the target audience in a particular area. Hence, we can agree that they are advertising trucks or trailers that are typically mobile and have information placed on each side for the audience to see. Furthermore, mobile billboards are the boards attached to a vehicle to drive around a predetermined route. This overcomes one of the challenges of the static billboard because viewers may not see it for consecutive days. Importantly, many people in different locations will be able to see the advertisement. A famous example of the mobile billboard is the "Go Home or Face Arrest" Campaign by the UK's Home

Figure 5.2 An example of a static billboard along a major road
Source: Spaceoutdoor.co.uk.

Office in 2013. The campaign was piloted in six London boroughs but was later pulled because it proved highly divisive (Wintour, 2013). Also, during the Covid-19 pandemic, locations with high numbers of cases were targeted with Covid-19 alert advertisements on mobile billboards saying, "this is a high risk area". This campaign is meant to target an area for a short period, and this saves the cost of permanently (at least for 3 months) putting up a poster on a billboard. The specific message on this mobile billboard can be shared around and driven to any other strong hotspot of the virus. In addition, these mobile billboards can also come in LCD screens which allow the images to be changed as the vehicle is driven around. This also overcomes the rigid and static nature of static billboards.

Multiple slides

These are billboards that change posters at a predetermined interval. The billboards are electronically powered to show these images. The billboard may have three different advertisements in a roll at it is changed at a predetermined time. These allow three brands (with different messages) to share the same billboard. Instead of being static and people getting bored, they see the advertisement at different times. The downside is that the brand may not be able to control the other two sharing the space. It could also be distracting, especially for viewers who want to take time and read the advertisement. Besides, because these slides are printed and installed at the same time, the three brands are stuck together for the duration of the campaign. That brings in the disadvantage of static billboards. Another thing about this is that with the limited time and attention span of the audience, it is difficult to get a larger volume of information across in a shorter time. However, a strategically placed advertisement can aid your multiple slides to rope in your target audience. However, the common issue is that the content of an advertisement is split in multiple slides, and it is difficult to create sync between each message being passed across to the readers who might not have time to see the whole message.

Digital billboards

These types of billboards have LCD screens which allow the images to be changed in real-time; though they may be physically static, their images are dynamic. This allows for animated video and more creativity. This type of billboard is generally not much more expensive because the bulk of the cost comes from renting the space rather than production. Advertisers can give the media space owner a JPEG file of their advertisement and it is placed on the billboard. They do not have to pay to print the large format and install. An example is Motion@Portfolio by JCDecaux. The flexibility, technical capabilities and creative scope of these state-of-the-art landscape video screens ensure viewers experience the most innovative, involving and memorable OOH campaigns.

Interactive digital billboards

Interactive digital billboards build on the feature of the digital billboard, which allows the advertisements to be changed, but, in this case, the interactive billboard feeds on real-time data to update itself. It is used in supermarkets or travel hubs where real information about other customers' activities are fed in to develop the message. These billboards are more dynamic, responsive and engaging. A popular one is British Airways' billboard that updates in real-time, displaying the flight number and origin. The billboard uses custom-built surveillance technology to pull off the feat (Wasserman, 2013).

As earlier stated, billboards are sited in strategic places to attract people's attention. These places include retail stores, airports, train stations and even buildings. Some have considered retail as a form of billboard, but this is not correct. The fact that billboards are in a retail store does not make it another type of billboard. The locations are selected to attract and engage target customers. Billboards are situated around supermarkets and shopping malls to serve as another final reminder about the product. To entice consumers into visiting a store or purchasing a product that is in relative proximity to where they saw the advert. Likewise, there are billboards at airports and train stations where many people are congregating, and they can see the advertisement.

As a matter of innovation, the media space owners are investing in making their billboards very responsive and reliant on data. They can provide this information to the brands and advertising agencies about the effectiveness of their board.

Case study 5.1

JCDecaux launches LDN!

JCDecaux, the world's largest outdoor advertising company and the United Kingdom's number one, today announced its vision for the outdoor landscape in London – the London Digital Network or LDN. JCDecaux will take over the world's largest bus shelter advertising concession from 1 January 2016 and start to build a network of 1,000 digital screens (JCDecaux, 2016).

The digital bus shelters will comprise 84" screens, the biggest of their kind ever deployed at scale and nearly 40% larger than the existing screens. The screens will be deployed in the capital's major retail zones where £1 in every £5 of the UK's retail spend takes place.

As part of the LDN roll out, JCDecaux will look to completely digitise Oxford Street, installing double-sided digital bus shelters along Europe's most important shopping street. Vital to the thriving heart of London, Oxford Street attracts shoppers, tourists, commuters and residents.

In order to deliver optimised LDN campaigns, the channel will be supported through big data and a new supply-side platform called SmartBRICS. Retail spend data from Consolidated Analysis Center, Incorporated (CACI) social media feeds and frame-by-frame audiences from Route outdoor media analytics can be used to target campaigns to optimise audience delivery. The SmartBRICS engine will enable campaigns to serve the right copy to the right screen in the right location at the right time.

Additionally, JCDecaux will launch Connected London, an exclusive panel of 5,000 Londoners who will provide daily data on mindset, attitudes, brand preferences and lifestyle. This new community will provide essential insight into what makes Londoners tick and how they can be targeted via the LDN.

Besides, the design and development of the sites are getting more creative. In as much as the advertisement on the board is impressive, the design of the billboard can also attract attention. In 2018, JCDecaux unveiled *The Kensington*, a curvilinear ribbon of matt steel, framing a curved digital screen, located on West Cromwell Road, London – the key route linking central London and Heathrow Airport. Zaha Hadid Design designed it. *The Kensington* provides brands with a unique communications' channel in the capital that combines the latest in digital screen technology with a spectacular, curved double-ribbon stainless steel design.

Case study 5.2

Heated debate from air conditioning billboard

Billboard advertising is one of the only remaining media of advertising which is intrusive. Audiences have a choice of whether they're going to click on a digital advertisement online, flip the page of a newspaper, ignore the leaflet or have a cup of coffee during the TV advert break. But with billboard advertising, the customer has no choice but to view the large poster placed on a busy junction or road network. Therefore, billboard advertising (also known as a hoarding advertisement in the United Kingdom and many other countries around the world) is an extremely good yet very wide and large outdoor advertising structure that is used by advertisers to help brands get their messages to their customers. These advertising media present large advertisements to passing drivers and pedestrians alike.

We have previously seen our clients receive nationwide press coverage due to a single poster going live. In the 2019 summer heat, a client placed a booking, and their marketing team created a poster campaign they believed to be relevant to the time for display on one of the 48 sheet (6m x 3m) backlights in Nottingham. Within seven days of this poster going live, with the message "Your wife is hot", the advertisement was re-produced throughout the media in news articles for its controversial message "which provided the brand with a miserable amount of exposure (*Evening Standard*, 2019).

Whilst the nature of the advertisement was indeed a controversial campaign, and the client received a hugely positive response from the message, billboards give a platform for brands to advertise towards their target customers in an environment where the customer is in a position to make an impulsive purchase. This makes billboard advertising very effective to large consumer brands such as food and beverage because they can target customers directly before the point of purchase, such as outside a supermarket/convenience store. Also, brands benefit from exclusive ownership of their advertising hoarding. Brands advertising through social media have no choice but to share this platform with direct competitors.

Henry Thomas
Head of Sales and Development
Space Outdoor

Poster

This is a smaller version of a billboard. These posters are often printed in newspapers and can be as large as A0 paper size. Posters are often targeted with the message of "POST NO BILLS HERE". This is because posters do not have to be pasted on a big board, requiring planning permission. No doubt, there are negative attitudes towards posters when pasted in inappropriate places. These can be seen to desecrate the street. Posters can be used by small or medium enterprises who may not have the financial resources to buy a big space. Music promoters are also known to use posters to draw immediate attention to their event. Provided posters are pasted in the right place, they can be very engaging and impactful as well.

Street level

These are posters displayed on street level, pasted on walls, hoardings or bus stops. These allow pedestrians to see. This may not be used by big and popular brands who can use bigger billboards.

Hoarding

Hoardings are often used on construction sites; instead of leaving the hoardings (the board that is used for fencing the development) vacant, they are often pasted with posters about the new development. Computer-generated images are printed and posted on the boards. Considering advertising is about communication, the developers are using these advertisements to create awareness about their ongoing development. These advertisements provide an indication of how the house will look upon completion (Mogaji, 2021). Using this platform (the boards) as a media to advertise can be more effective than putting the advertisement on the radio or newspaper, as people, passing by, can see the development.

Floor graphics

These can be used indoors, especially in supermarket, retail stores, train stations or airports. They are pasted on the floor for people to see as they walk. This can be considered a form of ambient advertisement as seen with the design created by Saatchi & Saatchi, Indonesia for Frontline.

Lift

While recognising that people may be bored while they are inside a lift, waiting to get to their floors, advertisements are also placed in the lift, in the form of posters which can be

Figure 5.3 Leaflet for Cakes by Tee
Source: author.

changed regularly. This can be very creative and impactful, especially in retail stores which can be another reminder about new products to buy in-store.

Leaflet

This is a smaller form of a poster; they are not pasted on any surface but often distributed by hand (see Figure 5.3). They can also be referred to as flyers and handbills. Often these media are in A5 or A6 paper sizes. A leaflet is another form of paper advertisement that is used by advertising agencies to communicate the message of the brand or client. It is usually intended for wide distribution of information and typically distributed or posted in a public place. However, it is sometimes sent through the mail or handed out to recipients in person. They are distributed at bus stops, train stations or places with high foot traffic. These leaflets are also left at stores, hospital reception or places where people congregate. People can pick up a copy, read it and keep it. This can be effective in providing information about an event or activities happening locally; it can be dropped through letter boxes, but people may consider it as junk mail and not be willing to engage with it. As a creative approach, the design should be attractive, appealing and presented with a message that can grab attention. Importantly, these could also be printed on thicker paper to allow a sense of prestige. There is no guarantee, however, that it will not be thrown away.

Figure 5.4 Mock-up design of an advertisement on a typical London bus
Source: author.

Figure 5.5 Mock-up design of an advertisement on a typical London bus
Source: author.

Transport

These are media spaces on transportation networks. They may include trains, buses, taxis and even bicycles. Often the landlord (owner of the taxi, for example) will have to work with an advertising agency (possible a media planner) to rent their space out. The advantage of these media is the coverage. The buses, for example, go along a route every time. It has both the benefit of the mobile billboard and the ability to target customers. For example, if your customers live in a particular area, you might want to place your advert on the buses that go through that area. If a new retail store has opened within the community, they may decide to place an advertisement on the bus that plies the route around the new supermarket.

There are two types of transport media.

On-transit

These are media places on public transport, and they are visibly seen by people outside as the vehicle moves around. Remember the advertisement I did for my student in Chapter 1 (see Figure 1.3); just like any advertisement, it is possible to have it on public transport to go along the route and living areas of the target audience. Figures 5.4 and 5.5 illustrate a mock-up design of my advertisement on a typical London bus, creative efforts (as discussed in Chapter 4) are, however, needed to redesign the advertisement to fit the platform (side panel of buses). Trams and taxis, as a form of public transportation, can also serve as a platform for disseminating advertisements. This on-transit advertising is not just limited to public transport but also to individuals who may want their cars branded with a message. Wrapify, MyFreeCar and Carvertise propose to pay drivers to wrap their vehicles with advertising and then drive as usual.

In-transit

These media spaces are inside the transportation medium. This could be the advertisement at the back of the seats on a budget airline, the advertisement inside the train carriages or the bus. This allows the viewers to take time and engage with the advertisement. The bus is not moving away from them, they are inside and can read the advertisement. This can contain considerably more text compared to on-transit media. In-transit media can also include advertising on the back of the bus or train ticket. These allow the passenger to engage with the advertisement in their typical environment. With in-transit advertisements, advertising agencies can also place adverts or posters or jingles on different compartments inside the bus. This is observed by passengers as the bus moves.

Points of sale

Points of sale are displayed media often located in stores when the customer is about to make a purchase. Advertisers present their brand message at the point when the consumer is making the decision to buy (Willems et al., 2017). The customer now has a visual memory of the advertisement. Some advertising agencies and media planners may consider digital billboards at the entrance of stores as points of sale.

There are two general forms for points of sale, depending on their mobility.

Figure 5.6 Static point of sale advertisement at entrance of ASDA retail store, Canterbury, UK
Source: author.

Static

These are displays that do not move. They are permanently located in a place during the period of the campaign. Static advertisements are advertisements that do not change for any reason. It is a plain and simple method of advertising. Advertising agencies choose static advertisements when they want to create awareness around their brand and reach a large audience. These can be located by the tills or around the supermarket. They are positioned strategically for consumers to see when making a purchase or walking around the store. These advertisements are only available to those who walk around the aisle or use the checkout tills. Figure 5.6 shows a static point of sale advertisement at the entrance to a retail store – an opportunity for companies to remind the customers entering the store about their brands.

Static points of sale advertisements also include placing an advert for a product in the store on TV (for example, the JML TV advertisement that appears in some retail stores in the UK). Advertisements on the fuel nozzle at petrol stations can also be considered points of sale advertisements.

Mobile

These are displays on shopping trolleys, baskets and carrier bags. Consumers go around with these messages popping out at them on their shopping trolley as they look around. Consumers get to see the advertisements on a more regular and personal level. While advertisements in a static point of sale stay in the supermarket, advertisements on a mobile point of sale often follow the customers. The advertisements can influence their decision.

Street furniture

These are displayed media that are available on street furniture. They are different from posters as they are legally constructed and permitted to have an advertisement posted on them. Jean-Claude Decaux invented the concept and business model of "street furniture", with bus shelters financed by advertising, and this has been well adopted across the world. Street furniture has the potential to attract the attention of people passing by the bus stops. It also has the additional benefit of being in places where people may be waiting, giving them plenty of time to notice the advertisement.

There are many examples of such street furniture.

Bus shelter

This is the most common and visible form of street furniture media. It allows advertisements to be pasted on the side panel of a bus shelter. As commuters wait for their bus, they can engage with the advertisement. As far as DOOH media is concerned, real-time data can be used to populate the media. Advertisers can make it very engaging and interactive. JCDecaux completed the synchronisation of four visual display clusters (VDCs) on its digitised Oxford Street network in London. The bus shelters near Marble Arch, Selfridges, John Lewis and Orchard Street (outside Selfridges Foodhall) have been synchronised, meaning that each screen within a pedestrian's line of sight shows the same advertisement at precisely the same time, which changes instantaneously. Synchronisation dramatically increases the impact and noticeability of the Oxford Street network in London. Figures 5.7 and 5.8 illustrate different examples of bus shelter advertising platform.

Figure 5.7 Mock-up design of an advertisement on a bus shelter
Source: author.

Roundabout

Drivers takes their time when approaching a roundabout, and are bound to slow down as they navigate the roundabout. This gives the driver and passengers the opportunity to see the advertisements. This street furniture is better used by local brands that can direct customers to their stores. It could say "My brand is at the second exit". These are often placed on metal signposts at the roundabout.

Welcome sign

Another form of street furniture is the welcome sign to a city or town. This street furniture attracts the attention of drivers and passers-by as well, and this allows brands to

Figure 5.8 Mock-up design of an advertisement on a typical London bus shelter
Source: author.

use it to advertise. These displays are more for brand integration and to keep the brands in the mind of the people.

Phone box

Phone box advertising is another medium used by advertising agencies to ensure cost-effective adverts for brands. It is intentionally used by advertising agencies so that the advert can be seen by a large number of people within city centres and towns. It primarily uses the internal and external parts of a phone box for advertising a brand, product or service. While the use of mobile phones has impacted how phone boxes are being used, advertisers have adopted them as a medium to showcase the brand's messages. These phone boxes are strategically located, obviously for people who want to make phone calls but also for pedestrians walking nearby and seeing the message. This does not fit into the category posters because they are legal structures that have been adopted for advertisements.

Designers will need to be aware of the shape of the phone box and design the advertisement to fit the side panels. This advertisement may not necessarily fit another media. It is important, however, to understand that it is often used to support a campaign, as part of integrated marketing communications and to remind those who have seen the advertisement on TV and their social media.

Furniture

Besides allowing people to sit and rest, furniture also allows marketing communications. As part of street furniture, chairs, especially in town centres, parks and other public places are often used for advertising campaigns. JWT, United Kingdom designed one for KitKat, making a bench in the form of a KitKat.

Cinema

Cinema offers a platform for advertisement which is considered out-of-home. It is also considered a displayed advertisement, albeit displayed indoors, in a cinema. Digital Cinema Media (DCM) is the market leader in UK cinema advertising, providing some 3,428 screens at 522 sites for advertisers. According to DCM, the top spenders in UK cinema are entertainment and leisure, motors, finance, telecoms and government, social and political. Top advertisers in UK cinemas are Amazon, McDonald'', Apple, BGL Group and Sky (DCM, 2020).

Cinema media reaches a huge target audience each month. Those who have come to watch a movie are served with advertisements on a massive scale (more prominent than their usual TV) and the cinema adverts still have the usual creative elements – in fact, more so and at a better level. The visuals are more prominent, the sounds are surround sound, which is better and can be integrated into the euphoria of the cinema experience. The message is being delivered to a captive audience. People paid for their ticket, and they want to be there. It is an uncluttered media environment suitable for presenting the brand's message.

Cinema can be used as part of an integrated marketing campaign, potentially with print, radio, television and other media; besides the location of cinemas is often close to supermarkets and other high-profile retail areas, making the advertisement close to the point-of-purchase. Cinema advertisement also has a very low avoidance score because there is little else to do while in the cinema; moreover, it cannot be skipped (like YouTube) and many see the advertisements as part of the cinema experience. Advertisements can be targeted by a demographic profile based on the geographic location of the cinema. A brand can be sure that people who live around the area have come to watch the movie.

A downside to cinema advertisement is that people may decide not to show up in time for the advertisements. Most people know that the advertisements will precede the actual movie. Advertisements typically roll for 15 to 20 minutes before a film begins. If your advert shows early in the run, it may only be seen by a few people who came in early. Making such an advertisement and placing it in a cinema may be very expensive for a small brand. Furthermore, its results and impact are difficult to measure. It may not be surprising that people have forgotten the advertisement by the time they have watched a 120-minute exciting movie.

Print media

Traditional media such as newspapers and magazines have been walloped by advertisers switching their campaigns to online platforms such as Google and Facebook. Print is one of the dominant media and has contributed significantly to the development of media (Dash & Belgaonkar, 2012). Magazines and newspapers are two of the main forms of print media, and they both have their distinct strengths and weaknesses. Print media are perceived as more informative than broadcast advertisements (Somasundaran & Light, 1991). Print media has also been found to be associated with informational advertising strategies while television advertising is perceived to be more suitable for transformational advertising strategies and provides more entertainment value (Mittal, 1994).

Newspapers

Newspapers have often being neglected in marketing commutations research. With more attention on television and magazines, newspapers are still one of the dominant media and have contributed significantly to the development of media (Dash & Belgaonkar, 2012). Unlike magazines, newspapers are more frequent; they are published daily and provide daily opportunities for advertisers; readers do not have to wait for a week to keep up to date with news (Mogaji, 2015). The degree of attention is also described as the level of involvement, and the amount of energy devoted to apprehending and understanding the messages (William & Arthur, 1992) is considered higher in newspapers. Television is considered entertaining but low involving while print advertising which includes newspapers and magazines is considered high involving where the readers' involvement in an information search is not interrupted (Gong & Cummins, 2020; Tan & Chia, 2007).

Mogaji (2018) suggested that reading an advertisement in a newspaper is a matter of choice, unlike the intrusive nature of television advertisements where the viewer has limited choices. Smit (1999) believed newspaper readers could get involved in the information and read the message at their own pace. This corroborates the findings of News (2014) which suggested that reading a newspaper is a slower burn experience, associated with stronger levels of engagement and emotional intensity and more readers spend more time on advertisements in printed newspapers than on tablets. Consumers actively seeking information may find newspapers more relevant than TV because they can be more informative. There are opportunities for more text (information) than can be provided by TV or radio.

Research by Newsworks (2015) in partnership with University College, London and PHD, a media and communications agency, suggests that the tactile nature of newspapers increases reader confidence, satisfaction, reliability and trust in advertised brands. The research was conducted among 272 participants in three groups, where one group read the printed version of the newspaper, another read it on the computer, while the last group read it on their digital mobile tablet. The research found that touching the advertisements in the newspaper made the brand feel more trustworthy and sincere; it increased customer satisfaction and likelihood to recommend.

The creative possibilities for newspapers cannot be underestimated; as Sampson (2015) concludes, newspapers "continue to offer and develop a wide range of exciting options for brand communication – tip-on, wraparounds, takeovers, special editions". Though the dwindling readership is of concern, the newspaper is still relevant and so also the advertisements therein, thereby justifying the need to understand how financial services are using

Figure 5.9 Mock-up design of an advertisement on the back page of a newspaper
Source: author.

the medium to reach out to their customers. Figure 5.9 shows a mock-up design of an advertisement on the back page of a newspaper.

Magazines

Magazines are picture publications, with stories, poems or essays, that are released or issued from time to time. They are periodically issued and usually target a certain set of readers. A magazine is bound in a paper cover and made in an appealing manner. Magazines offer another platform to advertise and disseminate the message on behalf of the brand. Magazines are for a specific audience who are highly interested in the topic. For example, *Cycling* magazine will be of interest to those who cycle and any brand trying to target a cyclist is better off placing an advertisement in *Cycling*.

Magazines do have a different layout with beautiful photographs and illustrations which are quite captivating. Magazines are classified by the frequency of publication – weekly, monthly, bimonthly or quarterly. Magazines can be bought through subscription. This is called *paid circulation*, where publishers sell their subscriptions. Publishers can identify if their readership is falling by the number of subscribers they have. Some magazines are distributed free of charge. These are *controlled-circulation* publications. They know the number of magazines they print and are freely distributed. This free distribution could be to the general public at train stations for example. This form of circulation is funded by advertisers who have paid to get their message out. Because readers are not paying for the magazine, they have time to read and possibly keep the magazine. *Stylist* is an example of those that are distributed freely at London train stations. Another form of controlled circulation could be for a member of a community or organisation. This serves as an opportunity to keep stakeholders updated about progress within the organisation.

Magazines are often better designed and printed than newspapers. They are printed on glossy paper which is attractive and may also attract readers to engage with the advertisements therein. The advertisements are printed to appeal to the reader. Magazines have both visual and touch creative elements. Readers can feel the quality of the print, an indication of the quality of the message. Magazines are also targeted towards specific readers and there is a high degree of audience selectivity (Fill et al., 2013). These magazines are oriented towards specific subject matter of interest and specific locations, and audiences are more likely to engage with the content (including the advertisements).

Unlike newspapers, whose content is no longer news by the next day, magazines last longer and are more durable. Advertisements in magazines does have a longer "shelf life". Advertisements placed in magazines can still be found relevant many months after the advertising has been placed. Magazines are not discarded every day like newspapers. Besides, there is the pass-on readership effect for magazines where people pass the magazine to somebody else to read, and this also increases the reach of the advertisement. The design flexibility of magazines is also an added advantage, and there are opportunities to be creative with the content. Perfumed scent strips have been inserted into magazines to bring the advertisements to a different and personal level. This design flexibility also allows for advertisements to be customised and used across many platforms.

The over-segmentation (targeting people of similar niche interest) is considered a limitation to an advertisement in magazines. This makes it inappropriate for mass communication. It only targets a selected member of the market. Also, there is a long lead time to have an advertisement in a magazine, as they are printed ahead (unlike newspapers that get printed every day), so advertisers must submit their advertisement well in advance to allow it to appear in the magazine, which may also affect the timing of the campaign. However, this medium can be used for a product launch, where a company puts an advertisement in a magazine at a period when a new product is being launched. The company can target the period when the magazine will be published/issued and offer to place an advert inside the magazine or on the front cover. That way the brand will be able to reach many customers.

The position of an advertisement in a magazine could also be a limitation, especially if the brand has not been able to secure a premium space – the advertisement may be placed at the back where readers may not engage with it. It can also be expensive to place an advertisement in a magazine taking into consideration the high-resolution photography that needs to appear in the advertisements, the glossy paper and production and distribution costs.

Direct mail

This is a printed advertisement that is sent to the customers directly. It is an effort to personalise a print advertisement. Names and contact details may have been bought from an electoral list, or the individuals have provided their names for the companies. These are often sent through the post. Direct mail is different from leaflets and handbills that are shared on the street. These advertisements, which can also be in the form of a letter to make them look genuine, can be useful in driving sales as they are delivered directly to the reader who may find the message relevant at that time. However, it can also be considered messy with poor images, especially if it has not been appropriately designed, and can thus be considered junk mail. There are also concerns around ethics and privacy as consumers may wonder how the brands got their details to send them the advertisements.

Summary

Advertisements are presented via different media. These includes broadcast media, display and print media. The design has been done, and this chapter explores the dissemination of these advertisements. The media is not an advertisement. The media could be used for many other things, but advertisers have found those platforms useful for engaging with the audience. It is also essential to recognise media space owners and those who go out to look for spaces and develop them in order to accept advertisements. They get the planning permission, install the displays and rent the space out to advertisers. Some media companies develop advertisements for commercial TV to allow advertisers place their message. Publishers print and distribute free magazines in order to sell advertising space. These opportunities abound. It will not be surprising as well to see advertising agencies having their own media companies. It all comes down to creating a platform that people will engage with, either when they are bored (like when using a lift or waiting for a bus) or when they feel excited as they have decided to go to the cinema. The lack of measurable engagement on traditional media is a limiting factor, and this may change the advertising landscape as advertisers will look for other media (possible digital media) that can offer them what they want.

Understanding the features of the media is essential in developing the advertising campaign. Grass and Wallace (1974), comparing print and TV as platforms for communicating adverts, suggested that readers exposed to adverts in newspapers or magazines can choose to spend much more time reading the adverts compared to when watching a commercial on television which is limited to the running time of the commercial. It is, therefore, possible that print adverts may be more effective than TV commercials, but again, it depends on the products or services that are being advertised and the embedded creativity to convey the message.

This chapter has explored a different platform that can accept advertisement. It is possible to strategically convey messages to various people at different times and in different places. While practitioners may think traditional media is dying, it is not, but rather evolving and infusing digital technology to enhance their performance and give value to the brands and agencies. The technology, however, should not take away the creativity and need to understand the features of these media. Billboards are now relying on data to give real-time updates and information. AdSmart is targeting individuals with different advertisements and direct mail is going digital.

The fact that there is a printed advertisement to go on a billboard does not mean it will fit on a telephone. Creative designers need to be aware of these features and media planners to be aware of how best to integrate the message, to reach the right people, to accommodate suitable creative elements and to make the whole process as affordable as possible. Here, negotiation skills come in. Creativity in these campaigns is essential, as discussed in the previous chapter; it is more important than ever as many brands are competing for the attention of the viewers. The design should be captivating and easy to read for the target audience, who may be driving round the roundabout or on the motorway. This also recognises the integrated marketing communication strategy of the campaigns. Advertisement is not just limited to traditional media – it is integrated with many other media. Outdoor advertisements should be designed to create attention, for people to share on social media and talk about. This gives better value for the advertising spending. Creativity is now even moving beyond the design of the advertisement to the design of the media as seen with *The Kensington* design, and a curvilinear ribbon designed billboard.

Revision questions

1. Why should an advertising practitioner be aware of traditional media?
2. Do you think outdoor media are placed in places where people get bored?
3. What are the differences and similarities between radio and television as media for advertising?
4. What are the differences and similarities between newspaper and magazine media for advertising?
5. What are the differences and similarities between billboards, posters and flyers as media for advertising?
6. Would you consider some products to be better advertised on traditional media?
7. Considering traditional media, where would you best advertise a new collection from a fashion designer, mortgage product from a bank and dental service for teenagers?
8. How would you describe the infusion of digital technology into traditional media?
9. How would you describe the future of traditional media?

Student activity

Creating a recruitment advertisement

You are forming a group as part of your task. The group should take the shape of an advertising agency, but you are not complete yet as a team. You need the services of a copywriter and graphics designer. You are therefore expected to create an advertisement to recruit from your class members.

- These advertisements will be designed on A4 paper.
- Remember you are designing two adverts: (1) for a copywriter who likes to write and (2) for a graphics designer who likes to draw. So be aware that the layout and creative elements in the two advertisements will differ.
- You should not use any computer software but create it by drawing and writing.
- You will be posting this advert on walls in the class for prospective candidates to have a look.

References

Cantor, J. & Venus, P., 1980. The effect of humor on recall of a radio advertisement. *Journal of Broadcasting & Electronic Media*, 24(1), pp. 13–22.

Dash, M. & Belgaonkar, P., 2012. Comparative effectiveness of radio, print and web advertising. *Print and Web Advertising*, 1(1), pp. 2–9.

DCM, 2020. *Cinema Advertising*. [Online] Available at: www.dcm.co.uk/advertising [Accessed 8.8.2020].

Evening Standard, 2019. [Online] Available at: www.standard.co.uk/news/uk/air-conditioning-billboard-with-your-wife-is-hot-slogan-sparks-heated-debate-a4196091.html.

Fill, C., Hughes, G., & De Francesco, S., 2013. *Advertising: Strategy, creativity and media*. London: Pearson Education.

Gökerik, M., Gürbüz, A., Erkan, I., Mogaji, E., & Sap, S., 2018. Surprise me with your ads! The impacts of guerrilla marketing in social media on brand image. *Asia Pacific Journal of Marketing and Logistics*, 30(5), pp. 1222–1238.

Gong, Z. & Cummins, R., 2020. Redefining rational and emotional advertising appeals as available processing resources: Toward an information processing perspective. *Journal of Promotion Management*, 26(2), pp. 277–299.

Grass, R. C. & Wallace, W. H., 1974. Advertising communications: Print vs. TV. *Journal of Advertising Research*, 14(5), pp. 19–23.

JCDecaux, 2016. *Synchronisation of Oxford St.* [Online] Available at: www.jcdecaux.co.uk/news/synchronisation-oxford-st [Accessed 8.8.2020].

Kotler, P., 2003. *A framework for marketing management.* Delhi: Pearson Education India.

Merritt, A., 2017. *The Impact of Alexa and Google Home on Consumer Behavior.* [Online] Available at: https://chatbotsmagazine.com/the-impact-of-alexa-and-google-home-on-consumer-behavior-c5753d838a38 [Accessed 7.7.2020].

Mittal, B., 1994. Public assessment of TV advertising: Faint praise and harsh criticism. *Journal of Advertising Research*, 34(1), pp. 35–54.

Mogaji, E., 2015. Reflecting a diversified country: A content analysis of newspaper advertisements in Great Britain. *Marketing Intelligence & Planning*, 33(6), pp. 908–926.

Mogaji, E., 2018. *Emotional appeals in advertising banking services.* London: Emerald.

Mogaji, E., 2021. Disclaimers in real estate print advertisements. In: M. Maiguny & S. Rosengren, eds. *Advances in advertising research (Vol. XI). Designing and communicating experience.* Berlin: Springer Gabler.

News, 2014. *Neuroscience: Tablets on the brain.* [Online] Available at: https://newscommercial.co.uk/insight/neuroscience-tablets-on-the-brain [Accessed 8.8.2020].

Newsworks, 2015. *Touching is believing.* [Online] Available at: www.newsworks.org.uk/Platforms/Touching-is-believing/75580 [Accessed 5.5.2020].

Sampson, J., 2015. *The power of touch shouldn't be underestimated.* [Online] Available at: www.newsworks.org.uk/opinion/tactile-newspaper-ads-are-more-effective- [Accessed 2.2.2020].

Smit, E., 1999. *Mass media advertising: Information or wallpaper?.* Amsterdam: Het Spinhuis.

Somasundaran, T. & Light, C., 1991. A cross-cultural and media specific analysis of student attitudes toward advertising. In: *Proceedings of the American Marketing Association's Educators' Conference*, pp. 667–669.

Tan, S. & Chia, L., 2007. Are we measuring the same attitude? Understanding media effects on attitude towards advertising. *Marketing Theory*, 7(4), pp. 353–377.

ThinkBox, 2019. *Define your marketing objectives.* [Online] Available at: www.thinkbox.tv/getting-on-tv/5-steps-to-getting-on-tv/1-define-your-marketing-objectives/ [Accessed 9.9.2020].

Wasserman, T., 2013. *Clever British Airways billboard tracks airplanes as they fly overhead.* [Online] Available at: https://mashable.com/2013/11/25/british-airways-billboard/?europe=true [Accessed 8.8.2020].

Willems, K., Brengman, M. & van de Sanden, S., 2017. In-store proximity marketing: Experimenting with digital point-of-sales communication. *International Journal of Retail & Distribution Management*, 45(7/8), pp. 910–927.

William, L. J. & Arthur, J. K., 1992. Observations: Do overall attitudes toward advertising affect involvement with specific advertisements? *Journal of Advertising Research*, 32(5), pp. 78–83.

Wintour, P., 2013. "Go home" billboard vans not a success, says Theresa May. *The Guardian.* [Online] Available at: www.theguardian.com/politics/2013/oct/22/go-home-billboards-pulled [Accessed 8.8.2020].

6 Advertisements shared through digital and emerging media

This chapter recognises that digital is very much integrated into marketing communications. It further emphasises that social media is not the only form of digital media. The chapter discusses various forms of digital media and how advertisements are being channelled through them. While acknowledging social media plays a massive part in digital marketing, other types of emerging media are also discussed. Location-based advertisements (LBA), online behavioural advertising (OBA) and near-field communication (NFC) are topics discussed in this chapter – uniquely, how they can all be integrated to enhance the marketing communication campaign. Besides, programmatic advertising on Facebook, Amazon and Google are discussed.

Learning outcome

At the conclusion of this teaching, students will be able to:

- Describe the features of digital media platforms;
- Recognise the difference between digital media devices and digital media platforms;
- Give examples of different digital media platforms;
- Describe location-based advertising and online behavioural advertising;
- Explain the need to understand the features and creative capabilities of digital media.

Introduction

The advertisement has been designed. It is now a physical product that needs to be delivered. In the last chapter, we discussed how advertisements are delivered through traditional media. Traditional media has value and we know it is not dying but evolving and still being used, *but* there are limitations to its capabilities in disseminating advertisements on behalf of brands. Advertisers are looking for the best media to deliver their message – media that consumers still engage with, media that can give insight and measurable data, media that can deliver. Traditional media is not guaranteed to do this.

Importantly, as consumer behaviours are changing, there are bigger expectations from the brand and advertisers for the media. Consumers are engaging with media differently, and this puts pressure on the media to step up their game or lose advertising revenue. If type of media is losing viewers or readership, the numbers will no longer be attractive to advertisers and therefore there is need to explore other media that can effectively deliver the message and, even more important, at a cheaper level and rate – why spend such a huge amount of money on TV when I can get a better reach on another medium?

And here we are with digital media and its features which have attracted the interest of advertisers. Here digital media is considered a *platform* for *sharing advertisements*. It is important to consider the keywords here.

- Platform – this is a noun. It is an animate noun that represents a physical thing. It is something that can be seen and engaged with.
- Sharing – this is a verb. It is an action word. It involves a process. An engagement between the advertisement to be disseminated and the platform to accept it. They accept digital information and effectively disseminate it.
- Advertisements – a noun. A physical thing. That can be felt (see case study 1.1). It has been produced by the advertising agencies (with the intention for it to be shared digitally). It needs a platform (the media) to make it complete its cycle.

Digital media is not limited to just online or internet-connected devices, though that is very important. There are digital media which still offers a platform without access to internet.

Digital media is not limited to mobile phones. There is more to digital media than what consumers engage with on their mobile phones There are opportunities for non-mobile digital media platforms.

This chapter will focus on digital media as a platform to disseminate the advertisements that have been created (or will be created) (Mogaji et al., 2020c). Different digital media devices and the platform (upon which advertisements are displayed) are discussed. It is important to recognise that there is a difference between a digital media device and a digital media platform. The smartphone could be a device, but it may not have social media applications on it, i.e. a platform. Two emerging technologies (in the wake of vast amounts of data and computer programming) are also covered: location-based advertisement (LBA) and online behavioural advertising (OBA). Prospects and limitations of digital media are explored and then rounded up with key considerations for a practitioner exploring digital media. So you are going to learn a lot about the different platforms of advertising.

Considerations for digital media

Here are some key considerations for digital media as we explore it in the context of a platform for disseminating advertisement.

The internet in digital media

The role of the internet cannot be overemphasised when digital media is being discussed. The internet makes digital media unique. It offers the media the ability to be mobile. This ensures that advertisements can be seen on the move and are not just limited to one location or one device. Internet-enabled digital media offers huge opportunities for advertisers and media space owners. It is not surprising that traditional media is incorporating internet technology in its offering as it tries to remain relevant.

Data in digital media

The vast amount of data being generated, increased use of mobile devices, cloud computing and the internet highlight the continued interest in digital media as a platform for sharing advertisements. A large amount of data generated by the consumers provides an insight into their behaviour. Customer analytics makes up 48% of big data use in sales and marketing (Columbus, 2016) which highlights new sources of data about the customers. Advertisers can seize the opportunity to use this data to personalise and target advertisements (Boerman et al., 2017). Marketers have never had this form of data from the customers. No doubt, these are big data collected over different touchpoints.

Consumer behaviour in digital media

Consumers do not have to write down a number after watching a television advert before making a purchase. They are spending less time reading newspapers. Consumers' engagement with media is evolving. While the internet has contributed to this evolvement, consumers' engagement and interest in digital media offer great opportunities for advertisers (Mogaji, et al., 2020a). The way consumers engage with advertisements on media is changing, and this has spurred more innovative ways of breaking the media clusters and serving advertisements to individuals who are more likely to engage with it. Consumers are changing, and advertising media is changing as well (Kumar & Gupta, 2016). We will always be served with advertisements (as brands will always want to communicate); the way brands will do this will keep evolving with consumer behaviour.

Social media in digital media

Social media may often be confused with digital media. Once social media is mentioned, people may think it can be interchangeably used with digital media. This is not so. There is a difference between social media and digital media. Social media is a form of digital media, and it is not the same as digital media. There are many forms of digital media and social media is one of them. Though social media is very popular and adopted by different brands, it is essential not to ignore other forms of media that can be used as well to disseminate a message effectively (Marlowe et al., 2017).

Digital media devices

As discussed earlier, the focus of this chapter is on digital media as platforms that can be used to share advertisements, suggesting that advertisers can place their developed advertisements on these platforms to reach out to people. These media platforms are hosted on several devices which allow the consumers' interaction with the media.

These devices include:

Mobile phone

This device has phone, maps, browser, camera text messages, email, games, and so many applications in everyone's hand. Consumers are always engaging with the mobile phone while on the go, relaxing at home and even in some private spaces. These open opportunities for advertisements to be served through any digital media on the phone. Since consumers are always near the phone, they are more likely to see the advertisement.

Tablet

This is closely related to mobile phones in terms of accessibility and mobility, but it should be noted that it has a bigger screen size which gives an opportunity for an enhanced media experience. The screens offer a larger real experience than smartphones do. Likewise, tablets are mobile but often used in leisure and not always on the go like a mobile phone. Most people have tablets to replace their desktop computers at home. They also use their tablets at home when relaxing and not for work purposes.

Computer

Unlike mobile phones, computers are not often mobile, with the exception of laptops. Desktop computers remain inside, and though still able to access the internet, the purpose is different. An advertisement which may require action while on the move may not be relevant to this medium. In addition, websites can be purposefully designed for desktops, and offer a different user experience which may not be available on mobile phones.

Games

This digital media device is an electronic game that can be played on a computing device, such as a personal computer, gaming console or mobile phone. Depending on the platform, video games can be subcategorised into computer games and console games. Social networks, smartphones, tablets and access to the internet have further shaped the prospects of video games as a platform for sharing advertisements. There are new categories such as mobile and social games. The UK Interactive Entertainment Association (UKIE, n.d.) reported that the Asia-Pacific region leads the global market with 52% of the market share. Europe, the Middle East and Africa have 21% share of the market. Mintel estimated the United Kingdom's mobile gaming market was worth £993 million in 2018. This market value represents an 11.7% rise from 2017 and is a continuation of its strong growth since 2013 (Mintel, 2018). "Grand Theft Auto V" is the most profitable entertainment product of all time with 90 million sales worth $6 billion, more than any other single media title in history, and it continues to sell (Cherney, 2018). There are people congregating to play games around the world and this offers advertisers an opportunity to place an advertisement in the gaming ecosystem. It should, however, be noted that video games are only a platform and it is not compulsory that advertisements will be presented on all games. As we have websites and television stations that do not take advertainments, some games also do not feature advertisements.

Outdoor media

Outdoor media advertising, also called out-of-home advertising is advertising experienced outside the home of a consumer. It is strategically placed where people can see it and this also uses technology in reaching its audience. This advertising technique incorporates mobile and internet technology with traditional media to form a device which can allow digital media files. Billboards and bus shelters offer a platform which allows advertisements to be shared digitally. This platform aligns with mobile networks, the location of mobile users and relevant data to inform the advertisement. While mobile phones and tablets may offer an advertisement on a personal level, these digital billboards can complement that to ensure the messages are effectively delivered.

The digital media platform

It is important to note that the digital media device does not necessarily serve as the platform. You can have a mobile phone and not receive an advert on it because your Bluetooth is not on, or you have not shared your location or installed the appropriate app. While the device is needed, there are specific platforms which serve as the media upon which advertisements are being shared. While there are variations across the platform, there are possibilities of the same advertisement being shared on different platforms. The subsequent sections explore various forms of digital media platform.

Social media

Social media can be defined as a group of technologies that foster engagement where individuals are active participants in creating, organising, editing, combining, sharing, commenting on and rating Web content, as well as forming social networks through interacting and linking with each other (Chun et al., 2010; Criado et al., 2013). These technologies include social networking (e.g., Facebook), microblogging (e.g., Twitter) and multimedia sharing (e.g., YouTube). Social media is no longer new. Organisations are increasingly adopting social media for strategic corporate and organisational communication and public relations (Macnamara & Zerfass, 2012). It has been hailed as transformative, which allows brands to engage with their stakeholders (Mogaji et al., 2016).

Social media include but are not limited to:

Facebook

Facebook is presently the largest social networking site in the world and one of the most widely used. It connects friends and relatives to create a network. Brands can have their profile pages and engage with those who have liked their pages. Users can share comments, upload their images, and engage with the university.

Twitter

Twitter is a social network and media platform where users communicate with 280-character messages, along with photos, videos and other content. Twitter is also not just a social networking platform, it is also a microblogging service through which users chat, like and follow a thread of post and interact with each other through what are known as "tweets". On Twitter, registered (whether verified or not) users can like, post or retweet something said by another and through that can make a message go viral. However, unregistered Twitter users cannot comment or tweet but only read the tweets of other registered users. Twitter is known for real-time discussions on breaking news stories and trends. Brands have their profile, (which can be verified), they follow other profiles, and they are followed as well. Brands can send tweets, and they can retweet tweets, converse through direct messages and reply to tweets. This is an affordable and reasonably easy yet fast way for brands and individuals to send their adverts out to users as there are billions of users of Twitter who are scattered around the world.

Instagram

This is a free online photo–video sharing app that is independent of, but owned by Facebook. It allows for the addition of several filters, editing and sharing options. Brands can have their verified profile and share photographs, videos and stories, which they use as a mode of engaging with their followers. Conversations can also be carried out using direct messages, which are private conversations.

Snapchat

A photo- and video-messaging app launched in 2011. It enables the user to chat with friends by using pictures. Users can add filters, text, drawings or emoji to their content before sending it to their recipients. Individual messages last only up to 10 seconds before they are entirely removed from the company's servers. This feature gives the user control over their post and makes it unique and attractive to its users.

LinkedIn

Acquired by Microsoft in 2016, LinkedIn is one of the most popular professional social networking sites. It is used worldwide by all types of professionals and serves as an ideal platform to connect with different businesses, and locate and hire ideal candidates. Individuals have their page, which serves as an online CV, and they can share video, images and live streams with their connections. Brands also have their own page where they share different content, including job vacancies.

WhatsApp

This is another social media technology which joined Facebook in 2014 but continues to operate as a separate app, with a laser focus on building a messaging service that works fast and reliably anywhere in the world. This is linked with specific telephone numbers and allows chat and phone calls. More than 1 billion people in over 180 countries use WhatsApp. Businesses have their pages and can communicate with brands. It is often integrated as a chatbot and AI assistance on websites. There is now WhatsApp Business, a type of WhatsApp that allows brands to set up their profile in a formal way. This also allows them to interact with their prospective customers in a professional manner. There is a "status feature" on WhatsApp which allows users/brands to place advertisements and inform people on their contacts list about a product.

YouTube

Operating as one of Google's subsidiaries, YouTube is the world's largest video-sharing social networking site that enables users to upload and share videos, view them, comment on them and like them. This social network is accessible across the globe and even enables users to create a YouTube channel where they can upload all their personally recorded videos to showcase to their friends and followers. Since YouTube deals primarily with videos, it might require a user to spend money on creating engaging content (adverts) which will be positively accepted by consumers.

TikTok (DouYin)

As short-form videos are gaining increasing popularity through social media, TikTok is another growing mobile video-sharing social networking service owned by ByteDance, a Beijing-based Internet technology company founded in 2012. TikTok positions itself to focus on quirky videos, most of which have not been too professionally or aesthetically produced (Wang, 2020); these videos can be used to endorse and demonstrate different products and brands. As of August 2020, Microsoft is considering acquiring TikTok in the United States, subject to a complete security review.

There are many more social media platforms for different purposes. Likewise, these social media platforms allow different advertisement formats. The fact that they are all social media with the capabilities of accepting advertisements does not make them all the same. It is important to understand the different features of these media and then develop advertisements to fit the media.

Case study 6.1

Audi's community driven digital advertising approaches for India

Audi is amongst the world's highest selling premium luxury car brands. It originated from Germany where the company has established the business across different countries and it is known as the sporty car of premium futuristic designs. Looking at the growing demand for luxury products in Asian countries, India and China, specifically, are lucrative markets for premium luxury cars; especially India, being a hub of the fastest-growing millionaires in the world and a market which is known for profit making investments (Bhandari, 2013).

Audi cars have been in India since 2004 but the company established its Indian wing with headquarters in Mumbai, Maharashtra in March 2007 (CarDekho, 2020). Initially, Audi targeted only the big cities in India during their launch (Bhandari, 2013). However, now tier-2 and tier-3 city audiences are contributing to the majority of the sales as ultra high network individuals in these cities have emerged and are willing to flaunt their achievements and possessions (Barlaskar, 2020). Importantly, Mercedes Benz and BMW entered the Indian market before Audi and are immediate competitors of the company. While being positioned as a young, dynamic and innovative brand, Audi is targeting the digital advertising approaches of a young segment of the Indian population (age group of 31–40 years), especially with the use of hashtags.

In efforts to be a futuristic brand and appeal to the young generation of India, Audi launched the flagship SUV – the Audi Q8 – in March 2020 under the campaign #8thDimensionReimagined in collaboration with eight illustration artists to create an impact through the design language, performance and exclusivity of the new SUV (ETBrandEquity, 2020). Second, Audi launched an after-sales service-focused campaign #ReadyToDrive on their website and social media handles from 17 August to 30 September 2020, to strengthen the company's customer service-driven positioning. Lastly, during the COVID-19 pandemic where lockdown made consumers spend more time on social media, Audi launched its two car models online and also launched engagement and customer-service driven social media campaigns such as #AudiTogether – a full online service booking and customer-assistance with the message "We are in this together" and a "Do's and Don'ts" campaign, giving out tips for car care during the lockdown. To engage the digital audience, it also came up with #FourRingsChallenege, where the audience recreated the rings of the Audi logo with things such as coins etc. available at home (Nagar, 2020). It also received social media traction for its post "keep safe distance" where Audi separated the iconic four rings to signify social distancing (Audi, March 2020).

To conclude, Audi is looking towards a digital future, focusing on community building as the world of advertising and brand communications will have to be more about serving consumers and people first, rather than just about the brand, especially with the new technology via mobile phones.

Prof. Varsha Jain, Professor of Marketing, Co-chairperson, Doctoral Level Program and Research Chairperson, MICA, India
Mr Vashishtha Joshi, Research Associate, MICA, India

Internet browser

The ability to browse the internet opens the opportunity for advertisers to serve prospective customers with advertisements. Internet browsing can be on a smartphone, tablet or even desktop. It is not necessarily linked to any mobile applications. Sometimes, it is used for advertising as adverts will pop up on the screen of users periodically.

Email

Email offers a platform for advertisers to reach out to customers. As individuals, we are often engaged with our emails, and it is not surprising to see advertisements being served.

Embedded email

This platform allows advertisements in the form of an email to be embedded into the message thread of the user. The advertisement is placed as part of the email. This is often for free email accounts provided by Yahoo, Outlook or Gmail. These advertisements are also identified with the word "AD" to show that they are not part of your email but an advertisement. The advertisements are also bound to change on a regular basis, and they are shown based on the interest or past browsing session of the email owners.

Direct email

These allow advertisements to be sent as direct mail into the mailboxes of customers. These are often sent to those who have subscribed or given their emails to the company.

Personal data and information legitimately collected online by companies can be used to design and personalise advertisements that appeal to the consumers' emotions and are shared online. This process differs from highly personalised and rational data such as age, gender and location which Aguirre and Davies (2015) found to have a reduced click-through rate. This often comes in the form of newsletters.

Website

Websites offer a huge platform and real estate for advertisement. Different parts of the website can allow advertisements. If consumers are visiting the website there are more likely to be advertisements showing on it. This is not compulsory, however, as some websites do not run advertisements as they do not rely on income from selling advertising pages to remain viable. Just like car owners who have signed up with Wrapify and allow brands to place adverts on their cars for which they get paid, website owners get paid for putting advertisements on their websites. As an advertiser, you must pay to advertise on a website. The payment, however, depends on many factors, including the size of the advertisement, the duration and level of engagement (viewership) on the website. While it may not be easy to negotiate with different websites, there are brokers who serve as middlemen between website owners and brands and they use programmatic, which is a process of buying advertisement spaces automatically, using data to decide which to buy and how much to pay for them (Palos-Sanchez et al., 2019). Programmatic provides a single view of the consumer and single point of media planning and buying across all digital media channels and allows marketers to leverage their own data, media and technology (Dawson & Lamb, 2016). Programmatic advertising ensures that targeted advertisements are optimised and delivered as anticipated (Mogaji et al., 2020b).

Different forms of media spaces are available for advertisements on websites. They include but are not limited to:

Displays

These media allow graphics advertisements to be placed. They allow images, text and even videos and are displayed around the website. These displays include banner adverts, which are often rectangular in shape (Figure 6.1), positioned at the top of a page or blog post. They can also appear at the bottom of the page. There are Skyscraper adverts that appear on the side of the website (Figure 6.2); they are like banner adverts that are turned around. Also, there are square or rectangular adverts that appear next to or in the content of the website (Figure 6.3). These displays accept the same creative elements, but there is variation in size, which also affects how the messages will be arranged and designed on the banner.

Figure 6.1 Banner display advertisement
Source: author.

FREE

ADVERTISING ON
DIGITAL MEDIA

LECTURE
TO BE
DELIVERED BY

DOCTOR
EMMANUEL
MOGAJI

THURSDAY
4TH NOVEMBER, 2021

KW315

11AM

Figure 6.2 Skyscraper display advertisement
Source: author.

Pop-ups

The dynamic nature of the platform makes it unique. As indicated, it "pops up" or appears when consumers visit the page. The popping up and instantly appearing on a webpage makes it possible to get the attention of the viewer. A displayed advertisement can also be made to pop up. Media platforms are programmed to appear when you first open a page or after a certain amount of time has passed, such as a second or two. This can be used to gain viewers' attention to a specific promotion, discount or deal or to subscribe for information. As a limitation, these pop-ups can be blocked with ad-blocking software, which means that even though the advert is on that platform, it has not been shared effectively.

Overlays

This type of media is like a pop-up as they are dynamic, but overlays operate a little differently. Unlike pop-ups that appears without any trigger, overlays cover the whole webpage through an interaction with the mouse. This allows the brand to have the full attention of the viewer while engaging with the website. This looks like the full coverage of a newspaper advertisement.

In-text adverts

This platform allows advertisements to be shared as links between content. This is also referred to as inline advertising. As readers are engaging with the content of the webpage, they are more likely to see the text. Many programs automatically insert text adverts based on keywords chosen. More so, since they are links, there are possibilities of clicking it to get more information about the message. This, however, can be distracting, especially for those who are much involved in the text and they may decide to ignore the advertisement. However, provided it is something related to the content of the website, there are possibilities of following the link.

Native adverts

Unlike having an advert within an article on a website, there are possibilities of presenting an advertisement in the form of an article. This is called native advertising. This allows advertisements to have the look and feel of the site on which they appear. Brands can sponsor a blog post and publish it on the website. Though they may declare it as an advertisement, its look and feel make it more engaging and readers may engage with it,

Figure 6.3 Rectangle banner display advertisement
Source: author.

thinking it is part of the website. This also highlights a different creative approach. Instead of the usual images and graphics for the display and pop-up advertisement, native advertisement is text-based – the content creation is a form of blog post to give any advice or highlight the benefits of a product or service.

Paid search

When you do a search, there are some results that appear which look like an advertisement above the search results. This applies to search engines and search results. It is considered a form of native advertising as the advertisements have the feel and look of the search results. It is worthy of note that paid search is simply a digital advertising method that many search engines like Bing and Google use to help advertising agencies show their ads on their search engine results pages (SERPs). Many paid searches are designed to operate on a pay-per-click model. This means that an advertiser doesn't have to pay for an advert on paid search until an internet user clicks on the advertisement and views it. These advertisements are paid for, to appear based on the search engines and the search keywords

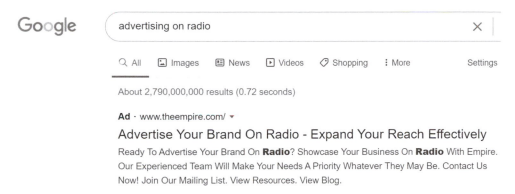

Figure 6.4 Paid search result on Google
Source: author.

that have been used according to the interest of the browser. These paid searches normally have the word "AD" in front of the text (see Figure 6.4), although it is not surprising that people will ignore the "AD" and still click on the link (advert). Google Ads and SEO are important creative considerations for paid search.

Smartphones

This device allows different platform among which are those that are specifically situated on the mobile phone.

Text messages

This platform offers brands the opportunity to engage with the audience directly. It can also be considered a form of direct mail as it is sent to the individuals. Consumers are still able to receive text messages/SMS as a form of advertisement (see Figure 6.5). There are possibilities of customising the message to appeal to the receiver. Likewise, there are possibilities of brands customising their name on the message to make it appear genuine. Importantly as well, the advertisement can be location based. That is, it will be sent to those that are within the area as they may relate better to the advertisement. These forms of advertisements are cheap as you can send bulk SMS to the customer, but there are limitations with getting the prospective customers' numbers (these should be collected ethically and with the owners' consent) (Bamba & Barnes, 2007). In addition, there are limitations with how well people may engage with it, especially since WhatsApp may offer a better platform to send text messages and at a relatively cheaper price.

Bluetooth advertisements

Like SMS, this can be location-based. This suggests that people who are passing through a geo-fenced location may receive a message on their phone through their Bluetooth).

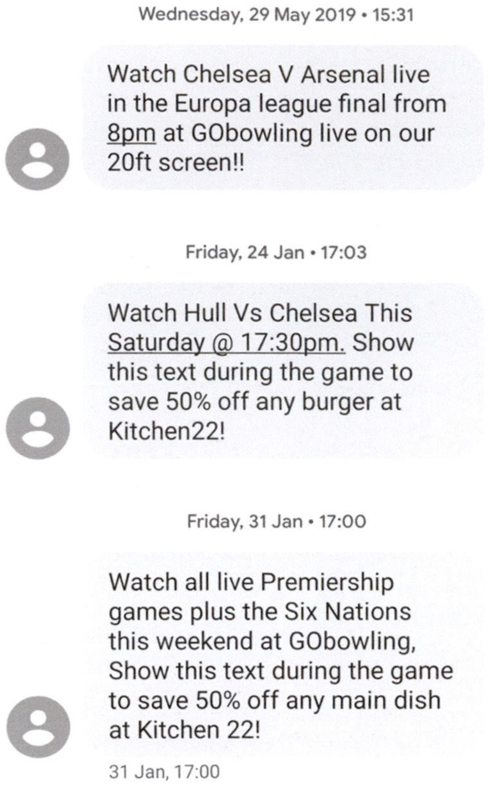

Wednesday, 29 May 2019 • 15:31

Watch Chelsea V Arsenal live
in the Europa league final from
8pm at GObowling live on our
20ft screen!!

Friday, 24 Jan • 17:03

Watch Hull Vs Chelsea This
Saturday @ 17:30pm. Show
this text during the game to
save 50% off any burger at
Kitchen22!

Friday, 31 Jan • 17:00

Watch all live Premiership
games plus the Six Nations
this weekend at GObowling,
Show this text during the game
to save 50% off any main dish
at Kitchen 22!

31 Jan, 17:00

Figure 6.5 Text message advertisements
Source: author.

Unlike text messages, this Bluetooth messages allows more creative elements to be integrated with the message; it gives information about promotions and sales happening, and provides real-time information. For example, if a store is having a sales promotion, it might send a Bluetooth message to everyone passing in front of their store (Page et al., 2018). This platform can be effective, provided it is not intrusive, and it is something that people can engage with instantly and decide. This can be better for low involving products or services whereby people do not have to take their time to decide. The downside of this advertising technique is that people may not have their Bluetooth on to accept the message.

App advertisements

A mobile application can be free to download for users. However, you may be expected to pay for some applications. It is likely you get served with an advertisement if you have not paid for a software application. The mobile application offers another platform for advertisers to reach prospective customers. This advertising technique allows advertisers to put an advert around the mobile application. This can be effective as the advertisers can target those who have downloaded the application; the level of engagement with the advertisement can also be tracked. The downside to this approach is that people may find it instructive and may just click the advertisement to carry on with what they want to do. While it can be argued that the advertisements are purposefully targeted, there is an indication of intrusion and lack of engagement.

Computer games

As indicated earlier, the vast amount of people engaging in video games offers brands opportunities to show them the advertisements. While the gaming and e-sports industries are being transformed into premium revenue engines, advertisers are able to tap into pop culture through games either with PC gamers, online games or console gaming, including Xbox and PlayStation. In-game advertisements have been considered suitable for reaching men between the ages 16 and 34 who uses games as a means of relaxing and entertainment instead of watching TV. For advertisers, it offers an opportunity to engage hard-to-reach audiences across screens and gain access to unique product placements.

Advertisements for computer games can be presented in two forms:

In-games

These are advertisements in the form of product placements in the course of the game. Many players across the world are playing the game and seeing the advertisements that have been designed as part of the game (see Figure 6.6). Several games utilise billboard-like advertisements or product placement to create a realistic gaming environment. Companies like Anzu.io use programmatic technology real-time data to serve up digital adverts to gamers in a seamless, hyper-targeted way.

These advertisements are integrated directly into natural spaces within video games, allowing advertisers to deliver campaigns at speed with reach and scale. This is referred to as blended in-game advertising, where advertisements are integrated into the gameplay as part of the environment. These in-game advertisements could be static or dynamic.

Static in-game advertising (SIGA)

These advertisements are integrated during the development and production stage of the game. It does not require internet access but cannot be changed once the game has been developed. Everyone playing the game will be seeing the advertisement.

Dynamic in-game advertising (DIGA)

This offers the opportunity to update and change the advertisement in real-time for different players around the world. It has the option of geo-targeting continent by country, region, city and age targeting. DIGA often takes the form of placements such as billboards, posters and hoardings situated throughout a 3D video game environment. The creative adverts that are served are unblockable by gamers or audiences, are non-intrusive and highly visible, meaning brands and advertisers can rely on instant, up-to-date information at any time.

Figure 6.6 Example of in-games advertisement
Credit: Anzu.io.

On-games

This platform allows the brand to advertise during the game or at intervals. This can be effectively provided as it is something people are interested in – that is why it is essential to understand this advertising technique, the media and how best to engage them. A player who is interested in continuing the game may not be interested in the advertisement that has been served. GoogleAdMob serves as the broker between game developers and advertisers. The platform sells advertisement space in real-time to programmatic buyers. It allows in-app advertisements, with actionable insights and powerful, easy-to-use tools. The platform allows developers to integrate native, rewarded, banner, video and interstitial adverts seamlessly into their application.

Advergaming

This type of in-game advertising takes the form of fully functional games that are developed for the sole purpose of promoting a company, brand or product. RapidFire offers the creation of such advergames (RapidFire, n.d.). Companies can promote their products through the elements integrated into a game. This increases brand awareness and encourages users to talk about the game and consequently, about the products advertised. The game may also be distributed freely as a marketing tool. Mexican food chain Chipotle teamed up with academy award-winning Moonbot Studios to develop an animated short and iOS game promoting sustainable farming (*The Week*, 2013). America's Army: Proving Grounds is the official game of the US Army, an innovative first-person action PC game series that provides an inside perspective into military combat. This free military game focuses on small unit tactical manoeuvres and puts you to the test in a wide variety of new America's Army maps and AA fan favourites.

On a positive note, it can increase brand awareness as it makes users interact with the product. It can also stir positive word of mouth as people who enjoyed the game might talk about it. It is also suitable for any business, as it's all about engaging with the customers, and this can also have long-term results. The icon on the customer device serves as an icon. The characters remain memorable as well. The downside, however, is the cost of the design and development. Since this is not a game to be sold, the brand will incur the cost of design. And this may also affect the quality which may discourage people from engaging with the game. A brand might want to save money and develop a cheap game with poor quality interface and design. Users may not be interested in the game, especially if they have played better ones. The cost of promoting the game is also a limitation for the brand.

The prospects of gaming advertisements are high, and there are many people around the world playing the games; technology allows us to integrate advertisements in real-time into video games for the console, PC, and mobile platforms. It can be scalable and allows for geo-targeting, age targeting and frequency capping. However, there are limitations with the perception of the advertisement by those playing the games, and often they do not want distracting advertisements when they have already paid the retail price and/or a monthly subscription fee. People want to enjoy themselves playing the game and advertisements can sometimes become intrusive. However, this does not negate the benefits of the advertising platform.

Smart speakers

This is also a platform that is becoming an integral part of consumers' days today and may be influencing advertising practises. Two in five consumers find voice ads to be more engaging than traditional banner ads or TV ad spots, according to an Adobe study of over 1,000 consumers. And a similar number finds them less intrusive, too (Koetsier, 2019). Smart speakers may just rely on the top search result to give results for the consumers. For example, if someone is asking *Alexa* for the best restaurant in town, the speaker may as well just read out the top search on Google. So, as user adoption increases – mainly of Amazon Echo, Google Home and Apple HomePod – the reach for audio advertising via these devices also grows (Gilliland, 2019). Krauth (2018) predicted what advertising on smart speakers looks like, making it more engaging and interactive than radio advertisement.

Billboards

This may be considered a traditional form of media, but there are growing prospects and possibilities of its integration with digital technology. Digital billboards can update and provide information in real-time. They can also be integrated into the location-based advertisement. A more personalised approach to location-specific advertising involves the use of beacons. For example, some companies use Bluetooth low energy beacons to send consumers specific promotions directly to their smartphone when they are in the vicinity of a new product. Another tactic is to attach computer chips to flyers and then tether these chips to specific billboards. These billboards can also be integrated with *proximity marketing* which allows customers with mobile phones to get served with relevant promotions when they are within a location. Likewise, two-dimensional bar codes such as QR codes (quick response codes) and NFC Tags (near-field communication) can be integrated with digital billboards to target the customers effectively.

Emerging technologies

Due to increasing access to the internet, the amount of data being generated and changing consumer behaviours, there are emerging areas of technology and digital marketing that can be explored.

Location-based advertising

The expanding diffusion of GPS-enabled smartphones and wearables and increasing capacities to collect and handle big data (McAfee et al., 2012) in real-time is offering advertisers the opportunity to target consumers in their location. This is described as location-based advertising (LBA). It is defined as "targeted advertising initiatives delivered to a mobile device from an identified sponsor that is specific to the location of the consumer" (Unni & Harmon, 2007, p. 28). LBA bridges the physical world with the digital world, providing contextual marketing communications and promotions to customers, reflecting their preferences, geographical locations and the time of day (Schade et al., 2018). Therefore LBA integrates mobile advertising directly with target services. The technology is used to pinpoint the consumer's location and then provide location-specific advertisements on the consumer's device.

LBA could be used in different locations and for different businesses. Hyper-contextual targeting sends out a contextual message to people in a location. If a retail store is opening in the neighbourhood, LBA allows advertisements about that context (new store) to be sent out to targeted individuals in the postcode.

Geo-aware targeting displays the mobile advertisement to prospective customers in a location (which could have been geo-fenced) to a possible customer who is close to a location. There are also possibilities for place-based LBA which sends messages to customers at a certain time and location. This could be Uber, for example, sending out an advertisement to people after a football game or music show. The people are targeted because they are in a location (stadium) at a time (after the match) and they may want to consider taking Uber. Geo-conquesting is another form of LBA which allows a brand to target a user when they are physically in or around a competitor's store. This could be to bring them in to get a better offer. For example, ASDA could set a geo-conquesting LBA around Sainsbury's location, displaying advertisements to those around Sainsbury's that ASDA has a better offer and they can also be served with coupons or promotional offers.

Location-based advertising can be a complex system. Location data may be easy to find, but customers may not be willing to share their locations. Consumers' intention to subscribe to LBA is hindered because of privacy concerns and the idea that people often do not see value in the advertisement, although there are indications that consumers may share their location data for cash rewards, location-based discounts or loyalty points. However, once the customer's location is hidden, the advertisement may no longer be targeted. Johnson (2017) reports that the complexities in ad targeting reaching a sizable audience are challenging and questions about the accuracy of the location-based firm's data, which relies on bits of information pumped through technology platforms, have not made LBA worked well for brands.

Recognising these challenges, it is important to leverage different information for reaching the customers accurately, transparently and effectively. This may necessitate the need to work with agencies that are specialists in LBA, leveraging location intelligence for relevant media campaigns that drive real results. Examples of these companies are PlaceIQ, NinthDecimal and Nuviad. Though Schade et al. (2018) identified three key stakeholders in an LBA context: (1) LBA providers (e.g., Google, Facebook, Telefonica, Vodafone), (2) advertising companies (e.g., McDonald's, Starbucks) and (3) consumers that use LBA (i.e. LBA users), it is important to identify another stakeholder, which is the advertising agency, albeit there is a high possibility they are working with the brand and will be liaising with the LBA providers on behalf of the brand.

Online behavioural advertising

It is no longer news that advertisers are increasingly monitoring people's online behaviour and using the information collected to target them with relevant marketing communications. This phenomenon is called online behavioural advertising (OBA). Boerman et al. (2017, p. 364) defined OBA as "the practice of monitoring people's online behaviour and using the collected information to show people individually targeted advertisements". Advertisers see it as part of the future of advertising, one of the most important new ways of reaching targeted audiences (Boerman et al., 2017; Kumar & Gupta, 2016).

With regard to data used to create OBA, Boerman et al. (2017) argued that personalisation is based on the types and amount of personal data being used. The types of personal data include browsing data or search history while amount refers to the intensity and combination of that information. Boerman et al. (2017) noted that OBA differs from other types of online advertising because of the covert nature of collecting personal data as this may be harmful and unethical, as consumers are unaware of the tactics advertisers put in place to collect the data. There have been concerns raised about privacy as this involves collecting, using and sharing personal data and consumer responses toward OBA (Baek & Mariko, 2012).

There are several players involved in OBA and third-party tracking, including ad servers, agencies, ad networks, exchanges, data aggregators and demand-side platforms. The demand-side platform (DSP) can be considered the most important stakeholder as it helps disseminate these advertisements to different platforms based on online behaviour. DSP is a system for advertisers to purchase and manage ad inventories from multiple ad sources through a single interface. This is normally done using intelligent software which bids on the inventories using an auction process. This makes the buying and selling of ads cheaper and more reliable. This whole setup is termed "programmatic advertising", and the bidding process by which ad placements are auctioned within micro-seconds is called "real-time bidding (RTB)".

Often consumers feel the advertisements are boring, intrusive or not interesting at all and thereby they put up a defence mechanism by using ad blockers, skipping the advertisements or just ignoring them (Mogaji & Danbury, 2017) and this has economic implications as the advertisements are not received as intended. Baek and Mariko (2012) found that this ad irritation increases ad scepticism, which consequently leads to more avoidance of OBA. However, there is evidence that advertisements that target individuals with their interest receive a higher level of engagement. Tucker (2014) found that Facebook ads which appeal to a person's interests led to higher click-through rates and likewise Aguirre and Davies (2015) showed that moderately personalised Facebook ads increased click-through rates; this highlights the possibilities of embedded emotional appeals in personalised advertisements to reach out to prospective customers, as Mogaji (2018) found that lack of interest and congruency with personal values are some of the reasons why advertisements are ignored.

Online behavioural advertising (OBA) is conducted by using third-party tracking. This means a tracking device – in the form of, for example, a cookie – is used to collect and analyse the behaviour of a computer user. There are also indications that third-party tracking is collecting information from many other sources and sharing the information. While there are concerns around the ethical implications, OBA offers brands the opportunity to serve prospective customers with advertisements they are more likely to engage with. This includes contextual advertisements which allow individuals to receive an advertisement when visiting a website. Consumers are more likely to click on the advertisement because it closely relates to their interests. In addition, the level of engagement through OBA can convert visitors to customers. Those who feel the advertisement has been considerate and relevant are more likely to engage further with the brand and thereby contribute to a positive impact on the brand's return on investment (ROI).

Augmented and virtual reality (AVR)

Augmented reality technology has already gained popularity, so more and more users are enjoying it. Many companies have already embraced this cutting-edge technology for their ads. Today, marketers benefit greatly from using augmented reality (AR) in advertising. Let's see what advantages AR has for marketers and advertisers (Gleb, 2020). The first and most important advantage of AR ads is that they help brands and advertising agencies to create a certain emotional connection with customers. Augmented reality ads are so interactive and realistic that consumers feel like they're playing an engaging video game. This builds an emotional connection, increasing brand awareness and encouraging customers to make purchases. Another benefit is the possibility of virtual try-ons (Kim & Kim, 2014). Your consumers can try on many different items with AR: glasses, shoes, clothing, jewellery, watches, etc., without leaving their homes. This makes AR ads a powerful tool for driving sales and increasing revenue, especially in the age of e-commerce.

Near-field communication (NFC)

Near-field communication (NFC) is a technology that enables a device to communicate with another at a maximum distance of around 20cm or less (Curran et al., 2012). This technology is a specification for contactless communication between two devices often used in contactless payment and smartcards on transportation systems where smartphones and other handheld devices can tap into a device at close proximity and receive information. There will be 1.6 billion NFC-enabled devices by 2024 and a market value of $47 billion by that same year (STMicroelectronics, 2019) which highlights the growing prospects of NFC.

Advertisers have also been using NFC to further share and disseminate their communication messages with the target audience, especially through the combination of smartphones and bus shelters. NFC brings the benefits of digital advertising strategies to physical and traditional media. It addresses consumer preference for speed, convenience and control (NFC, 2020). Bus shelter owners (like JCDecaux, Exterion and Clear Channel) install the NFC technology in the form of a small patch/tag beside the bus shelters. Advertisers can complement the bus shelter advertisement with technology that provides additional information about the advertisement. An action is triggered every time the tag is tapped by another NFC-enabled device (JCDecaux, 2011). Advertisers typically program this action to "open a website" which displays additional content regarding the brand or product. Importantly, it provides a more interactive experience based on proximity (Joshi, 2020).

JCDecaux (2011) noted that action triggered by NFC on bus shelters for an advertisement can include:

- Access to additional mobile content like visiting a webpage linked to the advertisement on the bus shelter, providing simple and straightforward customer engagement.
- Social media interaction which prompts visitors to "Like" a brand on Facebook, follow the brand on Twitter or Instagram and check into the location.
- Contact information which allows the consumer to save the email address, phone number, website of the brand for future follow-up. This contact information can also

include direction to a store or direction about how to do a task or use a product. To promote their new product line in London, Ralph Lauren had NFC tags on advertisements displayed in the window of Harrods, a luxury retail store. When customers tap the NFC with their mobile device, they are provided with a map of Harrods and navigation to the section where the Ralph Lauren collection is located.

- Custom vouchers for consumers who tap with their phones. They can be prompted to download a voucher that can be used in store. This can also include special contests and discount offers. In 2012, Orange launched the UK's first mobile contactless retail reward scheme described as "Quick Tap Treats", in partnership with the EAT restaurant chain.

- Payment can also be made on the spot for services advertised on the poster. China Mobile Hong Kong launched "NFC enabled services which support NFC mobile payment services" provided by designated banks/institutions.

The increasing awareness about NFC campaigns coupled with the increase in NFC-enabled smartphone users is bound to increase the scope for application of NFC-based ad campaigns in the coming years (Joshi, 2020). While the NFC campaign has its benefits and advantages, there are challenges with customer engagement; often NFC advert campaigns are targeted at those who are mobile, walking or waiting around bus shelters. More so, some customers may be reluctant to use the technology, especially as it concerns data protection, scanning information in a public place and security with regard to mobile payment. There are also challenges with the speed of data transfer between devices which may be due to the Wi-Fi or Bluetooth connection, or the customer's phone may not be able to process huge data. Figure 6.7 shows a bus shelter billboard in Balham London with the NFC tag.

Figure 6.7 A bus shelter billboard in Balham, London with the NFC tag
Source: photo by author.

Case study 6.2

KFC's Hot Shots Box Meal

KFC was launching their "Hot Shots Box Meal" in the UK and created an out-of-home (OOH) campaign using outdoor media sites. KFC worked with Posterscope, one of world's leading location-based marketing specialists and part of Dentsu Aegis Network, Proxama (now Location Sciences), a data intelligence company that verifies the accuracy and quality of location data used in proximity-targeted advertising, and Clear Channel, one of the UK's leading OOH and DOOH media owners. This campaign was not just an ordinary OOH campaign as they were strategically placed in outdoor locations and integrated NFC to deliver intuitive experiences to digital native and mobile-first customers.

Posterscope (advertising agency through their media planners) places an advertisement for KFC introducing the "Hot Shots Box Meal" on a bus shelter (owned by Clear Channel). Posterscope programmes the NFC tag that has been provided by Clear Channel to contain information about the nearest KFC, providing direction to the KFC and providing the customers with coupons which they can use in the KFC restaurant. So, when customers are standing at the bus shelter, they see the advertisement and are prompted to touch the NFC with their mobile phones. Utilising over 400 of Clear Channel's NFC-enabled UK outdoor media sites, consumers are encouraged to tap or scan for directions to their closest restaurant which is an effective technique for bringing in those customers who are on the go and need to find a good place for a quick meal.

The use of NFC allows KFC to integrate the power of digital media with traditional outdoor advertisement. With most smartphones with the NFC app, web-browsing capabilities and GPS, brands can have an understanding of how consumers are engaging with the advertisement. The media planners have measurable insights about the number of times people touched the NFC at a particular location and their subsequent action. Likewise, consumers can get more information, especially about products and services that may require instant decisions. This may be applicable for restaurants; retail stores that need the footfall of target customers usually put the NFC tag on a billboard closer to their store.

Prospects of digital media

Cheap

One of the greatest advantages of digital media is the cost, compared to traditional media. Traditional media offers a platform for mass media, and it is expensive to reach that mass media and a large number of the target audience, unlike digital media where advertisers can just pay to reach the targeted audience. The cost makes it more viable for businesses, especially small brands, to share their advertisements on social media without going through the hassle of having TV or newspaper advertisements, which are far costlier than digital media advertisements.

Accessibility

Advertisements shared on digital media are accessible anytime and anywhere. The message is not limited to time on TV, a slot on radio or monthly deadline for magazine advertisements. Consumers are engaging with these digital touchpoints every day, and they see the advertisements on their mobile phones, on websites when browsing and even on social media. These advertisements are seen on the go and on mobile phones – they are versatile and can easily be distributed at any time of day to the actual target consumers. The platform simply allows advertisements to be served anywhere and anytime, irrespective of the location (country) or time zone.

Targeted

Again, compared to the mass advertisement approach of traditional media, there are possibilities of personalising and targeting advertisements to reach prospective customers. Digital media makes it easy to target individuals and offer them advertisements that they may find relevant. If you have been making plans for travelling, you won't be surprised to see an advert for travel insurance. This may not be relevant for everyone (as when shared on traditional media), but it is personalised for those individuals who really need it.

Measurable

Digital media offers data and analytical insight to justify its value. Advertisers can see the exact number of people who have engaged with the advertisement, and it gives insight into how effective the advertisement is which allows the brand to improve it if need be. Brands can identify which of the digital media platforms is bringing the most sales and thus can invest more in such media. Unlike TV or newspapers, where data may not be accurate and effectively gathered, digital media offers insight that allows brands and advertisers to decide what to do and gives the media owners the opportunity to showcase their values.

Limitations of digital media

Access to the internet

Access to the internet is still a luxury for some customers. Not everyone has daily and uninterrupted internet access. In some developing countries, customers will switch off their data (internet access) so that their mobile phones will not download data in order to conserve the limited internet data they have. The consumer may not have enough money for data, or the government might not have installed broadband cables in the area where they live, or the available internet might be in English or passcoded, and therefore not useful to all. This offers some limitation for digital media, especially in developing countries. Likewise, in some developed countries, not all customers have access to the internet, and they may not be able to access digital media and therefore are not being targeted. So, digital media is still a platform that can accept advertisements but, in some cases, those advertisements may not be shared, due to limited access to the internet.

Access to hardware

Closely related to the lack of internet is also the lack of hardware to engage with the digital media. Particularly, access to smartphones may hinder how people engage with advertisements. No doubt this may no longer be relevant in a few years' time when everyone can afford a smartphone, but till then, it needs to be recognised. Unlike traditional media which is often readily available, where consumers may not necessarily buy any of the media before they see an advertisement, digital media expects consumers to own a form of media upon which they will be accessing the digital media. This is not surprising as tech companies are offering some of their hardware for people to use, through which they can access their data and serve them with relevant advertisements. Reynolds (2018) reports that big tech firms like Google and Facebook are battling to connect the half of the world's population who don't have internet access, but their solutions might not be best for the people they're trying to help.

Distraction

There are many other things going on in digital media – it is not solely for advertisements – and therefore people may be distracted by the many other things they are doing on the digital platform. For example, on Facebook, you are more interested in catching up with your friends, and you may find advertisements distracting at the time; likewise, reading a blog post with so much interest, the presence of an advertisement may be distracting. Digital advertising located by the roadside might distract the attention of a driver from concentrating on driving, thus, the driver will not be able to understand the message of the advert due to his/her attention primarily placed on driving and reaching his/her destination in time. This is a minus for digital advertising.

Ethical consideration

Considering the amount of data being generated through digital media and how brands are feasting on the data to serve consumers with relevant information, there are always concerns around the ethical implications of the data being collected and how the data is being used. The European Union General Data Protection Regulation (GDPR) highlights a limitation for digital marketing – cookies are placed on the website, and if consumers are making the decision not to be tracked, this presents a limitation for the brand. There are also concerns about people feeling brands are invading their privacy with advertisements, especially, when they keep getting emails that they do not want or subscribe to. It must be acknowledged, however, that in some cases, explanations are offered (as with Google Ads) and customers may unsubscribe from any direct mail they are receiving.

The availability of data

There are challenges for collecting and using data, especially considering GDPR. Data is essential in understanding the customers, their journeys and for developing the advertising campaigns. Personalised and automated content creation and sharing will not be possible if the data are not available. When customers are not willing to release relevant information, there are limitations to how effective digital media will be. There are indications of people turning off their Bluetooth and using Adblockers to reduce the number of advertisements they are being served. As advertisers, it is important to ensure that there is value in the advertisements being shared.

Brand safety

Delivering brand messages in a brand-safe environment is a key priority for advertising agencies. Companies have withdrawn their adverts from social media sites because they were placed alongside values they do not support or condone. Walt Disney Co. is said to have pulled its advertising spending from YouTube, joining other companies including Nestlé SA, after a blogger detailed how comments on Google's video site were being used to facilitate a "soft-core paedophilia ring". Some of the videos involved ran next to ads placed by Disney and Nestlé. Also, a CNN investigation found that ads from over 300 companies and organisations – including tech giants, major retailers, newspapers and government agencies – ran on the YouTube channel (CNN, 2018). One of the companies, Under Armour, once paused their advert on YouTube, noting they have "strong values-led guidelines in place" for advertising on social media. With programmatic often responsible for automating the buying of the digital media spaces, there are chances that brands' messages could be placed on media platforms they do not want to be associated with.

Moving on as advertisers

To highlight the importance of this chapter, there are key considerations that must be noted as an advertising student, especially for those considering a career as media planner – those responsible for buying the media spaces for the advertisements that will be developed.

Understand that the media exist

Many digital media platforms have been presented. This is for your information, to know what is available as a platform to disseminate the advertisement. This list is inexhaustible, and many may not have been covered, many may not have been developed now but will be available when you start your career. Irrespective of that, it is important to understand what exists out there now. You should be able to identify different digital media platforms that can be used for advertising. You should not just limit yourself to social media. There are many more platforms out there. Your understanding of these opportunities may be the difference in making an effective advertising campaign.

Understand the features

Understanding the media that exists is not enough – you should understand the different features and how they can be used to complement your marketing campaign. As advertisers, it is important to understand what makes each of these platforms unique, their advantages and disadvantages, and how the creative elements may be incorporated. The advertisements to be shared through Bluetooth may be different from those shared on a mobile device. Some advertisements that are presented on a desktop as side banners or skyscraper display advertisements may not be applicable on a mobile. It is paramount to know these features as they relate to the products that will be offered, the creative elements that will be adopted, the audience on the platform and how effective it will be in reaching out to prospective customers. In addition to understanding the features of advertising media, you must understand the target audience as well if you want to succeed as a professional advertiser.

Understand the creative elements

Understanding the features will also inform the creative elements that will be used. The creative elements may be visuals, including use of images and text and audio including sound and voice-overs. Some advertisements like those featured in newspapers, may not be able to integrate sound as a creative element, likewise some advertisements will have a different typographical approach due to the shape and size of the advertisement display. Some advertisements will have to be in a square format for one minute to fit Instagram while some will be in rectangular format for three minutes on YouTube. Understanding these creative elements also involves working with the creative team to get the right graphics for the right media. Though the same advertising storyline may be used throughout the campaign, there are possibilities for it to be adopted to fit the different media on which the advertisements will be shared.

Understand how to get on it

With the understanding of the features and creative elements, it is important to understand how to get on these media. This involves recognising the gatekeepers and media owners. For some media like Facebook or Twitter, an individual can place an advertisement on the platform, selecting a target audience and deciding how long the campaign should run. Google Ads offers a smart, easy online advertising platform that allows advertisers to pay to display their messages to web users. Google Ads ensures customers only pay for results, like clicks to their website or calls to their business. There are other third-party providers such as Oath, AppNexus, Taboola and Outrains. AppNexus is an American multinational technology company operating a cloud-based software platform that aims to enable and optimise programmatic online advertising personalised ads and Outbrain helps brands and agencies connect with one-third of the world's consumers, engaging with content on the open web. Recognising the role of these companies and when to contact them for a deal is important.

Understand how to evaluate it

Being able to get data and analytical insight is one of the benefits of digital media. It is therefore important for advertisers to make the best use of this feature, to understand how it can be used in making an effective decision. Advertisers should be able to identify how well their campaigns are doing on different platforms, to understand which campaign to intensify or stop. Cross-platform measurement and understanding the impact of marketing investment is necessary when making informed business decisions in an increasingly complex media environment. Depending on the size of the agency or the digital media being used, analytics are important. Insights about Facebook and Google Ads can be checked by individuals. There are companies like Comscore that help leading media properties, brands and advertisers to discover and act upon new opportunities to drive business growth, and Madtrix, providing analytics with automated data platform. It is important to the advertising agency (or the designer for a smaller agency or SME) to manage, track and optimise their campaign, evaluating the impact of media and marketing efforts to improve ROI and make future decisions with confidence.

Summary

The chapter has explored digital media as a platform to disseminate advertisements. It is important for practitioners to recognise the abundance of media in the digital space and how best they can be used to disseminate brand messages. The chapter highlights the difference between the digital platform and the digital media. Various examples of digital media platforms were presented, including social media, internet browser and computer games. Emerging technologies such as LBA, OBA and virtual reality were also discussed.

Importantly, the prospects and limitations of digital media have been presented. With the opportunities presented by digital media, the vast amount of data being generated and access to fast internet and bandwidth, advertisers have great prospects for targeting customers with the brand messages effectively. However, the limitations with hardware, internet access in developing countries and the ethical implications need to be considered. The chapter concluded with action plans and consideration points for advertising practitioners as they explore these media platforms.

Revision questions

1. How do you think consumer behaviour has changed how advertisers use traditional media?
2. What is the difference between a digital media device (smartphone) and digital media platform (social media)?
3. What are the differences between traditional and digital media?
4. What do you understand by location-based advertisements?
5. What do you understand by online behaviour advertisement?
6. What do you understand by near-field communication?
7. Would you scan an NFC tag at the bus stop? Why wouldn't you do it?
8. What are the benefits of digital media? What makes it unique?
9. What are the limitations and challenges of digital media?
10. Would you consider a digital billboard as digital media? Discuss.
11. Why should an advertiser be conversant with the digital media platform available?
12. How do you think brands can leverage voice to sell their products and services?

Student activity

Using digital media to disseminate information about student union activity

Your group has been tasked with helping disseminate the advertisement about the forthcoming New Student Fayre and Trade Show. The event is meant to welcome new students and introduce them to services within and around the university. The print advertisement has been designed and printed on a poster, but they want it shared electronically, so they need your advice for sharing the advertisement on:

- Social media – Facebook, Twitter, Instagram, LinkedIn and TikTok
- Location-based campaigns using text messages and Bluetooth
- Near-field communications at seven bus shelters around campus.

For each of these platforms, what adjustment or inclusion would you advise the student union to do to their print media?

Remember, you are only providing ideas and suggestions and not redesigning the print advert. So consider the size for an advertisement on social media, the size of messages on SMS and the call to action and action to be triggered when students tap on the NFC tag.

References

Aguirre, A. & Davies, S., 2015. Imperfect strangers: Picturing place, family, and migrant identity on Facebook. Discourse. *Context & Media*, 7, pp. 3–17.

Audi India, 2020. www.audi.in. (Online) Available: www.audi.in/in/web/en.html [Accessed 26.8.2020].

Baek, T. & Mariko, M., 2012. Stay away from me. *Journal of Advertising*, 41(1), pp. 59–76.

Barlaskar, H. A., 2020. *Audi customers are young and prefer driving on their own*. Gaurav Sinha, Audi India. www.afaqs.com. (Online) Available at: www.afaqs.com/news/advertising/audi-customers-are-young-and-prefer-driving-on-their-own-gaurav-sinha-audi-india [Accessed 26.8.2020].

Bamba, F. & Barnes, S., 2007. SMS advertising, permission and the consumer: A study. *Business Process Management Journal*, 13(6), pp. 815–829.

Bhandari, B., 2013. *Fast-growing millionaires in India are coming to Audi. Business Standard*. Retrieved from: www.business-standard.com/article/management/-fast-growing-millionaires-in-india-are-coming-to-audi-110020200039_1.html [Accessed 26.8.2020].

Boerman, S., Kruikemeier & Zuiderveen Borgesius, F., 2017. Online behavioral advertising: A literature review and research agenda. *Journal of Advertising*, 46(3), pp. 363–376.

CarDekho, 2020. *History of Audi*. www.cardekho.com. (Online) Available at: www.cardekho.com/Audi/history.htm [Accessed 26.8.2020].

Cherney, M., 2018. *This violent videogame has made more money than any movie ever*. [Online] Available at: www.marketwatch.com/story/this-violent-videogame-has-made-more-money-than-any-movie-ever-2018-04-06 [Accessed 8.8.2020].

Chun, S., Shulman, S., Sandoval, R. & Hovy, E., 2010. Government 2.0: Making connections between citizens, data and government. Information Polity. *Information Polity*, 15(1/2), pp. 1–9.

CNN, 2018. *Exclusive: YouTube ran ads from hundreds of brands on extremist channels*. [Online] Available at: https://money.cnn.com/2018/04/19/technology/youtube-ads-extreme-content-investigation/index.html [Accessed 8.8.2020].

Columbus, L., 2016. *Ten ways big data is revolutionizing marketing and sales*. [Online] Available at: www.forbes.com/sites/louiscolumbus/2016/05/09/ten-ways-big-data-is-revolutionizing-marketing-and-sales/#1bfc272b21cf [Accessed 8.8.2020].

Criado, J., Sandoval-Almazan, R. & Gil-Garcia, J., 2013. Government innovation through social media. *Government Information Quarterly*, 30(4), pp. 319–326.

Curran, K., Millar, A. & McGarvey, C., 2012. Near field communication. *International Journal of Electrical & Computer Engineering*, 2(3), pp. 371–382.

Dawson, P. & Lamb, M., 2016. Enhanced success with programmatic social advertising. In: *Programmatic Advertising*. Cham.: Springer, pp. 103–110.

ETBrandEquity, 2020. *Audi launches campaign for Audi Q8 debut in India*. ET Brand Equity. [Online] Available at: https://brandequity.economictimes.indiatimes.com/news/marketing/audi-launches-campaign-for-audi-q8-debut-in-india/74578639 [Accessed 26.8.2020].

Gilliland, N., 2019. *Are smart speakers making audio advertising more enticing?*. [Online] Available at: https://econsultancy.com/are-smart-speakers-making-audio-advertising-more-enticing/ [Accessed 8.8.2020].

Gleb, B., 2020. *How augmented reality makes advertising interactive*. [Online] Available at: https://rubygarage.org/blog/augmented-reality-in-advertising [Accessed 8.8.2020].

JCDecaux, 2011. *JCDecaux OneWorld's Guide to NFC Outdoor Advertising*. [Online] Available at: www.jcdecaux.com/blog/jcdecaux-oneworlds-guide-nfc-outdoor-advertising#:~:text=NFC%20'tags'%20are%20devices%20that,regarding%20the%20brand%20or%20product [Accessed 8.8.2020].

Johnson, L., 2017. *What Marketers Need to Know About Location-Based Advertising and Where It's Headed*. [Online] Available at: www.adweek.com/digital/lets-slack-about-location-based-marketing/ [Accessed 7.7.2020].

Joshi, C., 2020. *6 Companies Nailing it With NFC Campaigns*. [Online] Available at: https://blog.beaconstac.com/2019/03/5-companies-nailing-it-with-nfc-campaigns/ [Accessed 8.8.2020].

Kim, Y. & Kim, W., 2014. Implementation of augmented reality system for smartphone advertisements. *International Journal of Multimedia and Ubiquitous Engineering*, 9(2), pp. 85–392.

Koetsier, J., 2019. *Good news for Amazon, Google: 39% find voice ads on smart speakers "more engaging" than TV, online*. [Online] Available at: www.forbes.com/sites/johnkoetsier/2019/02/26/good-news-for-amazon-google-39-find-voice-ads-on-smart-speakers-more-engaging-than-tv-online/#679f90397639 [Accessed 8.8.2020].

Krauth, O., 2018. *What will advertising on smart speakers look like?*. [Online] Available at: www.techrepublic.com/article/what-will-advertising-on-smart-speakers-look-like/ [Accessed 2.2.2020].

Kumar, V. & Gupta, S., 2016. Conceptualizing the evolution and future of advertising. *Journal of Advertising*, 45(3), pp. 302–317.

Macnamara, J. & Zerfass, A., 2012. Social media communication in organizations: The challenges of balancing openness, strategy, and management. *International Journal of Strategic Communication*, 6(4), pp. 287–308.

Marlowe, J., Bartley, A. & Collins, F., 2017. Digital belongings: The intersections of social cohesion, connectivity and digital media. *Ethnicities*, 17(1), pp. 85–102.

McAfee, A., Brynjolfsson, E. & Davenport, T., 2012. Big data: The management revolution. *Harvard Business Review*, 90(10), pp. 60–68.

Mintel, 2018. *Mobile Gaming – UK – October 2018*. [Online] Available at: https://reports.mintel.com/display/910220/ [Accessed 8.8.2020].

Mogaji, E., 2018. *Emotional appeals in advertising banking services*. London: Emerald.

Mogaji, E., Balakrishnan, J. & Kieu, T., 2020a. Examining consumer behaviour in the UK Energy sector through the sentimental and thematic analysis of tweets. *Journal of Consumer Behaviour*. https://doi.org/10.1002/cb.1820.

Mogaji, E. & Danbury, A., 2017. Making the brand appealing: Advertising strategies and consumers' attitude towards UK retail bank brands. *Journal of Product & Brand Management*, 26(6), pp. 531–544.

Mogaji, E., Farinloye, T. & Aririguzoh, S., 2016. Factors shaping attitudes towards UK bank brands: An exploratory analysis of social media data. *Cogent Business & Management*, 3(1), p. 1223389.

Mogaji, E., Olaleye, S. & Ukpabi, D., 2020b. Using AI to personalise emotionally appealing advertisement. In: *Digital and social media marketing: Advances in theory and practice of emerging markets*. Cham.: Springer, pp. 137–150.

Mogaji, E., Soetan, T. & Kieu, T., 2020c. The implications of artificial intelligence on the digital marketing of financial services to vulnerable customers. *Australasian Marketing Journal*, https://doi.org/10.1016/j.ausmj.2020.05.003.

Nagar, A., 2020. *Audi India to reduce print advertising, to double down on digital*. [Online] Available at: https://bestmediainfo.com/2020/05/audi-india-to-reduce-print-advertising-to-double-down-on-digital/ [Accessed 26.8.2020].

NFC, 2020. *NFC vs QR code*. Wakefield, MA: NFC Forum.

Page, B., Anesbury, Z., Moshakis, S. & Grasby, A., 2018. Measuring audience reach of outdoor advertisements: Using Bluetooth technology to validate measurement. *Journal of Advertising Research*, 58(4), pp. 456–463.

Palos-Sanchez, P., Saura, J. & Martin-Velicia, F., 2019. A study of the effects of programmatic advertising on users' concerns about privacy overtime. *Journal of Business Research*, 96, pp. 61–72.

RapidFire, n.d. [Online] Available at: www.rapidfire.com/portfolio/advergaming/.

Reynolds, M., 2018. *Facebook and Google's race to connect the world is heating up*. [Online] Available at: www.wired.co.uk/article/google-project-loon-balloon-facebook-aquila-internet-africa [Accessed 8.8.2020].

Schade, M., Piehler, R., Warwitz, C. & Burmann, C., 2018. Increasing consumers' intention to use location-based advertising. *Journal of Product & Brand Management*, 27(6), pp. 661–669.

STMicroelectronics, 2019. *Smarter end-to-end supply chains. Combining blockchain and NFC/ RFID technologies*. Geneva, Switzerland: STMicroelectronics.

The Week, 2013. [Online] Available at: https://theweek.com/articles/460005/interview-brilliant-minds-behind-chipotles-haunting-scarecrow-ad.

Tucker, C., 2014. Social networks, personalized advertising, and privacy controls. *Journal of Marketing Research*, 51(5), pp. 546–562.

UKIE, n.d. [Online] Available at: https://ukie.co.uk.

Unni, R. & Harmon, R., 2007. Perceived effectiveness of push vs. pull mobile location based advertising. *Journal of Interactive Advertising*, 7(2), pp. 28–40.

Wang, Y., 2020. Humor and camera view on mobile short-form video apps influence user experience and technology-adoption intent, an example of TikTok (DouYin). *Computers in Human Behavior*, 110, p. 106373.

Theme 3
Engaging the message

7 Advertisements reflecting the values of the target audience

In this chapter, we will be covering how advertisements should reflect the values of the target audience. With advertisements shared through the media, consumers are engaging with the brands' messages, and there are attitudes towards the advertisements and the brands. This chapter highlights different possible perceptions of the audience, how they engage with media and their possible reactions towards advertisements. Traditional media could be the platform for the older generation whilst new media could likewise be the platform for younger generations. This chapter further reiterates the differences between traditional media and new media, recognising the need to complement both platforms to achieve the set objectives. The sociology of advertisements is introduced in this chapter, highlighting how advertisements are received by a diversified audience, and how they reflect the inherent values within society. This introduces students to the need to design advertisements that reflect the values of their audience and will be of interest to students reading culture through advertisements.

Learning outcome

At the conclusion of this teaching, students will be able to:

- Describe the reach and implication of advertisement towards a diverse audience;
- Recognise the different protected characteristics in advertisement;
- Describe the filtration process in advertising;
- Explain the implications of reflecting the values of a society;
- Describe the role of brands and advertisers in developing an inclusive advertisement.

Introduction

The advertisement has been designed and embedded with creative elements that will make it appealing to the viewers. The advert has a physical product and has been delivered through both traditional and digital media. Now the consumers are engaging with the advertisement. The viewers are receiving the messages that the advertising agencies have sent on behalf of the brand. Now the anticipation begins.

How will the consumers react to this message?

Advertisers are curious and eager to develop advertisements that will convey a message and be received as intended by the consumers. It makes the job of the advertisers easier, and the brands are happy about it as well. But oftentimes, it is not always that easy. While consumers' behaviour may be changing, our engagement with media is evolving. As individuals living in a society surrounded by other people, the perceptions of consumers about advertisements cannot be fully established.

Fletcher (2010) argued that the tripartite of advertising (advertisers, media and agencies) ought to include a fourth element: the public. This is the group that the critics of advertising are concerned about when they question the morality and benefits of advertising. This chapter recognises this issue – the difficulty in effectively delivering a message that everyone would like and act on. It theoretically explores the debate on whether advertisements should "mirror" and reflect what is happening in the society or the society should be "moulded" based on what the advertisers are conveying (McDonald et al., 2020). Further reiterating the challenge of which has the most significant power – the society shaping what advertisers can put or include in the advertisement or the advertisers taking creativity by the horns to deliver the message that goes against the norm of the society.

While it might be challenging to achieve this overall acceptance and consensus, this chapter explores the diverse nature of the targeted audience as a conceptual background to highlight these challenges (Mogaji, 2015). Understanding how diverse the audience is, advertisers can be mindful of how they develop their advertisements. The chapter also explores different considerations advertisers need to be aware of as they develop their campaign to reach out to diverse audiences. Importantly, the implications of the strategic approach are also presented, especially for the advertising agencies developing the message and the brands funding the message. The chapter concludes by providing practical action plans for the advertising practitioners and students in developing campaigns that will engage with as many people as possible in the audience.

The reach of the advertisement

It is crucial to understand how far and wide a brand wants to send the message. It is also essential to be strategic and concerned about the right audience and society that the message is being directed to by a brand that has commissioned an advertising agency. The global strategy of brands can also imply how they reach out to society. Dunkin' Donuts apologised after it ran an advertisement in Thailand featuring a woman in "blackface" make-up. The advert, which was used to promote the doughnut giant's "charcoal doughnut", was called "bizarre and racist" by a leading human rights group (*Guardian*, 2019). Take note, this is an American company with a franchise in Thailand. The use of blackface – which historically was used by non-black performers to represent a black person – has a known racial discriminatory connotation in America; while Dunkin' Donuts may not use it in America, it was used somewhere else without them knowing that the world is now a global village, and an offensive advertisement can be tracked down around the world. German skincare brand Nivea also had to apologise and remove an advert that was deemed discriminatory (BBC News, 2017). The advert for its invisible deodorant range said "white is purity" across an image of a woman. The advertisement was posted on the firm's Facebook page, geographically aimed at its followers in the Middle East, even though the company has over 19 million fans globally on its page, and they all have access to the post.

While big and global brands may be concerned about how to localise or standardise their advertising strategy as they reach the diverse audience in their market, smaller brands and brands in the small and medium enterprises (SME) category may not go down that route, as they are not excused from reflecting the societal values in their advertisement. It is essential for advertisers (on behalf of the brands) to recognise and understand the shared values that define society – hence, they should incorporate this ethos in their campaigns to align with the society and essentially go beyond any demographic limitation.

The diverse society

While the diversity in the society may be relative – some countries are more diverse than others. For example, the United Kingdom recognises gay marriage in their law – it is part of the society which advertisements should reflect. In contrast, in some African countries, this is not recognised, therefore it is understandable if advertisements do not indicate that. It might be considered a creative gamble if an advertising agency were to propose such an idea for a brand in a country where gay marriage is not allowed. Advertising, like any other form of mass communication, makes a significant contribution to shaping social values and attitudes but is also a reflection of the cultural and societal values inherent in a society (Holbrook, 1987). Kay and Furnham (2013) suggest that any stereotypes present in advertisements represent the societal attitudes towards, and perceptions of, certain beliefs or groups. This further identifies the need for advertisers to understand their society and how to reach out through marketing communications effectively.

These understandings and reflections of societal values are profoundly rooted in and expressed through the creative elements of the advertisements which include the storyline of the advertisement, the conversation between the characters, the colours and music being used as well. It is all an effort towards authenticity that the society can feel and associate with. It is important, as well, to portray the modern and diverse society in which the customers live, which they see around them, reflecting the different communities, real people and real issues.

Advertisements should recognise their reach and limit, making a creative effort to align with the values of the society in the way they do things. This is undoubtedly different for different countries, but the most important thing is to recognise these inherent values and consider integrating them in their advertisements. It could be the cultural way of cooking, taking care of the family, marriage ceremony, national holiday or pets. These are often the abstract identity of the society; people have generally accepted that that is the way things are being done.

No doubt this may evolve, and advertisement is also expected to change with it. Previously, in the United States of America, slave owners were advertising their sales, selling slaves and willing to pay bounty on slaves that had escaped; now, such advertisements do not exists any longer; the country has evolved. Also, the stereotypical position of women has been to take care of the family and the home in the past, and we have seen different advertisements featuring women doing the cleaning and laundry – this is no longer accepted in today's society.

Aligning with acceptable cultural and societal values is essential for the effectiveness of an advertisement. Though it might be a creative challenge, it is worth the effort. The people see the advert, and it strikes a chord; they feel associated and more prone to engage. United Bank of Africa (UBA) is one of the biggest banks in Africa. The bank is based in

Nigeria and has many branches across the continent of Africa. WizKid is a famous Nigerian musician who is also a brand ambassador of UBA. There is an Instagram post which United Bank of Africa used to integrate the music lyrics of the artist (Wizkid) to deliver financial education for their followers. Importantly, they adopted the words in a way to show how they understand the musicians, to align with many other people around the world who appreciate the music, but they decided to use the lyrics in pidgin language as sung by the musicians. These align with the cultural values of Nigeria whereby musicians often speak in pidgin English, which is a colloquial form of the proper English but, notwithstanding, the bank incorporated it to develop their financial education. Those who know the lyrics can relate to the message. The bank has not just used the image of their brand ambassador to deliver their message but also his lyrics which the target audience can relate with.

The Space Case Finolex advertisement highlights the inherent value of spice in Indian culture. Most citizens will understand the importance of having the right spice with their meal. This includes the astronaut who is on a space mission and getting set to eat his lunch, when he discovers that there is no pickle left and exclaims "achaar khatam" (Pickle is over). The message reaches the control room on Earth, and everyone in the control room begins to panic; this gets to the Prime Minister, the issue gets media attention and everyone tries to find a solution on how to send the spice to space. Surprisingly, the astronaut's mother and domestic help, Ramu Kaka, devise a solution, gathering Finolex fans together to blow Ramu Kaka up into space. Though the advert was about a fan, it is interesting to see how they have embedded it with the inherent value placed on pickle which the society can relate with. Perhaps someone thinks if Finolex fans can help avoid a "national disaster", then they can be useful in their home. The advertisement was developed by Boing Agency.

The protected characteristics

While the values in a diverse society are considered abstract, fluid and evolving, some values are incorporated and recognised in the law of the land. As earlier stated, diversity in society is relative, and it differs from one country or region to another. Race, gender and age are often considered as critical elements of diversity in a society but the UK Equality Act of 2010 (Gov.uk, 2020), covers nine characteristics. The Equality Act provides a legal framework to protect the rights of individuals and advance equality of opportunity to all, legally protecting people from discrimination in society, based on the identified nine protected grounds, including age, gender and sexual orientation. However, there is more to diversity in the United Kingdom than ethnicity and disability; the law recognises a civil partnership, and people cannot be discriminated against because of their religious beliefs, sexual orientation or age. Table 7.1 presents and describes the nine protected characteristics.

The possibilities of associating messages in the media with perceptions of societal values have led researchers to examine the social consequences of these images (Mogaji, 2015). Johnson and Grier (2011) conclude that the depictions in advertisements can influence the way members of a group that is the subject of the stereotyped portrayal perceive themselves. At the same time, they can also shape the perceptions and beliefs of the out-group members towards stereotyped viewers. Highlighting and understanding these protected characteristics offers advertising practitioners the strategic insight to develop an

Table 7.1 Description of the protected characteristics under the Equality Act 2010

Protected characteristics	Description
Age	A person belonging to a particular age (e.g. 32-year olds) or range of ages (e.g. 18–30-year-olds)
Disability	A person has a disability if s/he has a physical or mental impairment which has a substantial and long-term adverse effect on that person's ability to carry out normal day-to-day activities
Gender reassignment	The process of transitioning from one gender to another
Marriage and civil partnership	Marriage is defined as a "union between a man and a woman" while same-sex couples can have their relationships legally recognised as "civil partnerships"
Pregnancy andmaternity	A condition of being pregnant or expecting a baby. Maternity refers to the period after birth, including treating a woman unfavourably because she is breastfeeding
Race	A group of people defined by their race, colour and nationality (including citizenship) ethnic or national origins
Religion and belief religion	Religion and belief – religion has the meaning usually given to it, but belief includes religious and philosophical beliefs including lack of belief (e.g. atheism)
Sex	A man or a woman
Sexual orientation	Whether a person's sexual attraction is towards their sex, the opposite sex or to both sexes

Source: Equality and Human Rights Commission.

inclusive advertisement that can be appealing and engaging to the diverse audience. Findings from Mogaji's (2015) analysis of UK print advertisements showed that the diversity of the country (as presented through the Equality Act and the protected characters) is not reflected through newspaper advertisements, as models of some of the protected characteristics were sparingly featured in the advertisements.

While there are nine protected characteristics, it is essential to examine their practicalities in an advertising context. It is also important to understand how these characters can be creatively presented to the target audience. On that note, the focus will be on six of the characteristics which are (1) Age, (2) Disability, (3) LGBTQ, (4) Race, (5) Religion and belief religion and (6) Sex. Sexual orientation is contextualised in terms of marriage and civil partnership. It may be argued that gender reassignment is a personal issue which may sometimes require medical attention, and therefore may not be deemed appropriate to be featured in an advertisement (Mogaji, 2015). The image of a pregnant woman is seldom featured in the advertisement. It appears that this is a social issue with different opinions which brands do not want to be involved in.

Age

This involves creating an advertisement that has different characters from different age groups. To create an advertisement that is not just for young adults but also for older people, the advert must be presented in a way that it represents all ages and caters for the needs of every target audience. Creatively, this may mean having a grandfather and granddaughter together in an advertisement, reflecting a society where the older generation can still make contributions. This also has implications for advertisers as they have to cast models of different ages as well, and not just work with models of a young age, so inadvertently, this can also affect the storyline and the concept behind the message.

Importantly, effort should be made towards connecting with different age groups through the creative execution of the advertisement. Each age group has its features and distinctive characters which shape how they engage with the advertisement. There are the Boomers and mature members of the society who have more time and disposable income and are eager to engage; they are also adopting technology to keep in touch with their families. As they go through different life stages, the advertisement should reflect the values they hold tightly. This could be spending time with their grandchildren, their health needs, or losing loved ones and friends. There are also Generation X, the Millennials, Generation Z and children. Advertisers should recognise this diversity in age groups in the society and creatively approach them with marketing communications they can relate with.

Disability

Disability should not be a hindrance in featuring in an advertisement. There are many less able individuals in society, and making a creative effort in featuring individuals with a disability is crucial in reaching out to a diverse audience. Maltesers is a brand that is very good at reaching out to the disabled members of the community. Reaching out to the blind, they have created an advertisement using the Malteser for Braille. Reaching out to the Deaf, they have created an advertisement using sign language and no voice-over or background music – "Theo's Dog". Reaching out to those who are physically disabled, they have created an advertisement featuring a woman in a wheelchair – "New Boyfriend". The brand has been created and acknowledged for this creative effort. Maltesers and AMV BBDO (their Advertising Agency) won the first edition of the Channel 4 Diversity in Advertisement competition in 2016 with an irreverent, comic slant on disability.

Mogaji (2015) found that only four adverts in over 1,200 samples had a reference to any form of disability. These include an advertisement for a bank with a man wearing a hearing aid and another for a law firm showing a man in a wheelchair. No individual with developmental, mental or any other physical disability featured in any of the advertisements, making these groups severely underrepresented. The report suggests that disabled people feel underrepresented by TV and the media, which highlights an implication for advertisers to be more diverse in their approach.

Creatively incorporating these characters in a campaign is, however, crucial so as not to portray them in a demeaning, insensitive or offensive manner. The Maltesers advertisement featuring a woman in a wheelchair who described a spasm during a romantic moment with her boyfriend was one of the most complained-about advertisements in the UK in 2017 as some people felt it was offensive to portray the woman, who was in a wheelchair, in this manner. The Advertising Standards Agency (ASA) did not uphold the complaint, and it was ruled that "the advertisement was championing diversity and did not think that it denigrated or degraded those with disabilities" (ASA, 2018).

LGBTQ

While recognising that in a diverse society marriage is more than just a man and a woman, it is therefore essential to see advertisements reflect these values within the society. However, beyond the male and female set-up of a marriage, there are a growing number of lesbian, gay, bisexual, transgender and queer (LGBTQ) couples in a diverse society and this should be reflected in advertisements (Grau & Zotos, 2016). Perhaps for advertising mortgages or travelling, where couples are meant to appear together in an advertisement, advertisers should be expected to look beyond the traditional male and female characters as husband and wife; the modern family is diverse, and so, therefore, the advertisement should reflect this. Thomas Cook shows a gay kiss to indicate a "modern population", representing the needs of the consumers. This, however, depends on the law of the land.

To avoid such backlash, companies hesitated to feature LGBTQ couples in their advertising as they feared upsetting a large segment of consumers, so they resorted to running what's known as gay-vague advertising (El Hazzouri et al., 2019), which takes a more covert approach. These advertisements feature LGBTQ-related images that can be understood differently by distinct consumer segments. Gay-vague advertisements have proven popular with LGBTQ community members while avoiding a backlash from straight consumers. However, as society has become more accepting, mainstream brands have started featuring same-sex couples in their advertisements.

Cheerios served up a dose of love with their "The Cheerios Effect" campaign featuring two Québécois gay dads André and Jonathan as well as their newly adopted daughter Raphaëlle. Real is a Diamond featured a young lesbian couple, as one partner gives viewers an in-depth, loving perspective of the beauty of her better half. Lloyds Bank in the United Kingdom prominently features a same-sex couple during a proposal, in the middle of a crowded street – who are also shown embracing towards the end. The bank also had different still images of the same-sex couple with the words: "He said yes".

In a study published in the *Journal of Advertising*, North American consumers, on average, still express less favourable attitudes towards advertising featuring same-sex couples as compared to male–female couples (Um, 2014). As many people still feel discomfort with the idea of gays and lesbians, let alone seeing them in our day-to-day advertising, the study findings suggest that ads featuring homosexual imagery could lead to negative brand evaluation. This is especially true for more conservative consumers – those with a high social dominance orientation have the strongest opposition to such advertisements. El Hazzouri et al.'s (2019) study, which also examines how heterosexual consumers react to advertising featuring same-sex couples, found that heterosexual consumers reported higher levels of disgust in response to advertising featuring same-sex couples in comparison to mixed-sex couples, which results in more negative attitudes towards the advertisement and the advertised brand. YouGov, however, found that consumers in the United States, United Kingdom and Germany are more likely than the general public to act after seeing an ad. The data also suggests that LGBTQ consumers are more likely to act after seeing an ad than the average shopper (Hiebert, 2017).

As marriage is still considered a valid union between a man and a woman in some countries around the world, it is paramount for advertisements targeting customers in those countries to be aware, recognise and be mindful of their creative approach. Importantly as well, finding a balance between the frequency of both sexes is essential (Oakenfull et al., 2008). Anecdotal research suggests that gay men are more often featured in advertisements than lesbians. This presents implications for advertisers as they cast for characters to feature in their campaign.

Case study 7.1

Sunsilk

Sunsilk highlights the taboo that exists around being a transgender person in Thailand in its latest ad. Like thousands of girls in Thailand and across the world, Rock was born in a man's body. Sunsilk tells her life story from her hair. Every inch of hair is an essential milestone on her journey to womanhood. The longer it gets, the more feminine she is. The advert titled "Hair Talk" conceptualised by J. Walter Thompson Bangkok features the story of Rock Kwanlada, first runner-up Miss Tiffany Universe 2017. Kwanlada narrates her story about how, when growing up, her father wanted her to act like a boy despite knowing that she was inclined towards being a girl and loved to play with dolls. It was an instant hit on social media, with 2.5 million organic views within the first 48 hours. After two months, it had sparked a nationwide conversation around gender and stereotypes, gathering over 37 million views in Thailand alone. Sunsilk joins a lengthy list of Thai marketers, from insurance and telecom to packaged goods, that specialise in the art of "cryvertising", that, when done insightfully, can become a viral sensation. "Hair Talk" introduces a new Sunsilk product, formulated for long hair, through its star Rock Kwanlada, a young trans woman and beauty queen. The coming-of-age story, told from her hair's perspective, follows her early battle with bullies, her reluctant double life and her struggle for acceptance.

Race

Mogaji (2015) found that in the analysed newspaper advertisements, models of "white" racial appearance comprised 91% of the examined characters, while Africans featured only comprised 5.3%. The 2011 Census of the United Kingdom showed that white was the majority ethnic group at 86%, while individuals from black/African/Caribbean/Black British ethnic groups made up 3.3% of the total population of England and Wales (ONS, 2011), indicating that models of "white" racial appearance are overrepresented while black/Africans are underrepresented within UK print media advertisements.

This is often a tricky characteristic for advertisers to work with. While the focus may be on the black and ethnic minorities (BME) in the United Kingdom, there are also the creative challenges of working with the African-American and Hispanic communities in the United States. While the intentions are for genuine connection, there are possibilities for getting it wrong, which may influence the brand. This idea of race as a protected characteristic also covers the challenges of reaching out to the Chinese, Japanese, Korean, Indians and the myriad of other Asian cultures. One size may not necessarily fit all. Likewise, in another country with different tribes (not necessarily races), it is essential to see how the brand's message can be effectively communicated without being offensive or ignored.

HIV Prevention England (HPE) is the national HIV prevention programme for England. It is part of Terrence Higgins Trust and funded by Public Health England. HPE runs the annual National HIV Testing Week promoting HIV testing to gay and bisexual men and black African men and women in the United Kingdom. This suggests that they know their target audience and they need to be creative in reaching out to them. It is not surprising to see that they have assessed different individuals to convey the message. They have used images of people who look like those they are targeting. This is important because the target audience can feel and sense a relationship between themselves and the people in the advertisement. This aligns with the theory of meaning transfer (Miller & Allen, 2012; McCracken, 1989) which indicates that the embedded meaning in an image used for an advertisement can be transferred to the audience. HPE has used images of different gender, sexuality and race to reach out to the audience. Those same messages are still being communicated (the text and copy remain the same) but the images are changing. It is also important to highlight the image of the African man wearing different attire. The way of dressing makes him different from the other photos, and you can be assured that someone will find that as a connection to engage with the advertisements. These are conscious creative efforts that have been made by advertisers to send a message to a diverse society.

The University of Missouri Athletic Department created a social media campaign for the National Collegiate Athletic Association (NCAA)'s Inclusion Week to generate discussion and emphasize the importance of diversity and inclusion in student–athletes' success; while they attempted to reach out and showcase how diverse they are, it was a big failure as it was criticised as insensitive. The Tweet showed four students, two black and two white. The graphics featuring the white athletes highlighted their career ambitions. Gymnast Chelsey Christensen's said, "I am a future doctor". Swimmer CJ Kovac's said, "I am a future corporate financier". While the two black athletes – track and field athlete Arielle Mack's said, "I am an African American Woman" and Caulin Graves said, "I am a Brother". The post was criticised on social media for defining Mack and Graves by their race instead of their goals and accomplishments. The athletic department deleted the advert and apologised, saying "Earlier we made a mistake when we posted a graphic about our student–athletes. We apologise. Our intent was to provide personal information about our students, but we failed. We listened and removed the post." Reflecting diversity is not just about having the right image showing a mix of race or gender but also the choice of words. You want to ask why did the university (or their designer, copywriter or art director, whoever is responsible) choose those words for those (African-American) individuals.

As with any of the protected characteristics, it is essential to integrate race in the campaign, as seen with the University of Missouri Athletic Department social media campaign that failed because they had not effectively integrated and embraced diversity. There are many more examples of advertisements that have failed because race was insensitively and offensively integrated: as seen with the Kendall Jenner advert for Pepsi, the Dove advert with a woman, in changing her clothes, turning from a black woman into a white woman, and H&M's the "coolest monkey in the jungle" hoodie. While there is an increased call for diversity, advertisers must be very mindful as they approach these protected characters.

It is better not to include one than to add it wrongly and then get a backlash which may warrant the need to remove the advertisement.

Religion

Despite falling numbers, as recorded by the Office for National Statistics in the 2011 UK Census Data, Christianity remains the largest religion in a multi-faith England and Wales, yet the incidence of this religion in advertisements is negligible. Of all the characters analysed by Mogaji (2015), only two advertising for a fashion brand showed a prevalence of religion, being representations of a male priest and female priest wearing the traditional black and white robes. Mallia (2009) suggests that the presence of religious features in advertisements can arouse shock in consumers, and advertisers seem not to be adopting this approach. It appears that brands want to be politically correct and ethical, disassociating themselves from any religious affirmation so as not to offend anyone in such a diversified country. This seems to apply even more because the number of people with no religion has increased across all age groups according to the 2011 census, and these people now form the highest proportion of economically active people. Thus, emphasis on the need to exclude religious features in brand advertisements is quite understandable.

This, however, did not stop Amazon from adopting a multi-faith campaign in response to anti-Muslim rhetoric. The brand advocates for religious tolerance (and even friendship) with two old friends. Though the Priest and Imam practice different faiths, Amazon focuses on their everyday challenges and shared empathy. The response to the advertisement which came out in 2016 was positive as many people felt the advertisement showed tolerance with others. Likewise, for the 2018 Superbowl, Toyota chose the religious approach for their advertisement. A Catholic priest, a Rabbi, an Imam and a Buddhist Monk all get into the same car to go and watch sport and meet a couple of nuns, and the commercial ends with the "We're all one team" disclaimer.

While Amazon may have had success with theirs, some advertisements have been banned because their religious contents were deemed offensive. A gambling advertisement by Boylesports was banned for mocking Christ's crucifixion (Sweney, 2016). The advertisement was sent through email to punters and showed a hand nailed to a piece of wood against a desert scene with the strapline "nailed on bonus". ASA said that the timing of the advertisement at Easter, the "jokey" language and making light of the subject of the crucifixion was likely to cause serious offence to some readers. The Meat and Livestock Australia's (MLA) advertisement that featured a range of religious gods, deities and prophets was banned (Schipp, 2017). The ad sang the praises of lamb as the food of the gods, with a message of unity and bringing people of diverse backgrounds together. The fact that it featured opposing divinities and prophets, including Jesus, L. Ron Hubbard, Thor, Zeus and Hindi god Ganesha made it offensive to some people. Australia's Advertising Standards Board ruled that the advertisement was discriminatory to those of Hindu faith because Ganesha (in an advertisement for lamb) is believed to be a vegetarian. Religion is a sensitive and sacred matter, and advertisers must be strategic in integrating it into their campaigns. Therefore, before an advert is created, advertisers must conduct profound research to understand the intended message of the brand viz-à-viz the beliefs or worldviews of the target audience. This is because an advert which is supposed to be harmless and encourage consumers to buy a product or use a service can sometimes offend the consumers when it does not fully align with the religious beliefs and opinions of that same target audience.

Sex

Plakoyiannaki and Zotos (2009) noted that women in British magazine advertisements were portrayed as physically attractive sex objects. From a social learning perspective, groups exposed to images like this may continue to view all women in that manner even though such a perception is inaccurate. Bailey (2006) suggests this situation affords brand managers a medium through which to depict a better representation of women. This can also be applicable in portraying an ethnically diverse country like the United Kingdom, breaking the stereotypes and using advertisements to reflect an accurate representation of members of these groups.

The sex role in society is also referred to as the gender role – a social role encompassing a range of attitudes and behaviours which are generally considered appropriate, acceptable or desirable for someone based on the person's perceived or biological sex. This sometimes leads to stereotypes and ostracisation in a society. Some advertising agencies unwittingly reflect negative/harmful sex roles in their adverts – this is not encouraged. However, to curb that, the new rule in the ASA Advertising Codes bans harmful gender stereotypes (ASA, 2019). The rules state that advertisements "must not include gender stereotypes that are likely to cause harm or serious or widespread offence". This expects advertisers to look beyond the sexualisation of women and the stereotypically positioning of them for some tasks like cleaning and looking after the home. Two television adverts – one for Volkswagen and the other for Philadelphia (the cream cheese brand owned by Mondelez) – were banned by the ASA in their intended format following complaints from the public that they perpetuated harmful stereotypes.

Working with the protected characteristics

Advertisers need to work with and incorporate these protected characteristics in their advertisements and, in as much as they want to reflect the diverse modern society, property integration is essential to avoid any backlash. Three key points are noted for effectively working with the characters.

Understand the characteristics

Advertisers need to understand the different characteristics that relate to the reach of the advertisement. As earlier indicated, advertisers know the target audiences, society and country their advertisement will reach. Therefore a good understanding of the characters that are relevant to those countries is essential. For the United States, it could be the Hispanics, while in Nigeria, it could be the fact that gay couples are not an inherent value of Nigerian society. Understanding these characteristics also involves recognising them as individuals that need to be well represented and presented.

Understand their values

With the understanding of the characters comes the knowledge of their values. This is not just knowing that they exist and using them in a campaign but, rather, understanding what makes them unique. This could involve a form of research and data analytics to have a deep understanding of the group, to recognise their struggles and experiences which may shape how they want to be reflected in the media and advertisements. This is one thing that Pepsi got wrong with their advert. They did not recognise the value of protest to the black community while the Amazon advert understands the importance of prayers for the Imam and the Priest and the choice of the knee pad (of all products on Amazon) to convey their message of tolerance and love. Sometimes these values may not be visible. Those who are unfamiliar with these values (and who may be present on the creative team in the Advertising Agencies) might not be able to convey the advertisement message effectively. This highlights the importance of a diverse advertising team. Adverts must not only recognise but respect the values of every consumer in a target area and must also be highly inclusive.

Understand how to integrate

With the understanding of the values comes the strategic development of the campaign. This involves exploring how to integrate the characters into the storyline for the advertisement. Asking different but relevant persons if they would feature alone in the advertisement or as part of many other characteristics is an ideal way to integrate. This also involves casting and selecting the right characters to front the campaign. Again, as with the Pepsi advertisement, Kendal Jenner appeared not to be a good fit. The casting also involves selecting the right celebrity for a campaign reaching out to a specific group. The media placement to reach the audience is also essential. Creativity becomes important here – the thin line between an advertisement that will be well received and an advertisement that will be banned is how creatively different characters and ideas are used in the advert.

The diverse individual

While advertisers may be displaying advertisements on billboards or through social media, engagement with these advertisement is essential for both advertisers and brands. However, it is necessary to recognise that everyone engaging with advertisements is different (Northey et al., 2020). Their level of interest in the message will differ as well, and importantly, how they will engage with the advertisement. The advertisers may send an advertisement to the gay community (the diverse society) but cannot control how the individual audience will engage with the advertisement. This highlights the difference between societal diversity and the individual's positioning, which aligns with the congruency theory that suggests that advertisements should reflect what is in congruence with societal value (Zhu et al., 2019) and Schema theory that recognises individual's ability to process an advertisement based on their experience (Kim et al., 2019).

Diversity in the target audience involves many things, among which is the personality of the individuals. The way consumers engage with advertisements differs based on their nature. This is basically about the person they really are – especially about their personality. This personality can also influence how they engage with the message they have received. As with most things, we process advertisements based on our personal preferences. This acknowledges we are all individuals entitled to our own opinions, even though they may go against the cultural norm. Sometimes it cannot yet be explained why participants do not like a brand or are not interested in an advertisement.

An advertisement containing an image of a dog is more likely to engage a positive attitude and arouse positive emotions; however, it would not be surprising to see that someone disliked the advertisement because they had been bitten by a dog while growing up. An advertisement may have a celebrity as its brand ambassador, but some individuals may find the use of such model as inappropriate. This personality (which influences the attitude towards the advertisement) could also have been shaped by their life experiences and background: the country they grew up in, the products they used in their family while growing up, their religious beliefs, worldview, experiences in school and many other things. This list is inexhaustible, highlighting the difficulties in creating an advertisement that everyone will like.

Case study 7.2

Gucci's influencer driven advertising approaches for Indian consumers

Gucci is one of the oldest luxury fashion brands, established by Guccio Gucci in 1921. The company designs and manufactures most desirable luxury products such as leather goods, apparel, eyewear and fragrances which are sold across countries through a network of directly operated boutiques. After extensively catering to Indian customers in European locations for many years, Gucci decided to enter the Indian market in 2007 and the company's first store was a franchise in association with the Murjani Group. Later, in 2009, Gucci announced direct selling in Indian markets (Vasudev, 2016). Now, with four stores in the three metropolitan cities of India Gucci showcases the pinnacle of the Italian Craftsmanship. Importantly, the company's positioning is based on eclectic, contemporary and romance (Gucci, 2020b).

For Indian consumers, Gucci has come a long way from being just an Italian luxury brand, motivating the consumers with its signature "Double G" logo to a brand which now targets consumers who are "high earners but not rich yet" also known as "HENRYs" (Vasudev, 2016). To target such consumers, Gucci uses content-driven strategies – to understand these strategies we will discuss the five content-driven approaches used by Gucci, that focus upon: online PR, influencer marketing, using AR/VR on social media and Meme marketing, sustainable production, and supporting unprivileged talent.

HENRYs are the new tech savvy millennials and GenZs, who look for brands which showcase authenticity, reliability and sustainable practices across their communications. (Delloite, 2019). To retain such tech-savvy consumers, Gucci has maintained a top spot amongst the leading five brands in terms of online selling and engagement. To gain a competitive advantage with immediate rivals such as Louis Vuitton, Chanel, Rolex and Dior, Gucci has also created a mark on the luxury shopping websites such as TataCliQ, The Collective, LuxePolis and Elitify. The company also maintains top spot with the highest social mentions, being discussed over 11 million times per month, on average, in 2019 (Beauloye, 2020).

To create such an engagement, Gucci's content developed for the Indian market is different than that for the developed nations. The luxury brand glamour is associated with the culture of India where showcasing or owning luxury brand with big logos signifies affluence through materialistic possessions. North Indian markets are well known for such consumer behaviour which is also driven by influencers (Jain & Sheth, 2019).

This highlights the first approach where Gucci is mentioned in the song sung by famous Punjabi-Bollywood singer YoYo Honey Singh (Rathore, 2013). Adding to the online PR, Gucci is famous for being sported by Bollywood celebrities such as Deepika Padukone, as their airport look or during a film promotion shoot which is covered by fashion magazines (*Pinkvilla*, 2018).

Second, as a part of Gucci's publicity campaign in 2017, the company hosted an end-of-the-year party at a lavish hotel in Mumbai which was attended by Bollywood personalities. This was not only to talk about their then upcoming season collection or "Gift-Giving" collection but also to celebrate the launch campaign of their DIY services in India #GucciDIY (Vaidya 2017).

Third, Gucci teamed-up with social media application Snapchat for the "Gift-Giving" campaign to launch a new portal lens which transports users to a 3D world with holiday-themed AR elements (ANI, 2019). To appeal to GenZ, Gucci also adopted meme marketing to promote its new series of watches (Youngun India, 2020).

The brand also created a Twitter controversy when they included a royal blue turban in their autumn 2018 collection called "Indy Full Turban" which attracted negative publicity from the "Sikh community". The brand later apologized and withdrew the product from their collection and website (EtBrandEquity, 2019). Adding to this, Gucci looks forward to a very responsible and sustainable future.

This leverages Gucci's fourth approach where the company launched a sustainable collection in 2020 called 'Gucci Off-The-Grid' using only recycled, organic and sustainably sourced materials. (Gupta, 2020).

Fifth, Gucci supported "I Was a Sari" foundation by Stefano Funari where under-privileged women in Mumbai selling upcycled products made from used saris are being helped to become world-class artisans and gain financial independence (Gucci, 2020a).

With such activities the brand tries to create value-based positioning across digital media channels. To conclude, the future of advertising will be based on such influencer-driven communications where the brands will have to showcase their product uniqueness by highlighting their responsibility towards the society along with the enhancement of lifestyle among consumers.

Prof. Varsha Jain, Professor of Marketing, Co-chairperson, Doctoral
Level Program and Research Chairperson, MICA, India
Mr Vashishtha Joshi, Research Associate, MICA India

The filtration process

As earlier indicated, different factors can shape how an individual will engage with marketing communication that is sent their way. Through the filtration process, the target audience or consumer can sometimes distort, bar or generalise the message that a brand is trying to communicate in its adverts. This is why sometimes an advert is not as well received as the brand or advertising agency had projected. This is what Mogaji (2018) described as the filtration process in advertising. Consumers exposed to emotionally appealing advertisements that are transferred through various media channels are expected to decode the said advertisements to understand their message, and engage with marketing communications. In doing so, a filtration of emotional appeals occurs.

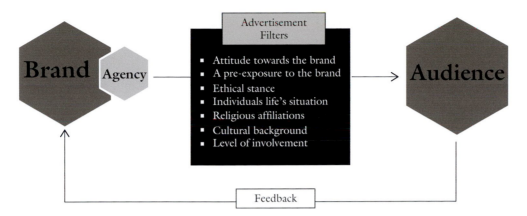

Figure 7.1 Key filters for advertisement
Source: author.

The filtration process in advertising is the process whereby consumers engage with advertisements and filters of the message, to deduce a meaningful conclusion, based on their individual preferences, ideologies or experience. Figure 7.1 presents key filters for advertisements; it builds on communications theory (discussed in Chapter 2) that highlights how consumers decode advertisements based on some filters according to their personal experience and personality as an individual. This is a unique and personal process, which is why two people can be exposed to the same advertisement but have different reactions to it. The idea of the filtration of emotional appeals also corroborates the findings of Misra and Beatty (1990), who highlight the "filtering model", suggesting that executional cues in advertisements that do not corroborate brand message or customer expectations will be filtered out and will not enhance the meaning-transfer process.

Advertisers make conscious creative decisions with their advertisements to appeal to viewers, using attractive copy and colourful images, all perfectly laid out, and anticipating an emotional reaction that will lead to a purchase. However, this route cannot always be guaranteed. The filtration of emotional appeal is often multilayered, involving various components, which can include the brand, the advertisement, the individuals being targeted and society. Consumers interpret the identified appeals from their ideological points of view, shaped by their own experiences and previous exposure to brands. The subsequent section discusses different elements of the filtration process.

Attitude towards the brand

An inclination towards the brand can influence how consumers engage with the advertisements. If it is a brand that is well loved and seen as credible, consumers are more likely to engage with its advertisements compared to a brand that has a damaged reputation. This also presents implications for advertising agencies to understand the brands they want to work with and whether they feel they can be associated with those brands. Following the negative media coverage about banks after the global financial crisis in 2008, there appeared to be an undesirable predisposition towards banks which inadvertently affected the attitude towards their advertisements. Individuals with strong political views and ideologies about banks are more likely to have a negative attitude towards bank advertisements and may not be interested in their message or the emotional appeals embedded therein. For example, an individual who believes that houses should be made socially available by the government may have a negative attitude towards any mortgage advertisements they are exposed to. This will also resonate with young adults who find it challenging to save enough money to buy their own houses. They see an advertisement for a mortgage and decide to ignore it, based on their understanding of banks not doing enough to help them get on the first rung of the property ladder.

Pre-exposure to the brand

Pre-exposure to the brand and other advertisements may also shape attitudes towards current advertisements. For example, where a customer has previously had a bad experience while visiting a bank or considered the banking atmosphere unattractive, they are likely to have a negative attitude towards the advertisement and filter it out. Similarly, if a customer has had a positive experience with the brand, they are likely to show more interest in the advertisement. Pre-existing knowledge about the brands can also shape consumers' attitudes towards these brands. This becomes important for brands that change their name or have been acquired. For those relocating to another country, pre-existing knowledge about a brand in their former country may be transferred to their new country. For example, a resident of Spain that has been exposed to Santander Bank, or someone from China that has been exposed to HSBC can have a positive attitude towards those brands when they arrive in the United Kingdom. From an advertisers' perspective, a positive attitude towards the agency can influence how people engage with the advertisements they make.

Ethical stance

Similarly, ethical issues surrounding a brand can also affect how consumers may engage with an advertisement. Likewise, the moral stance of individuals regarding how (sustainably) brands operate can also influence the filtration process. Consumers may see an advertisement (as sent by an advertising agency on behalf of a brand), process the message with their ethical stance, then the message is filtered out, making them not to want to engage with the brand. So, in this case, the fact that the consumers are getting the message is irrelevant – the important point is how well they are engaging with it.

Individual life situations

Individual life situations can also influence how people engage with advertisements, as Mogaji (2018) illustrated with the comments of a 71-year-old grandfather after being exposed to a bank advertisement featuring a mother hugging her daughter and a Nationwide advertisement where a young girl is running by the seaside. For each advert, the emotional appeals had been transferred through the images, and he recognised what the bank was suggesting. However, after the filtration process, there was a different attitude towards the advertisements. After the man lost his wife to cancer, seeing the advert of a mother hugging her daughter made him feel different, but the bank would not have been aware of this, or that the advert would no longer appeal to him. In a newspaper, he would be able to turn the page because it reminded him of his loss. This highlights that the creative element in an advertisement (like the images, colours and text) may trigger an emotion as consumers engage with it. This may eventually arouse either a positive or negative attitude towards the advertisement. An individual may get excited about the colour of the advertisement, and someone may get excited about the font and get more interested in the advertisement.

Religious affiliations

Religious differences among individuals or target audiences of an advert may influence the message the brand is trying to pass to the consumers. This is because, from different religious perspectives, people sometimes derive their understanding of a particular communication or message. Many times, consumers project their religious sentiment into an advert – this contributes to either positive or negative reception that an advert may enjoy from the consumers. Therefore, religious affiliation is a filter that can often be controversial and may not be considered a screen but it has been found to filter out emotional appeals as presented in the advertisements, leading to an indifferent or even negative attitude to the brand, primarily if the images or copy used did not conform to the individual's religious beliefs. Cases include interest for mortgages and the idea that banks can take pride in the fact that they lend customers money to achieve their dreams. With regard to the filtration of emotional appeals based on religious affiliations, there are cases whereby an advertisement has been negatively perceived; for example, in 2017, there were threats to boycott Tesco after a Muslim family featured in a Christmas advertisement (Belam, 2017) and a lamb advertisement was condemned by Hindus for depicting a vegetarian deity eating meat (Pavey, 2017). In 2015, Mulberry replaced Jesus Christ with handbag in their Christmas advertisement (Bushfield, 2015).

Cultural background

Cultural background is the context of one's life experience, vision and worldview as shaped by an individual's membership of groups based on race, sexual orientation, ethnicity, political class, socio-economic status, gender, language, exceptionalities, religion and geographical area (Wingate, 2015). The role that culture plays in the filtration process of emotions appeals cannot be overemphasised. In line with the meaning of transfer theory, there is a conventional path for the movement of cultural meaning in consumer societies (McCracken, 1989). This result presents the filtration moves along the meaning transfer route; the cultural background of an individual can shape how they engage with an advertisement. Meanings are acquired as part of a cultural society. For example, the colours used in an advertisement to make it emotionally appealing may be interpreted from their cultural point of view. If a colour was not congruent with their associated meaning, there would most likely be a negative attitude. In some cultures, people have often associated black with death, and in China they have a different understanding of the black colour. Likewise, images used in an advertisements may be interpreted through the customer's cultural background filters.

Level of involvement

A consumer's level of involvement has to do with the extent to which a consumer is interested in buying a product, associating with a product or service and/or consuming a product or service. As is understood, the level of involvement depends on the personal relevance or importance of the purchase and customers devote a considerable amount of time in processing information before making a choice (Park & Young, 1986). The level of knowledge and level of involvement has been found to influence the information processing of individuals and is considered central to the processing of emotionally appealing advertisements (Braverman, 2008; Hauff et al., 2014). The latest Apple iPhone may be advertised on the biggest billboard in the world – if the customer is not interested in buying a phone or even an iPhone, their level of involvement is low and there is little or no interest in the message. This highlights the need for advertisers to target an audience who are more likely to engage with the advertisement because they will need the product. This level of noise (according to communications theory) and distraction may also increase this lack of interest. This also presents another implication for advertisers with regard to media placement and ensuring the customers are getting the message with less noise and distraction so they can engage with the message as intended.

It is important to note that advertisers may not be able to change or effectively influence how people engage with an advertisement – a customer may like an advert today and dislike the same advertisement the next day. These filters are fluid, and they can be modified with better education, information and awareness. Notwithstanding, advertisers should make an effort to address these filters as much as they can creatively. While the filtration process is from an individual perspective (which the advertisers may not be able to solve), this section illustrates the values within a society that represent the view of the majority and how advertisers should align with it.

Implications of reflecting the values of the society

Social values are those ethics/ethos recognised by the society as good, useful and important to the society. These values form essential aspects of people's way of life, culture and their society as a whole. When these values are trampled on, the society frowns on the offenders and might punish them. This is because any threat to these social values is believed to be a threat to the existence of the society. This principle is also applied to advertising to the extent that the society or consumers find any advertisement that goes against society values as a repulsive advertisement, and therefore will not engage with it. There are many implications of reflecting the inherent values in a society in advertisements. Importantly, it is the RIGHT thing to do. An advertisement should reflect what is going on in the society, recognising the fusion of culture, the modern family beyond Daddy and Mummy and the less able individuals who are an integral part of that society. It should not always be about a size zero blonde female model – there is more going on within the diverse society where the customers live.

The subsequent subsections highlight critical implications among many of the brands and advertisers.

Engaging

A diverse advertisement is more likely to be engaging as people will like the advertisement and will talk about it and share it on social media. Everyone can see a bit of themselves in the advertisement and this further drives the conversation around the brand. An example is Amazon's Priest and Imam advert – it was unique, creatively presented and viewers found it worthwhile to engage with. It is also important to note that the engagement could lead to a positive attitude if people find it offensive. Importantly, such advert goes beyond the norm of the society, breaking the clusters and driving conversation. With the amplification available on social media, brands need to get their inclusive advertising strategy right.

Positive attitude towards the brand

Engagement leads to a positive attitude towards the brand. People want to know more about the brand, thereby building a positive connection with the brand. Consumers see such brands as socially responsible, recognising the differences in society and using their advertisements to send a message. When MacDonald's changed their Golden M arches logo into a W to honour women, there was a positive attitude towards the brand. Customers recognise an inclusive advertisement, it speaks to them, and they can relate to it. Customers will go far to support brands that share similar values.

Reaching a new market

Brands are aware of the untapped market for the LGBT and BME communities, the older generations, women and even Muslins. Brands should not ignore the influence and spending power of minority groups. Advertisers have the responsibility to effectively engage with these markets, reaching a new market and expanding the business of their brands. It is essential to deliver messages that these groups can associate with and will like. This does not necessarily mean developing new products, but rather, creating awareness using values that they adhere to. Nike did an advertisement to reach out to women; although they make shoes specifically for women's feet, they had never communicated exclusively to females. That led to developing the "She Runs The Night" campaign which became a ground-breaking one for Nike (*Marketing*, 2013). Here the brand moves beyond reaching out to men and using men in advertisements to specifically target women.

Well appreciated and no complaints

The embarrassment of being reported to the advertising regulators, getting an advertisement banned, having to make a public apology and withdraw the advertisement have critical implications for brands and advertising agencies. This has happened to many brands and is still happening because they have not strategically conceptualised and executed their campaign. This backlash, often from customers who feel offended, impacts the brand reputation and, indirectly, their sales as people are likely to boycott the brand. While some may argue that some brands may create an offensive advertisement on purpose to raise awareness and create buzz, it is essential to note that the effect may be more devastating than anticipated.

How advertisers and brands can reflect values

Research

Advertisers need to intensify their research to better understand their target audience. No doubt customer behaviour is evolving at a faster rate, and advertisers need to catch up, so research plays an important role. This may be from a focus group to understand the target audience, their values and beliefs or to use artificial intelligence and data analytics to have a holistic understanding of the audience. It is therefore not surprising to see that the big advertising agencies are recognising this growing demand for research-informed design and they are investing in acquiring and establishing data management and insight companies. In 2017, Dentsu Aegis acquired the Dutch performance marketing firm Oxyma Group. In 2018, IPG acquired Acxiom in a push to elevate data practices and address the onset of "outcome-driven marketing". WPP acquired the US data marketing business I-Behaviour Inc. as it looked to increase its investment in digital knowledge-based marketing solutions, while Omnicom launched Omni, a "people-based" precision marketing and insights platform designed to identify and define personalized consumer experiences at scale across creative, media, CRM as well as other Omnicom practice areas. Omni delivers a first-of-its-kind, single view of the consumer that can be dynamically tracked and shared across all marketing practices. This is all about understanding the customers through data management, analytics, data strategy and audience creation and serving them with relevant advertisements.

Diversity in the team

The creativity within a diverse team cannot be overemphasised. Agencies must have a diverse team to develop an advertisement that will appeal to a diverse audience. Brands as well need to recognise the need for diversity as they work with advertising agencies. A non-diverse team may be locked into one form of creative ideas which may be offensive to the target audience or public. When brands are not open to different or various interpretations of their adverts, that may affect them negatively. As a professional advertiser you should encourage brands to create a brief that allows use of a diverse team. Diversity is not about race in the design of a firm but also about gender, ideas, life experiences and even educational background. You must engage people who will think differently and explore ideas in reaching out to a diverse audience. This can also take the form of training for the staff, to make them aware of biases that may influence their thought process and, inadvertently, their design. Everyone within the team needs to understand the broad scope of diversity and inclusion and that it encompasses providing equal opportunities for all.

The Institute of Practitioners in Advertising (IPA) recognises the need for improving diversity within the advertising and marketing communications industry and works collaboratively with their members, to demonstrate the value of diversity to creativity and effectiveness. This includes tracking ethnicity and diversity progress via an online survey sent to all their member agencies (IPA, 2019). The Channel 4 Diversity in Advertising Award is also committed to improving diversity in advertising by offering a £1m airtime prize each year until 2020. Starbucks and its creative agency, Iris, were the winner of the 2019 Diversity in Advertising Award, which tasked entrants to focus on the lack of representation and stereotyping of the LGBT+ community in advertising (Channel 4, 2019). The brand received £1m worth of commercial advertising for its winning campaign which aired on Channel 4 from February 2020.

Recruitment is also crucial in diversifying the team and not recruiting from the same pool of creatives. There are agencies like The Elephant Room, making the advertising industry a more representative and inclusive place through their recruitment strategy. It is essential to hire beyond just ticking box exercises or hiring someone because they are a mate or the person who can fill the position the quickest. It is vital to remove unconscious bias and agencies should not just hire people who are similar to each other.

Brands need to be aware and educated about the need for inclusive advertisement. Nadim Salhani, the CEO for Dunkin' Donuts in Thailand, which is operated as a franchise, was initially angry about the blackface advert for the brand which was later pulled, saying, "It's absolutely ridiculous, "We're not allowed to use black to promote our doughnuts? I don't get it. What's the big fuss? What if the product was white and I painted someone white, would that be racist?" (*Guardian*, 2013). In 2013, the Indian unit of Ford Motor Company had to apologise for an advertisement showing former Italian Prime Minister Silvio Berlusconi with a group of bound women in the boot of a car (BBC News, 2013). The owner of the detergent which advertised with a black man walking in and getting washed a different colour told BBC Chinese's Grace Tsoi that he did not realise it was racist until it was pointed out to him: "I don't know much about the advertisement", "To be honest, I didn't really pay that much attention to the advertisement" (BBC News, 2016). When brands are aware, they can also question and seek to understand the diversity within the advertising agency working for them because when the agencies have a narrow view of what's happening within the world, their output (to the brand) will be limited as there are people that go underrepresented.

Seek assistance

In developing an advertisement that reflects the value of society, advertising agencies need to seek assistance when in doubt. This is all effort towards making sure the message is well conveyed and received as intended by the brand. It is important that a brand ensures that their delivery is top-notch and when they cannot give perfect delivery to their clients, they should seek help from other companies.

Assistance from professionals

There are professionals and consulting companies that can advertise an advertisement reaching diverse audience. These include Trade Bodies (for Advertisers) and Charities working with diverse audience. Often, they are well waste in each of the protected characters, and they can advise accordingly on the advertising strategies.

Assistance from other creatives

This may be more appropriate for a small advertising agency or a freelancer who may not have access to trade bodies or other creatives in the agency. This involves seeking assistance from other creative individuals, to share ideas, get their thoughts on the design and ask for feedback. This is all about having a different eye to look at the design. There is also the possibility of allowing someone who is not on the design team to have a look at the campaign; someone who has not been engrossed in the production details, who has an objective overview of the campaign, perhaps might see something the team has not observed.

Assistance from the customers

This could be a form of focus group or survey to understand the expectations of the consumers, invite them to have a look at the design and provide feedback. While the selected sample may not give generalisable results, it may, however, offer some additional insight that may not have been previously thought about by the agency.

Assistance from regulators

Regulators such as the Advertising Standards Authority (ASA) in the United Kingdom, Autorité de Régulation Professionnelle de la Publicité (ARPP), the French advertising self-regulatory organisation, or the Advertising Standards Council of India (ASCI) can assist agencies in ensuring that their advertisement aligns with the values of the society. These organisations are the self-regulatory voluntary organisations in the advertising industry. In most cases, any advertiser, advertising agency or media company can submit its non-finalized project to the regulatory bodies for checking and providing feedback.

Summary

Advertisements are expected to mirror the values of the society. Advertisers are expected to take cues from society and shape their advertisement to reflect these values to make their advertisement engaging and appealing to the audience. While it may be considered easy to send an advertisement to the society, it is essential to take note of three factors. Firstly, society is not homogeneous. It is diverse with different individuals engaging with different brands. While the advertiser is trying to reflect the values in society, it is also essential to recognise the diversity and the individuals who may have values different from those inherent in the society. Secondly, the global nature of brands offers a different challenge as they reach out to the audience. There is a need to decide on either localising or globalising advertisement campaigns. Recognising that the same advertisement may not work in different countries is also important. The perfect example of this is an advert by Volvo. Volvo has one advertisement for the United Kingdom and a different advertisement for Poland. Brands and advertisers need to recognise these differences as they develop and disseminate their advertisements. Thirdly, advertisers may sometimes want to go against the society norm to show how creative they are. Brands need to be mindful of this direction, as in some cases there may be a backlash because the society has refused to accept such idea, while in other cases it may be a huge success.

This chapter explored the consumers' engagement with the advertisement. This is often an area that the advertisers cannot control. They must do their best and ensure their best is good enough when the advert is received by the customers. As consumers are managing their media and being mindful of the advertisers that can reach them, it is paramount for advertisers to be more proactive and vigilant as they scramble to reach the right audience wherever they can find them. No doubt, feedback is vital for the advertisers and brands. This will enable them to learn and evaluate their strategies as they aim to reach out to the diverse audience.

Advertisements play an essential role within the society. The research by Mogaji (2015) concludes that advertisers and brand managers need to do more to creatively integrate the characteristics protected under the Equality Act with the mainstream marketing communication strategies, to make their marketing more relevant. The underrepresentation of these characteristics in the media confirms that the society does not have true equality of opportunity, at least to the extent expected, as the diversity in the country is not reflected well enough in newspaper advertisements.

Advertisers, therefore, need to recognise their role as custodians of values and ensure that it is well conveyed to the audience. Research is essential in understanding the audience and developing an advertising campaign that will be effective, and likewise the creative team behind the campaign should be diverse. If in doubt, advertisers should seek assistance from their colleagues, other professionals and the regulators.

There are repercussions if things are not done correctly; this may affect the brand and the advertising agency. The regulators might also be involved in checking that the agencies have abided by the code of conduct. While no agency wants to go through this reputational damage, the role of regulators in shaping advertising practises is essential and will be subsequently covered in the next chapter.

Revision questions

1. Why should advertisers reflect inherent cultural values in their advertisements?
2. What do you understand by protected characteristics? Are they applicable in your country?
3. How can advertisers work with and integrate protected characteristics in their campaigns?
4. How would you expect advertisers to reach out to the Boomers and mature people, Generation X, the Millennials, Generation Z and children?
5. What are the challenges of having an inclusive advertisement?

Student activity

Design an inclusive advertisement brief

Work within your group to understand what you all like and design an advertisement that encapsulates all your interests. You should come up with an advertisement brief that will appeal to everyone in the group (imagine you are giving the brief to an advertising agency). This will help you understand the challenges of creating an advertisement that everyone likes, and is willing to watch and share.

Each group member should identify their choice of:

- Pet animal
- Music
- Colour
- Media
- Interest.

So, if two out of four in the group like the image of a dog, you need to reach a consensus to ensure that you all use an image that everyone likes. Likewise, the choice of music should be what everyone likes and also the use of colour and media. Everyone may not like YouTube. You may want to agree and reach a compromise. Considering that you are all in the same class, shared interest in advertising may be an added advantage.

Your output should be a brief for an advertisement, highlighting the message you want to pass (your shared interest in the group), the images you want to use, the background music and colour and also the platform you want to use to share the advertisement with your target audience.

References

ANI, 2019. *Snapchat brings new Gucci-themed portal lens*. ET BrandEquity. [Online] Available at: https://brandequity.economictimes.indiatimes.com/news/digital/snapchat-brings-new-gucci-themed-portal-lens/72048229 [Accessed 26.8.2020].

ASA, 2018. *Top 10 most complained about ads from 2017*. [Online] Available at: www.asa.org.uk/news/top-10-most-complained-about-ads-from-2017.html [Accessed 8.8.2020].

ASA, 2019. *Ban on harmful gender stereotypes in ads comes into force*. [Online] Available at: www.asa.org.uk/news/ban-on-harmful-gender-stereotypes-in-ads-comes-into-force.html [Accessed 2.2.2020].

Bailey, A., 2006. A year in the life of the African-American male in advertising: A content analysis. *Journal of Advertising*, 35(1), pp. 83–104.

BBC News, 2013. *Ford India apologises for Berlusconi advert*. [Online] Available at: www.bbc.co.uk/news/world-asia-india-21921139.

BBC News, 2016. *What's behind China's "racist" whitewashing advert?* [Online] Available at: www.bbc.co.uk/news/world-asia-china-36394917.

BBC News, 2017. *Nivea removes "white is purity" deodorant advert branded "racist"*. [Online] Available at: www.bbc.co.uk/news/world-europe-39489967.

Beauloye, E. F., 2020. *The 15 most popular luxury brands online in 2020*. Luxe Digital. [Online] Available at: https://luxe.digital/business/digital-luxury-ranking/most-popular-luxury-brands/ [Accessed 26.8.2020].

Belam, M., 2017. *Threats to boycott Tesco after Muslim family features in Christmas ad*. [Online] Available at: www.theguardian.com/business/2017/nov/13/threats-boycott-tesco-muslim-family-christmas-ad.

Bushfield, A., 2015. *Mulberry replaces Jesus Christ with handbag in Christmas advert*. [Online] Available at: https://premierchristian.news/en/news/article/mulberry-replaces-jesus-christ-with-handbag-in-christmas-advert.

Braverman, J., 2008. Testimonials versus informational persuasive messages: The moderating effect of delivery mode and personal involvement. *Communication Research*, 35(5), 666–694.

Channel 4, 2019. *Channel 4 awards £1m Diversity in Advertising prize to Starbucks and Iris*. [Online] Available at: www.channel4.com/press/news/channel-4-awards-ps1m-diversity-advertising-prize-starbucks-and-iris.

Deloitte Report, 2019. *Global Powers of Luxury Goods 2019*. Deloitte. [Online] Available at: www2.deloitte.com/content/dam/Deloitte/ar/Documents/Consumer_and_Industrial_Products/Global-Powers-of-Luxury-Goods-abril-2019.pdf [Accessed 26.8.2020].

El Hazzouri, M., Main, K. & Sinclair, L., 2019. Out of the closet: When moral identity and Protestant work ethic improve attitudes toward advertising featuring same-sex couples. *Journal of Advertising*, 48(2), pp. 181–196.

ET BrandEquity, 2019. *"Turban" marketing "blues" haunt Gucci*. ET BrandEquity. [Online] Available at: https://brandequity.economictimes.indiatimes.com/news/marketing/turban-marketing-blues-haunt-gucci/69370320 [Accessed 26.8.2020].

Fletcher, W., 2010. *Advertising: A very short introduction*. Oxford: Oxford University Press.

Guardian, 2013. *Dunkin' Donuts apologises for "bizarre and racist" Thai advert*. [Online] Available at: www.theguardian.com/world/2013/aug/30/dunkin-donuts-racist-thai-advert-blackface.

Gov.uk, 2020. *Equality Act*. [Online] Available at: www.gov.uk/guidance/equality-act-2010-guidance [Accessed 7.7.2020].

Grau, S. & Zotos, Y., 2016. Gender stereotypes in advertising: A review of current research. *International Journal of Advertising*, 35(5), pp. 761–770.

Gucci, 2020a. *I was a sari.* Equilibrium. [Online] Available at: https://equilibrium.gucci.com/i-was-sari/?utm_medium=gucci.com&utm_source=gucci.com_int&utm_campaign=equilibrium_launch_june20&utm_term=equilibrium_website&utm_content=equilibrium_website [Accessed 26.8.2020].

Gucci, 2020b. *About us.* [Online] Available at: www.gucci.com/hk/en_gb/st/about-gucci [Accessed 26.8.2020].

Gupta, G., 2020. *Gucci launches a new sustainable collection, Off The Grid. Vogue.* [Online] Available at: www.vogue.in/fashion/content/gucci-launches-a-new-sustainable-collection-off-the-grid-jane-fonda [Accessed 26.8.2020].

Hauff, J. C., Carlander, A., Gamble, A., Gärling, T., & Holmen, M., 2014. Storytelling as a means to increase consumers' processing of financial information. *The International Journal of Bank Marketing*, 32(6), pp. 494–514.

Hiebert, P., 2017. *The benefits of advertising to LGBT consumers.* YouGov. [Online] Available at: https://today.yougov.com/topics/media/articles-reports/2017/06/08/benefits-of-advertising-to-LGBT-consumers [Accessed 8.8.2020].

Holbrook, M. B., 1987. What is consumer research?. *Journal of Consumer Research*, 14(1), pp. 128–132.

Institute of Practitioners in Advertising (IPA), 2019. *IPA publishes 2019 IPA Agency Census.* Online] Available at: https://ipa.co.uk/news/agency-census-2019.

Jain, V., & Sheth, J., 2019. *Consumer behavior: A digital native.* 1st ed. Delhi, India: Pearson Education India.

Johnson, G. & Grier, S., 2011. Targeting without alienating: Multicultural advertising and the subtleties of targeted advertising. *International Journal of Advertising*, 30(2), pp. 233–258.

Kay, A., & Furnham, A., 2013. Age and sex stereotypes in British television advertisements. *Psychology of Popular Media Culture*, 2(3), p. 171.

Kim, J., Choi, D. & Kim, H., 2019. Advertising nativeness as a function of content and design congruence. *International Journal of Advertising*, 38(6), pp. 845–866.

Mallia, K., 2009. From the sacred to the profane: A critical analysis of the changing nature of religious imagery in advertising. *Journal of Media & Religion*, 8(3), pp. 172–190.

Marketing, 2013. *She runs the night – strategy, execution results of Nike's groundbreaking campaign. Marketing.* [Online] Available at: www.marketingmag.com.au/hubs-c/she-runs-the-night-strategy-execution-results-of-nikes-groundbreaking-campaign.

McCracken, G., 1989. Who is the celebrity endorser? Cultural foundations of the endorsement process. *Journal of Consumer Research*, 16(4), pp. 310–321.

McDonald, R., Laverie, D. & Manis, K., 2020. The Interplay between advertising and society: An historical analysis. *Journal of Macromarketing*, https://doi.org/10.1177/02761467 20964324.

Miller, F. & Allen, C., 2012. How does celebrity meaning transfer? Investigating the process of meaning transfer with celebrity affiliates and mature brands. *Journal of Consumer Psychology*, 22(3), pp. 443–452.

Mogaji, E., 2015. Reflecting a diversified country: A content analysis of newspaper advertisements in Great Britain. *Marketing Intelligence & Planning*, 33(6), pp. 908–926.

Mogaji, E., 2018. *Emotional appeals in advertising banking services.* London: Emerald.

Northey, G., Dolan, R., Etheridge, J., Septianto, F., & Van Esch, P., 2020. LGBTQ imagery in advertising: How viewers' political ideology shapes their emotional response to gender and sexuality in advertisements. *Journal of Advertising Research*, 60(2), pp. 222–236.

Oakenfull, G., McCarthy, M. & Greenlee, T., 2008. Targeting a minority without alienating the majority: Advertising to gays and lesbians in mainstream media. *Journal of Advertising Research*, 48(2), pp. 191–198.

ONS, 2011. *Ethnicity and national identity in England and Wales: 2011.* [Online] Available at: www.ons.gov.uk/peoplepopulationandcommunity/culturalidentity/ethnicity/articles/eth nicityandnationalidentityinenglandandwales/2012-12-11 [Accessed 8.8.2020].

Park, C. W. & Young, S. M., 1986. Consumer response to television commercials: The impact of involvement and background music on brand attitude formation. *Journal of Marketing Research*, 23(1), pp. 11–24.

Pavey, H., 2017. *Lamb advertisement condemned by Hindus for depicting vegetarian deity eating meat.* [Online] Available at: www.standard.co.uk/news/world/lamb-advertisement-con demned-by-hindus-for-depicting-vegetarian-deity-eating-meat-a3628196.html.

Pinkvilla, 2018. *Deepika Padukone, Kareena Kapoor Khan, Ranbir Kapoor: These are the LUXURY brands Bollywood celebs swear by. Pinkvilla.* [Online] Available at: www.pinkvilla. com/fashion/celebrity-style/deepika-padukone-kareena-kapoor-khan-ranbir-kapoor-these-are-luxury-brands-bollywood-celebs-swear-431644 [Accessed 26.8.2020].

Plakoyiannaki, E. & Zotos, Y., 2009. Female role stereotypes in print advertising: Identifying associations with magazine and product categories. *European Journal of Marketing*, 43(11/12), pp. 1411–1434.

Rathore, V., 2013. *How Punjab singers are making big brands like Prada and Gucci famous. The Economic Times.* [Online] Available at: https://economictimes.indiatimes.com/industry/ services/advertising/how-punjab-singers-are-making-big-brands-like-prada-and-gucci-famous/ articleshow/20825063.cms?from=mdr [Accessed 26.8.2020].

Schipp, D., 2017. *Hindus get lamb ad ban as advertising watchdog does backflip.* [Online] Available at: www.news.com.au/finance/business/retail/hindus-get-lamb-ad-ban-as-advertising-watchdog-does-backflip/news-story/ff7528c4ae4cfdbc45fc77d1e67a10e6 [Accessed 8.8.2020].

Sweney, M., 2016. *Gambling ad banned for mocking Christ's crucifixion. The Guardian.* [Online] Available at: www.theguardian.com/media/2016/may/18/gambling-ad-christ-crucifixion-banned [Accessed 8.8.2020].

Um, N., 2014. Does gay-themed advertising haunt your brand? The impact of gay-themed advertising on young heterosexual consumers. *International Journal of Advertising*, 33(4), pp. 811–832.

Vaidya, R., 2017. *A peek inside the biggest Gucci party of the year. Vogue India.* [Online] Available at: www.vogue.in/content/a-peek-inside-the-biggest-gucci-party-of-the-year [Accessed 26.8.2020].

Vasudev, S., 2016. *The Gucci turnaround. LiveMint.* [Online] Available at: www.livemint.com/ Leisure/Vh7HdGRlGaeRvGosjgw35M/The-Gucci-turnaround.html [Accessed 26.8.2020].

Wingate, U., 2015. *Academic literacy and student diversity: The case of inclusive practice.* Bristol: Multilingual Matters.

Youngun India, 2019. *7 Brands that turned the tides with meme marketing.* Medium. [Online] Available at: https://medium.com/@youngunindia/7-brands-that-turned-the-tides-with-meme-marketing-26056bf6569f [Accessed 26.8.2020].

Zhu, X., Teng, L., Foti, L. & Yuan, Y., 2019. Using self-congruence theory to explain the interaction effects of brand type and celebrity type on consumer attitude formation. *Journal of Business Research*, 103, pp. 301–309.

8 Offensive or unoffensive

Regulating advertisements

As consumers engage with advertisements, there will be some who like them while others may dislike them. As there are individual differences, there are psychological traits that make individuals react either positively or negatively to an advertisement. It is possible that some may find an advertisement offensive because it does not reflect their values, and they may decide to complain about and report the advertisement. This chapter introduces you to the regulatory bodies responsible for ensuring that advertisements are truthful, honest and not misleading. You will be introduced to the advertising codes of practice that bind the industry. Examples of regulatory boards across the world are also presented with different examples of advertisements that have been banned or have received complaints. The ethical issues associated with advertisements and legislative control and various codes of practice are discussed. With this information, you are better prepared to work within the regulator's code of practice. Also, with the knowledge you are going to gain in this chapter, you will be able to minimise the margin of errors that usually characterise advertisements created by new and inexperienced advertisers. Furthermore, this chapter will help you with the information needed to create advertisements that perfectly observe the regulations, ethics and Code of Advertising.

Learning outcome

At the conclusion of this teaching, students will be able to:

- Describe what can make people find an advertisement offensive;
- Recognise the importance of the Code of Advertising Practice;
- Describe the self-regulatory organisations in advertising;
- Explain the general advertising principles;
- Describe the process of raising a complaint about an advertisement.

Introduction

The society has engaged with the advertisement. They have seen the creative elements that have been embedded in the advertisement. During this process, there are possibilities that some individuals, groups or other brands will find the message offensive or inappropriate (Auxtova et al., 2020). Some people may feel this advertisement should not be aired on national TV or printed in a newspaper. There are expectations from the society about the type of advertising messages that they should be receiving. This then leads to questions about who is responsible for monitoring advertising – the consumers watching it? The advertisers producing it? Or an independent third party?

This chapter explores the role of regulators in the advertising industry. It recognises that in some cases, advertisements may be considered offensive or inappropriate and someone needs to be a mediator between the creative designers and the conservative customers. Advertisers want to create a message that will make a lasting impression; they may wish to exaggerate some claims to make the message look impressive, but some consumers feel this is not honest. This lecture further explores what the regulators regulate, how they regulate and why regulation is essential.

As advertising students, it is crucial to be aware of the role of the regulators, the advertising code of practices which shape the creative process and the implications of flouting these rules. Just like any other profession, some rules must be followed in the process of delivering the message. Importantly, this is to ensure that customers do not find the advertisements offensive and, if perhaps they do, that advertisers have a regulator who can meditate on the matter.

Offensive or not offensive

Advertising that pushes the boundaries can sometimes be negatively received by the consumers. There are chances that some consumers may not like an advertisement. They find it offensive and would prefer not to be exposed to the marketing message. There is a negative attitude towards the advertisement and also towards the brand. There are many reasons why consumers may find an advertisement offensive. As discussed in the last chapter, society is diverse, and there are different opinions and perceptions about a message that inadvertently may give offence.

Portrayal

The way characters are portrayed in an advertisement can be offensive to some individuals (Liljedal et al., 2019). The portrayal of the advertisement has to do with the theme, colour, models, language and every other factor used to describe or represent the message being sent to the audience about the brand. This message can be in the form of either a spoken description, a dramatic character, or even a photograph or painting of the message being communicated by the brand and the advertising agency. While this is a creative decision by the advertisers, some consumers when exposed to it may feel sensitive about it. For example, the portrayal of women in a sexualised manner has often raised concern. There was the uproar about the "Are you beach body ready?" controversial weight-loss advertisement in London. People felt the choice of image on the massive neon yellow background was inappropriate. Likewise, McDonald's had to withdraw its TV advertisement that featured a boy asking his mother about his dead father after it was criticised for exploiting child bereavement. The fast-food giant apologised "for any upset" caused but had to remove the advertisement, created by Leo Burnett London. Creative elements embedded in an advertisement can trigger that negative attitude which further necessitates the need to be mindful in the design and development of an advertisement. An agency might think they have done an excellent job, only for the consumers to react against it because it has not portrayed a true reflection of their society.

Textual content

While images can be offensive, the textual content of an advertisement can also offend the sensibility of consumers. This content could be seen on social media or read in a newspaper. An example of this is the social media campaign created by the University of Missouri Athletic Department for the National Collegiate Athletic Association (NCAA)'s Inclusion Week which used different wording to describe the aspirations of the black athletes. Any advertisement which contains swear words or inappropriate use of a religious name also falls into this category. Misleading text on advertisements can also be offensive, especially when people feel they have been deceived.

Case study 8.1

McDonald's sponsored Instagram advertisement in New Zealand

In New Zealand, a McDonald's sponsored Instagram advertisement shows a photo of two McDonald's cheeseburgers, fries and a drink which has "No sugar" and Coca-Cola written on the outside of the paper cup. There is a big "$5" next to the food and drink. Across the bottom of the advertisement is the text: "McDonald's NZ Only on the Macca's App. Available Wed 25 and Thurs 26 September, 10.30 am – 10.30 pm, 2x cheeseburgers, small fries and small drink for just $5!" A. Brien (Complaint number 19/330 to New Zealand ASA) was concerned the advertisement was undermining the health and well-being of individuals because the food depicted does not meet the Ministry of Health Eating and Activity Guidelines and contains an excessive amount of energy for one meal. The Guidelines recommend foods with unsaturated fats, that are low in sodium, have little or no added sugar and are mostly "whole" or less processed. They also recommend plain water over other drinks. Issues were raised on social responsibility, health and well-being, truthful presentation and food and beverage claims.

McDonald's said the advertisement "doesn't encourage excessive consumption or show food that exceeds portion size". The statement further went on to say that "if the complaint was upheld it would be effectively banning the advertising of occasional food and beverages". Moreover, the regulatory body did not uphold the complaint because it was considered "a straightforward 'price and product' advertisement for an occasional food and did not promote a meal in a way that undermined the health and well-being of individuals".

Even though the advertisement was on Instagram, which is considered age-gated for those aged 18+, and they can make an informed choice about what they buy and eat, this case study highlights how consumers can notice small details in an advertisement and raise a complaint about it. This suggests the need for brands and advertising agencies to be very mindful of the claims they put in their advertisement.

Reflective questions

- How important is the textual content of an advertisement?

- Do you think it's important for consumers to complain about an advertisement that they find offensive?
- Have you found an offensive advertisement? What did you do? Did you share it on social media, complain to the brand or complain to the regulatory body?
- What is the responsibility of brands to create advertisements with a due sense of social responsibility to consumers and society?
- Do you think age-gated media (media that can be assessed by people of a certain age) is an excuse for brands and advertising agencies to develop advertisements that may be deemed offensive?

Verbal content

Verbal content in advertising refers to the use of words by the advertisers. The use of words in advertising makes and mars the delivery to and reception by the target audience of such advertisements. Recognising the diversity in the society, some individuals may not be able to read the textual content of an advertisement but can listen to its verbal content, albeit on radio or TV. A television advertisement for an Isuzu D-Max Ute in New Zealand shows a man taking his new UTE for a spin and saying "Geez, wahoo, I love this truck". M. Burke (Complaint number: 19/311 to New Zealand ASA), said: "The name of 'Jesus' was used inappropriately and disrespectfully". It was used to indicate how a common swear word may be used seemingly intending to emphasise how good the product is. This kind of inappropriate and disrespectful use of what is a holy name in the Christian religion is discriminatory.

Placement

The placement of an advertisement deals with how an advertiser can decide to choose to put their adverts out for the audience to see, hear or read. Placement targeting is usually considered as the best way to reach the right group of audience. Advertisement placements can be as broad as an entire website or as specific as a single social media post. The positioning of an advertisement in the media space can also make some consumers raise concerns about the advertisement. In this case, it is not about the design or creative element but rather the dissemination of the advertisement. Here is an implication for media planners on where and when to show an advertisement. There was a complaint about the promotion for Merkur Cashino on the back of a child's bus ticket, seen on 28 May 2019, which stated "£5 Free Plays on a machine of your choice with this ticket!" (ASA, 2019). The complainant challenged whether the advertisement was directed at those below 18 years by the selection of the media or context in which it appeared. Only one person complained about the advertisement, but it had to be dealt with as the rule states that gambling must not be directed at those aged younger than 18 years through the selection of the media or context in which they appear. The fact that it was placed on the back of a bus ticket was the main concern here because the complainant felt children would see the advertisement. The timing of an advertisement – the time of day the advertisement is to be shown, which contributes to the placements and media buying – can also make an advertisement offensive. For example, it may be inappropriate to show advertisements for certain products when children are watching TV. Parents may feel it is not right for such messages to be displayed during the day when children may see them.

Four people complained about a poster and billboard promoting a Hallowe'en event, seen in Norwich in September 2019: the poster stated, "Norfolk's Biggest Scare Experience . . . PRIMEVIL . . . SCREAMING WON'T HELP!" and featured an image of a lumberjack holding a chainsaw and wearing a bloodied hessian mask and apron. The advertisement text further stated, "Street Performers, Bar, BBQ, Hot Snacks, Live Music, Refreshments" and "17 Nights of Terror – 5 Frightening Haunts". The complainants challenged whether the advertisement was likely to cause fear or distress in children and might therefore be inappropriate for outdoor display. Marketing that was likely to cause fear or distress for young children should not appear where they would be likely to see it.

Two versions of an advertisement for the film *Hallowe'en* were screened on Virgin Media channels before 21:00. The Advertising Standards Authority received two complaints from Ireland concerning these advertisements. Both complainants felt the scenes shown during the advertisements were unsuitable to have been broadcast at the times in question during what they considered to be family programming. They both said that their children had been watching television at the time the advertisements were broadcast and one complainant said that her child was distraught and affected by the advertisements.

Product

The advertising of some products may be considered offensive as well. Especially as parents (and society) believe that some products such as alcohol, tobacco and some medications should not be brought to the attention of children through advertisements (Delgado & Foschia, 2003). As an advertiser, you must realise that the product is an object or system made available for consumer use by the brand; it is anything that can be offered to a market to satisfy the desire or need of a customer. It is now your job to ensure that the advertisement created for the brand to sell or introduce a product or service to a group of buyers really gets the word across to the right audience. You must ensure the advert is not placed in the wrong place, for the wrong audience or through the wrong media.

Outdoor posters for Blu electronic cigarettes (e-cigarettes) seen in the United Kingdom in July 2019 featured a stylised drawn character of a woman wearing sunglasses and holding an e-cigarette. The ad featured the headline claim "I blu do you?" alongside the claim "NEW MYBLU. HANDY AND EASY VAPING". Small text to the right of the image stated, "FOR EXISTING ADULT SMOKERS & VAPERS ONLY". Smaller text underneath said, "this product contains nicotine 18+ only. Not a smoking cessation product". People complained about whether the advertisement encouraged non-smokers and non-nicotine users to use e-cigarettes.

Instagram posts on Holly Ah-Thion's Instagram account, for Tequila Rose Distilling Co, an alcoholic liqueur company, were seen in the United Kingdom on 4 May 2019. The post featured an image of Holly Ah-Thion sitting on a sofa holding a shot glass filled with a pale pink liquid. A bottle of Tequila Rose Liqueur and another shot glass filled with a pale pink liquid were on a table in front of her. The image was accompanied by a caption, which stated "[#AD] Dressed for the occasion. One for me, one for you. Date night feat. @lovetequilarose. Tequila, but not as you know it . . . #TequilaRose Strawberry Cream, is pure creamy, strawberry, yumminess in a glass". The complainant challenged whether the ads, which featured alcoholic drinks, were inappropriately targeted at people under 18 years of age.

A national press ad, seen in the *Sunday Express* on 26 November 2017 was headed, "Enjoy a breath of fresh air". Text, in the style of an article, described how the device worked and how it could benefit people with different types of breathing problems.

A blue box titled "SCIENTIFICALLY-TESTED TO REDUCE BREATHLESSNESS**" featured text stating "In a recent clinical study in 23 people with COPD at University Hospitals of Leicester (NHS trust), daily use of Aerosure over an 8 week period resulted in a significant improvement in breathlessness." In the small print at the bottom of the page the text stated, "Two complainants challenged whether the claims that the Aerosure Medic device was 'SCIENTIFICALLY-TESTED TO REDUCE BREATHLESSNESS' and 'using clinically tested breathing therapy' were misleading and could be substantiated" (ASA, 2019). Claims such as "scientifically tested" or "clinically tested" for medications and medical devices often raise concerns from consumers. Advertisers need to ensure that their claims can be substantiated with evidence.

There are many more reasons for which consumers will find an advertisement offensive. Crucially, this can be summarised into anything that goes against the essence of good advertising which suggests that:

- All marketing communications should be legal, decent, honest and truthful.
- All marketing communications should be prepared with a sense of responsibility both to the consumer and to society.
- All marketing communications should conform to the principles of fair competition as generally accepted in business.

It may, however, be argued that these principles are relative. How would you describe a decent advert? What an agency finds to be suitable, consumers may feel is annoying. Legality varies across different countries. An advertisement may not contain a lie, yet not be truthful. Implementing these principles requires a laid down code of practice for all practitioners – a guide that officially describes what decency looks like and that can be adopted by everyone.

Code of Advertising Practice

The code sets the criteria for acceptable advertising and forms the basis upon which advertising is evaluated in response to consumer complaints and complaints between advertisers. A code of conduct in advertising is a set of rules that has been defined by a regulator. This code outlines the rules, norms, mode of operation and responsibilities or proper practices of an individual party or an organisation. It is widely endorsed by advertisers, advertising agencies, media that exhibit advertising, and suppliers to the advertising process. The code is not intended to replace the many laws and guidelines designed to regulate advertising but to complement and provide a guiding principle.

The Code of Advertising Practice sets out the rules that the marketing and advertising industry agree to follow, which indicates to the consumer and the public the steps that are taken to ensure compliance. In most countries, local advertising standards are based on the Advertising and Marketing Communications Code of the International Chamber of Commerce. Through self-imposed regulation, advertisements can be trusted, leading to the establishment of a perfect system through which recourse can be sought by those who may have been harmed or prejudiced by an advertisement.

Belgium and Sweden use the International Chamber of Commerce (ICC) Marketing Code in its original version, having translated it into the local language(s). The United States implements self-regulatory standards which have been developed independently of the ICC Marketing Code; while most other countries use national self-regulatory standards, which are at least in part inspired by the ICC Marketing Code. Specific provisions contained in local standards are typically agreed upon by an independent standards-making body within self-regulatory organisations (SRO) and subsequently updated regularly.

In the United Kingdom, there are two advertising codes – the Non-broadcast Advertising and Direct & Promotional Marketing (CAP Code) which is the rule book for non-broadcast advertisements, sales promotions and direct marketing communications, and the Code of Broadcast Advertising (BCAP Code) which applies to all advertisements (including teleshopping, content on self-promotional channels, TV text and interactive TV ads) and programme sponsorship credits on radio and TV services licensed by the Office of Communications, commonly known as Ofcom, the UK-government-approved regulatory and competition authority for the broadcasting, telecommunications and postal industries of the United Kingdom.

National adaptations are, however, often necessary to consider legal, social, cultural and economic specificities. For example, in Islamic countries where alcohol is not allowed, the advertising practices will reflect that. Likewise, the codes are also often complemented by sectorial guidelines addressing the marketing of specific products or services (e.g. alcohol, beauty products) or by issue-specific guidelines (e.g. on interest-based advertising, on advertising to children, on influencer marketing).

In UAE, for example, the Advertising Business Group (ABG) (ABG, 2020) advocates responsible advertising standards in the Gulf Cooperation Council. Though the standards reiterate principles already established under various existing legislation and regulations, they have introduced new rules governing advertisements and advertising content in the region. These include:

Respect for religion and political institutions:

The advertising content must be respectful of all divine religions and not offend Islamic beliefs. It must not disrespect the regime in the UAE and/or the symbols and political institutions thereof. Further, no content broadcast or published by a media corporation or outlet may disrespect the local and international policies of the UAE or disrespect the cultural heritage of the UAE.

Prohibited products/services:

The Advertising Standards explicitly prohibit advertising alcoholic beverages, tobacco, smoking and all banned products or services including banned narcotics and prostitution.

In Singapore, there is an emphasis on the family, not just immediate family but the grandparents. This is included in their Code of Practice under Social and Family Values (ASAS, 2018, p. 13).

Social values

* Advertisements should not:

    a) Downplay the importance of patriotism and national unity;
    b) Misinterpret national policies and goals for the benefit of any individual;
    c) Distort the perception of Singaporeans and the quality of life in Singapore;
    d) Distort the perceptions of citizens' influence on national issues;

e) Discredit or be derogatory to Singapore as a democratic country or in any other way.

    i.   Advertisements should not promote or condone rude and inconsiderate behaviour.

    ii.   Advertisements should not downplay the importance of having a caring and compassionate attitude for the less fortunate members of the community.

    iii.   Advertisements should not adopt or encourage a confrontational approach to resolving societal conflicts or differences.

    iv.   Advertisements should not exploit or fuel conflicts relating to national problems and controversial policies or issues.

    v.   Advertisements should be handled sensitively to minimise misinterpretation of intentions on ethnic issues.

    vi.   Advertisements should not jeopardise interethnic understanding or discriminate against any ethnic group or religion, or downplay the importance of mutual dependence amongst all groups.

Family values

- Advertisements should not:

a) Downplay the importance of the family as a unit and foundation of society;
b) Undermine the perception of the family as a place of comfort and security;
c) Discredit mutual love, affection and support amongst family members.

    i.   Advertisements should not encourage inconsiderate and disrespectful conduct amongst family members.

    ii.   Advertisements should not denounce or discourage the responsibilities of honouring, supporting and providing for one's parents and grandparents in their old age.

    iii.   Advertisements should not undermine the willingness among family members to stand by one another through ups and downs.

    iv.   Advertisements should not erode or downplay the importance of communication amongst family members in building trust and understanding.

These Codes of Practice (across the world) need to be enforced by a regulatory body – an organisation that is responsible for making sure that practitioners adhere to the principles. Importantly, as well, there is need for a mediator in situations where advertisers go against the rule. This highlights the many responsibilities of regulators of advertising practice.

Advertising regulators

As previously discussed, advertising is communicating a message – from brands through advertising agencies to consumers. It is essential that the news is truthful, correct and can stand the test of time. Trust is crucial as the message is being communicated. But as we all know, sometimes, a deceitful message may be coated in truth. You see the truth in an advertisement, and you decide to buy a product, only to discover that the product is not doing what it says on the tin. You feel cheated. It is also essential to recognise that people are making huge investments based on marketing communications they have received; if these messages happen to be false, there are detrimental effects for the customers.

Besides, as individuals, there are different perceptions about a message. While the message may be true, some individuals may find it offensive; perhaps how the truth has been presented they feel is not appropriate. In some cases as well, brands may feel the way the truth is being presented is affecting their business, causing them harm and, therefore, they have reservations towards the advertisement.

To mediate

These scenarios illustrate the reasons why consumers and advertisers need regulators. There are independent third parties who serve as mediators when a consumer accuses a brand of telling lies in the advertising, when a consumer finds an advertisement offensive because of its form of portrayal or when a brand feels its services are being tarnished. The regulator needs to hear both sides of the story and mediate between the parties (Beales, 1991). While there may be issues between advertisers and consumers, regulators can also deal with complaints of advertisers or advertising agencies about each other as a consequence of their commercial communication and promotion activities.

To lay the rules

To avoid a reoccurring need for a mediator, regulators are needed to set standards that guide both parties – advertisers and consumers. The consumers can see if advertisers have flouted the rules of the regulators (which is possible). Advertisers as well can shape their creative designs to align with the regulators' rules. The set of rules becomes a working document for advertisers, a guide for consumers and an arbitration platform for the regulators.

To enforce the rules

There will be situations whereby the advertisers will flout a rule, perhaps on purpose to create attention for their messages; consumers notice this, and they may decide to complain. Regulators are needed to enforce the rule and ensure that the advertisers address the concerns raised by the consumers. Regulators are required to show advertisers the rule book and let them know if and how they have disregarded the law that binds the party.

To support and advise

The role of a mediator is never-ending in as much as there is a need for brands to communicate with the consumers. There will always be reasons to mediate and enforce the law; to reduce this happening every time, regulators are needed to support and advise the advertisers (Rozendaal et al., 2011), to let them know what is in the rule book and how they can creatively communicate their message without offending anyone. Through a proactive education and outreach programme, regulators can keep the industry informed of regulatory and legislative trends. This can be effectively done through workshops, custom consultations and seminars for advertisers, agencies and other stakeholders.

Self-regulatory organisations (SRO)

While the role of regulators may be considered informal – to mediate and support – it is essential to recognise that regulators have significant roles to play in today's fast-changing media environment. Besides, advertisers have taken it upon themselves, at least in some countries, to establish organisations that can officially take up the role of regulator without relying on the government to enforce any rules (Feenstra & Esteban, 2019). These are the self-regulatory organisations (SROs).

Who are the SROs?

They are self-regulatory organisations (SRO)

The regulators are often not created by the government. They do not have a legal backing nor are they recognised by law, and they are not government agencies. They are independent and not funded by taxpayers or governments. This independent status is a critical factor in maintaining public confidence in the self-regulatory system. Instead, it is an organisation made up of advertisers coming together to regulate themselves. That is the reason they are referred to as self-regulatory organisations (SROs). They are an industry organisation that is supported by advertisers, advertising agencies and media organisations to maintain standards in advertising. The organisations are responsible for self-regulating the content of advertising in their countries with quality decisions and fair process.

The stakeholders recognise them

Advertisers regard themselves as bound by the Code, and willing to adopt the principles of the regulatory body. The strength of the self-regulatory system lies in the support and commitment of the advertising industry – advertisers, advertising agencies, media specialists, direct marketing companies, sales promotion consultants and the various media – print, radio, television, online, cinema and outdoor interests. Members of SROs are required to abide by the Code and not to publish an advertisement or conduct a promotion which contravenes Code rules.

They enforce the Code of Advertising Practice

Self-regulation means the adoption by the advertising industry of standards drawn up by and on behalf of all advertising interests. It involves the enforcement of those standards through the commitment and cooperation of advertisers, agencies and the media. SROs adopt and enforce, as far as reasonably possible, the existing and established Code of Advertising Practice among their members. They determine whether advertising contravenes the Code of Advertising Practice. The Code sets out the rules that advertisements are to comply with to ensure they are responsible

They ensure a sense of social responsibility in advertisements

SROs apply standards aimed at ensuring that advertisements are responsible from an ethical point of view. They ensure that advertisements and all forms of marketing communications are prepared with a due sense of social responsibility. Self-regulation encourages the industry to take responsibility to provide legal, decent, honest and truthful advertising communications to consumers. Moreover, ads should conform to the principles of fair competition, as generally accepted in business.

They provide an additional layer of consumer protection

While they may not be government organisations, these regulatory bodies offer an extra layer of consumer protection that complements the legal framework. They can listen to the grievances of customers who may have found an advertisement offending or misleading. They work towards establishing universal principles of best practice and greater convergence towards these common principles and safeguarding consumers' interests.

Services of SROs

Advisory services

SROs provide services to advertisers and their agents before the publication of an advertisement.

Pre-clearance

SROs assess advertainments as a mandatory pre-condition before they can be published. This service could be obligatory for sensitive sectors such as drugs and medical devices, ads directed at children or ads for financial services. This is provided by SROs in Canada, France, the Philippines and Italy. In the United Kingdom, pre-clearance is provided by Clearcast for Television Advertisement (www.clearcast.co.uk), and the Radiocentre is for radio advertisement (www.radiocentre.org). Clearcast halted Iceland's plans to reuse the Greenpeace "Rang-tan" film. The political associations of Greenpeace meant the supermarket had to change plans for its purpose-led Christmas campaign (Gwynn, 2018).

In some cases, advertising pre-clearance is often done to ensure compliance when producing advertisements. Advertising agencies and media owners who are in doubt over the acceptability of advertisements can contact their regulatory bodies to obtain advice and guidance. The regulators provide fee-based, objective and independent advertising copy review and an advisory service for practitioners. Advertising agencies and media houses are expected to pay for this service, and it is not often intended to be a clearing-house for the approval of all advertising.

Pre-clearance may be limited to the regulated advertising categories, depending on the capabilities of the organisation. In the case of Canadian's Ad Standard, they offer pre-clearance in five regulated advertising categories: alcoholic beverages, children's advertising, cosmetics, food and non-alcoholic beverages and health products (AdStandards.ca, 2020).

The Canadian Ad Standards has a logo that may be affixed to advertising materials that have been reviewed by and received approval from the clearance services. The logo may be used in all forms of media, provided that the advertisement has been reviewed and approved by Ad Standards in its final, as-produced. This helps build consumer confidence by communicating that the brand's message is compliant with all pertinent regulations in Canada.

The clearance can offer the following decisions:

Approved for production

This is given to a material when copy and visual claims are adequately substantiated. With this approval, advertisers may proceed to actual production, recording and printing.

Approved for production, with caution

This is given to a material when copy and visual claims are adequately substantiated but a specific visual, copy, claim, or its tone/mood/theme is sensitive and potentially controversial in nature. The material may proceed to actual production, recording or printing, but a reminder of care and sensitivity in the execution of the material is given.

Disapproved

This is given to a material containing copy, claims, visuals or elements that violate the Code of Advertising Practice. The material is therefore denied permission to proceed to production unless the advertiser/ad agency addresses the violating aspects.

Refer to panel

An advertisement may be referred to a panel when the subject or execution deals with sensitive themes and requires further or complex technical substantiation from independent sources or a third party, especially ads of product categories or services that deal with technology and health. Upon the recommendation of the panel, the advertisement may be approved for production, approved for production with caution, or disapproved.

Copy advice

Voluntary copy advice

SROs issue an opinion as to whether an ad complies with advertising standards before the publication of the advertisement, at the request of the advertiser, agencies or the media. There may be occasions when an advertiser, a media owner or agency is concerned that the proposed marketing communication, which is not subject to the Code, may offend. On request, SROs can give informal advice in such cases. The advice is provided on a confidential basis and is usually non-binding. It may include suggestions of amendments to ensure compliance with the rules. Copy advice can be a free service or a paid service, depending on the market and the type of ad/advertiser.

Compulsory copy advice

Marketers and advertising agencies that are known for disregarding advertising principles may be asked to provide compulsory copy advice. This could be for the advertiser who often deliberately flouts the Code, intending to generate complaints, PR and subsequent notoriety; in this case the SRO can request the advertiser and the media to submit for a stated period any of the advertisers' proposed marketing communications to check their compliance with the Code.

Educational service

SROs also make an effort to provide education services to practitioners and consumers. They raise awareness about ad standards and enhance compliance. They host forums, workshops and seminars to raise awareness of emerging industry and consumer issues about self-regulation and developments in advertising clearance.

Power of SROs

SROs are empowered to ask an advertiser or an advertising agency to amend or withdraw any advertisement that, in their opinion, is contrary to the Code (Harker & Harker, 2002). The organisation can also ask an advertiser or advertising agency to withhold such advertisement until it has been modified or in the case where the SRO has requested further information to decide whether an advertisement is contrary to the Code, pending receipt of such information and a decision.

The SROs are also often empowered to ask media owners to support their decisions. As a consequence of going against the advertising codes, the SROs can ensure the withholding of advertising space or time from advertisers, and the withdrawal of trading privileges from advertising agencies. There is also a sanction of adverse publicity which can bring a negative attitude towards the brand.

Funding SROs

SROs are independent organisations that need funds to run their activities. The funding ensures that SROs have the necessary resources to handle complaints and independently check advertisements. Besides, it helps SROs to provide pre-publication advice to advertisers, agencies and the media. There are three main categories in terms of how these organisations are funded.

Membership fees

Most SROs worldwide are funded through annual contributions from member firms and associations representing the advertising industry. The fees can take the form of a fixed amount or of proportional fees based on a sliding scale (with more significant members paying a higher fee than smaller members). There are also sometimes different membership fees depending on the type of businesses the members represent and depending on the kind of services provided. Canadian's Ad Standards membership is made up of over 230 leading advertisers, media organisations, advertising agencies and suppliers to the advertising sector. Members can take advantage of reduced fees when attending seminars, workshops and events, and receive discounted rates for clearance services. Members can use the Ad Standards member logo on corporate communications material.

Levy system

In this funding model, a small percentage of advertising costs goes to finance the operation of the SRO. This amount is typically collected by advertising agencies which act as intermediaries between advertisers and media owners (TV, radio, billboard sites, newspapers, websites) before it is transferred to the SRO. They are funded by a voluntary levy, or in simple terms a charge, on the cost of advertising space, i.e. the amount of money advertisers pay media owners, such as billboard sites, newspapers, posters, online etc., to run their ads. The UK ASA is funded through the levy system. They receive 0.1% on the cost of buying advertising space and 0.2% on some direct mail. For example, that means where an ad cost £1,000 to appear on a billboard, £1 of that would be collected and go towards funding the ASA. The levy is collected on behalf of the SRO the Advertising Standards Board of Finance (Asbof) and the Broadcast Advertising Standards Board of Finance (Basbof).

Combination of the membership and levy systems

This is a model in which the SRO charges for membership and receives levy from the advertisement.

Self-regulatory organisations (SROs) around the world

The organisational set-up of SROs, however, varies significantly from market to market. ARPP in France is the oldest SRO in the world. It was founded in 1935. The Canadian SRO was created in the 1950s, with four SROs following in the 1960s (in the UK, the Netherlands, Italy and El Salvador). The European Advertising Standards Alliance (EASA) members include the largest and oldest SROs in the world such as those in France, the United Kingdom and Spain. EASA is not a self-regulatory organisation in itself but acts as a coordination point for best practice in the implementation of self-regulation, as well as operational standards for its national SRO members.

The International Council for Advertising Self-Regulation (ICAS) estimates that there are at least 50 advertising SROs worldwide. Table 8.1 includes organisations which can broadly be described as SROs, according to the Global Factbook of Advertising Self-Regulatory Organizations ("Global SRO Factbook") which is a yearly publication of ICAS (Global SRO, 2018).

Table 8.1 List of SROs around the world

S/N	Country	Short name of SRO	The long name of SRO
1	Argentina	CONARP	Consejo de Autorregulación Publicitaria
2	Austria	ÖWR	Österreichischer Werberat (Austrian Advertising Council)
3	Australia	Ad Standards	Ad Standards
4	Belgium	JEP	Jury d'Ethique Publicitaire
5	Bulgaria	NCSR	National Council for Selfregulation
6	Brazil	CONAR	Conselho Nacional de Autorregulamentação Publicitária
7	Canada	Ad Standards	Ad Standards
8	Switzerland	FW	Swiss Commission for Fairness in Commercial Communication

S/N	Country	Short name of SRO	The long name of SRO
9	Chile	CONAR	Consejo de Autorregulación y Ética Publicitaria
10	Colombia	CCACC	Comisión Colombiana deAutorregulación de la Comunicación Comercial
11	Cyprus	CARO	Cyprus Advertising Regulation Organisation
12	Czech Republic	RPR	Rada Pro Reklamu
13	Germany	DW	Deutscher Werberat
		WBZ	Zentrale zur Bekämpfung unlauteren Wettbewerbs e.V.
14	Ecuador	SAC	Special Advertisement Committee
15	Spain	AUTOCONTROL	AUTOCONTROL
16	Finland	MEN	Mainonnan eettinen neuvosto (The Council of Ethics in Advertising Finland)
		LTL	Liiketapalautakunta (The Board of Business Practice Finland)
17	France	ARPP	Autorité de regulation professionnelle de la publicité
18	Greece	ASC	Advertising Self-Regulation Council
19	Hungary	ÖRT	Önszabályozó Reklám Testület(Hungarian Advertising SelfRegulatory Board)
20	Indonesia	DPI	Dewan Periklanan Indonesia
21	Ireland	ASAI	The Advertising Standards Authority for Ireland
22	India	ASCI	The Advertising Standards Council of India
23	Italy	IAP	Istituto dell'Autodisciplina Pubblicitaria
24	Japan	JARO	Japan Advertising Review Organization
25	Korea	KCSC	Korea Communications Standards Commission
26	Lithuania	LRB	Lietuvos Reklamos Biuras
27	Luxembourg	CLEP	Commision Luxembourgeoise pour l'Ethique en Publicité
28	Mexico	CONAR	Consejo de Autorregulación y Ética Publicitaria
29	Malaysia	ASA	Advertising Standards Authority
30	The Netherlands	SRC	Stichting Reclame Code
31	New Zealand	ASA	Advertising Standards Authority
32	Norway	MFU	Matbransjens Faglige Utvalg (the Food and Drink Industry Professional Practices Committee)

(Continued)

Table 8.1 (Continued)

S/N	Country	Short name of SRO	The long name of SRO
33	Peru	CONAR	Consejo Nacional de Autorregulación Publicitaria
34	The Philippines	ASC	Advertising Standards Council
35	Poland	RR	Związek Stowarzyszeń Rada Reklamy
36	Portugal	ARP	Auto Regulação Publicitaria
37	Paraguay	CERNECO	Centro de Regulacion, Normas y Estudios de la Communicacion
38	Romania	RAC	Romanian Advertising Council
39	Sweden	RO	Reklamombudsmannen
40	Singapore	ASAS	Advertising Standards Authority of Singapore
41	Slovenia	SOZ	Slovenian Advertising Chamber
42	Slovakia	RPR	Rada Pre Reklamu
43	El Salvador	CNP	Consejo Nacional de la Publicidad
44	Turkey	ROK	The Advertising Self-Regulatory Board
45	United Arab Emirates	ABG	Advertising Business Group
46	United Kingdom	ASA	The Advertising Standards Authority
47	USA	ASRC	Advertising Self-Regulatory Council. On 1 June 2019, the ASRC was merged into BBB National Programs (BBB NP)
48	Uruguay	CONARP	Consejo Nacional de Autorregulación Publicitaria
49	South Africa	ARB	The Advertising Regulatory Board
50	Zimbabwe	ASAZIM	The Advertising Standards Authority of Zimbabwe

Source: The Global Factbook of Advertising Self-Regulatory Organizations. International Council for Advertising Self-Regulation (ICAS) (Global SRO, 2018).

Assessment guidance

These are the criteria used to assess whether an advertisement is compliant with local standards.

Legality

This has to do with whether an ad is compliant with applicable laws or not. Advertisements should not contain anything that is illegal or that might incite anyone to break the law. Nor should they appear to condone or lighten the gravity of unlawful activities. Furthermore, advertisements should not contain anything that contravenes the ethical code of recognised professional bodies in the country.

Decency

This has to do with whether an ad is not offending standards of decency prevailing in the local culture or not. Advertisements should not contain anything offensive to the rules of decency prevailing among those who are likely to be exposed to them.

Honesty

This has to do with whether an ad is not abusing the trust of consumers or exploiting their lack of experience or knowledge. Advertisements should not abuse the confidence of the consumer or exploit their lack of experience, expertise or knowledge.

Truthfulness

This has to do with whether an ad is not including content that could mislead customers (e.g. as regards the actual benefits/characteristics of the product or service). Advertisements should not mislead in any way by inaccuracy, ambiguity, exaggeration, omission or otherwise. More specifically, advertisements should not misrepresent any matter likely to influence consumers' attitude to any product, advertiser or promoter; misrepresent any information to mislead consumers into believing any matter that is not true, such as the source of the product, quality of the product, obligation (or non-obligation) in using a trial product, and others; mislead consumers about the price of goods or services; underestimate the actual total price to be paid; mislead consumers to overestimate the value or mislead consumers regarding the conditions on the terms of payment such as hire purchase, leasing, instalment sales and credit sales.

(Social) responsibility

Social responsibility refers to whether an ad respects human dignity and is free of any form of discrimination, including race, national origin, religion, gender, age, disability or sexual orientation. All persons should be portrayed in a manner respectful of their dignity. No person should be commoditised.

Safety

Advertisements should not show a disregard for safety. In particular: (a) Advertisements should not contain any visual presentation or any description of dangerous practices or of situations which show a disregard for safety, unless justifiable on educational or social grounds; (b) Special care should be taken in advertisements directed towards or depicting children and young people and (c) Consumers should not be encouraged to drink and drive.

Fairness

Ensuring that an ad is not derogatory to the competition and is free of plagiarism. Advertisements should not be so similar in general layout, copy, slogans, visual presentation, music or sound effects to other advertisements or promotions as to be likely to mislead or confuse.

Right to privacy

Ensuring that an ad complies with (self)-regulatory standards on data protection for consumers.

Non-denigration

Advertisements should not unfairly attack or discredit other products, organisations or professions directly or by implication.

Non-exploitation of goodwill or intellectual property

Advertisements should not make unjustifiable use of the name, initials, logo and trade and service marks of any firm, company or institution. Advertisements should not take unfair advantage of another firm, person or institution's goodwill in its name, trade name or other intellectual property, or the goodwill earned by other's advertising and promotion campaigns.

It should be noted that this varies across different countries as not all countries adhere to all the principles. According to ICAS, truthfulness is the only criterion that is used across all markets. The United States does not consider legality, decency or (social) responsibility. Ireland does not consider legality while Australia also excludes honesty and right to privacy from their criteria. Likewise, Belgium, El Salvador, India, Mexico and Peru exclude right to privacy from their criteria. Belgium and South Africa do not consider fairness.

Advertising guidelines for protected sectors

There are guidelines in the Code of Practice that appeal to some specific industries. It is essential to be aware of this if you are working with brands in these sectors.

While marketers, agencies and publishers have primary responsibility for ensuring that everything they do is legal, advertising guidelines have limitations in some sectors. Advertisers working with brands in these sectors need to be aware of the following items:

- Medicines, medical devices, health-related products and beauty products
- Weight control and slimming
- Financial products
- Food, food supplements and associated health or nutrition claims
- Gambling
- Lotteries
- Alcohol
- Motoring
- Employment, homework schemes and business opportunities
- Tobacco, rolling papers and filters
- Electronic cigarettes.

Laws with a bearing on marketing communications

The Code of Advertising Practices aligns with many of the statutes, orders and regulations of the country. As seen with UAE, where alcohol is not allowed, this is embedded in the guideline. These laws have a bearing on marketing communications, and therefore they need to be considered while interpreting advertising practices. Some important aspects are governed by legislation enforced by local authority trading standards and environmental health officers; therefore marketers who break the law risk criminal prosecution or civil action.

For financial products, advertisers must have regard to the financial promotion restriction in Section 21 of the Financial Services and Markets Act 2000 and in the Financial Services and Markets Act 2000 (Financial Promotion) Order 2005 (as amended), as reflected in the rules and guidance issued and enforced by the Financial Conduct Authority (FCA). For food, food supplements and associated health or nutrition claims, the Code of Practice must be read in conjunction with the relevant legislation, including the Food Safety Act 1990, the Food Information Regulations 2014 and Regulation (EC) No. 1924/2006 on nutrition and health claims made on foods (the EU Regulation) as they apply to all marketing communications for food products. The EU Regulation is mandatory and seeks to protect consumers from misleading or false claims.

The Tobacco and Related Products Regulations 2016 prohibit the advertising of nicotine-containing electronic cigarettes (e-cigarettes) which are not licensed as medicines, but only in some media channels. The UK advertising codes stipulate the legal basis for types of claims marketers may make online and how they might avoid indirectly promoting prohibited products in the media subject to the Regulations through the marketing of non-nicotine or other products.

Regulated by another organisation

When another organisation regulates the sector, the guideline from advertisers is interpreted following the other regulatory body. For example, in medicines, medical devices, health-related products and beauty products, the rules apply to market communications and not to the products, which are regulated by health regulators such as the Medicines and Healthcare products Regulatory Agency (MHRA), Veterinary Medicines Directorate (VMD), the European Medicines Agency (EMA), and the Department of Health, UK ASA Code of Advertising Practice noted that marketing communications for those products must comply with the rules and professional codes of conduct of relevant professional bodies. Likewise, the Financial Conduct Authority (FCA) regulates financial services provisions, and their guidelines also expect advertisements to be "clear, fair and not misleading".

Age restrictions

For products with age restriction such as gambling and alcohol, there is special mention with regard to the guidelines which advertisers must be aware of. Importantly, marketing communications for these products should be socially responsible, concerning the need to protect children, young persons under 18 and other vulnerable persons from being harmed or exploited by advertising that features or promotes such products (Newall, 2017). These are also embedded into laws, as in the United Kingdom's Gambling Act 2005. For rules on marketing communications for lotteries, see Section 17. The legal framework for gambling in Great Britain, including the requirements for licensing operators, is set out in the Gambling Act 2005 and The National Lottery etc. Act 1993 (as amended). Marketing communications for lottery products that are licensed and regulated by the Gambling

Commission for National Lottery products should be aware of these conditions and special mentions in the Advertising Code.

Standardised measure

To avoid misleading and inaccurate claims, advertisements that require standardised measurement receive specific mentions. For example, alcoholic drinks are defined as drinks containing at least 0.5% alcohol; for the UK Advertising Code, alcoholic drinks are defined as drinks containing between 0.5% and 1.2% alcohol. This suggests that any drink with less than 0.5% can be advertised to children and sold as non-alcohol because the alcoholic content is below the standardised measure according to the codebook.

Also, for car marketers, the code warns that they must not make speed or acceleration the central message of their marketing communications. Marketing communications may give general information about a vehicle's performance, such as acceleration and mid-range statistics, braking power, road-holding and top speed. This is because the speed limit on UK roads is 70 miles per hour. If the car is advertised as being able to reach 200 miles per hour, it is deemed irresponsible and unsafe.

Obesity in adults is defined by a body mass index (BMI) of more than 30 kg/m2. The Code suggests that advertisers must be mindful of their claims in marketing communications for weight control and slimming foodstuffs, aids (including exercise products that make weight-loss or slimming suits), clinics and other establishments, diets, medicines, treatments and the like.

UK ASA defines anyone with over 30,000 social media followers as a "celebrity". This is to enforce advertising rules. This standardised number further highlights the need for influencers and marketers to know how to present their content if it is a form of advertisement.

General advertising guidelines

Children and young people: advertisements should not exploit the natural credulity of children or the lack of experience of young people and should not strain their sense of loyalty. Advertisements addressed to or likely to influence children or young people should not contain anything that might harm them mentally, morally or physically. Advertisements should not promote a lifestyle that is promiscuous or that denigrates or is detrimental to family values.

Matters of fact: all descriptions, claims and comparisons that relate to the issues of objectively ascertainable facts should be capable of substantiation. Advertisers and advertising agencies are required to hold such approval ready for immediate production when asked.

Use of research results: when a factual claim in an advertisement is said to be supported by the results of independent research, the advertiser and sales promoter should be able to show that those responsible for the research accept the advertisement as an accurate account of the study.

Use of testimonials: advertisements should not contain or refer to any testimonial or endorsement unless it is genuine and related to the personal experience of the party who provided the testimonial or endorsement. Care should be taken to ensure that testimonials based on fictitious characters are not framed to give the impression that real people are involved.

Quotation of prices: clarity – if reference is made in an advertisement to more than one product, it should be clear to which product or version any quoted price relates. Truthfulness – if the price quoted does not include the product in its entirety (for example, a lamp without its lampshade), this fact and the new cost should be stated with no less prominence than the price itself.

Associated purchases: if a product cannot be purchased without purchasing other product(s) from the advertiser or promoter, this fact must be stated with no less prominence than the product itself.

Use of the word "free": when a product is advertised or promoted as being "free", incidental costs, which will necessarily be incurred by the consumer in acquiring it, should be clearly stated. Advertisers should not seek to recover the cost of the product that they describe as free in any manner, including (a) Imposing additional fees they would normally not charge; (b) Inflating any incidental expenses they may legitimately recover; or (c) Altering the composition or quality, or increasing the price, or any other product which they require to be bought as a pre-condition of the consumer obtaining the "free" product.

Use of the word "discount": when a product is being advertised or promoted as to be sold at a discount (or similar description such as a bargain), the discounted price must be lower than its usual price and cannot be offered indefinitely. The word "discount" should not be used in the situation where the reduced price has become or would be reasonably perceived by the consumers as the usual price.

Comparisons: advertisements containing comparisons should not violate the principles of fair competition. Where a comparison is made between the respective cash values or prices of goods that are not identical, the advertiser should indicate that this is the case. All comparative advertisements should be so designed that they are transparent and fair, and there is no likelihood of the consumer being misled as a result of the comparison.

Availability of products: an advertisers should ensure that there is an adequate supply of their products to meet foreseeable demand generated by their advertisement or promotion. They should make clear any limitations of the product's availability unless such restriction is inherent and unique to the product.

Bait advertising: advertisers should not seek to entice consumers into a retailer's premise with no real prospect of selling the advertised or promoted goods at a price offered.

Guarantee: advertisements may contain the word "guarantee", "guaranteed", "warranty" or "warranted" or words having the same meaning only if the guarantee or warranty referred to improves the consumer's legal right. The full terms of the guarantee as well as the remedial action open to the purchaser should be set out in the advertisements or should be available for the purchaser to inspect before they are committed to purchasing. Any substantial limitations should be spelt out in the advertisement.

Identification of advertisers: the identity of the advertiser should always be clearly stated. Mail orders, direct response, exhibition, trade promotion and on-line advertisements should clearly state the permanent address of the advertiser.

Charitable causes: advertisements claiming that the purchase of a product will support some charitable cause should not mislead as to the share of proceeds that will go to charity.

Legibility of disclaimers: disclaimers have to be legible to the unaided eye of the target viewer. As a general rule of thumb, disclaimers should not be in a font size smaller than the smallest font used to make affirmative claims in an advertisement, subject to a minimum font size of 8.

Case study 8.2

Nigerians be warned: a political advertisement in Nigeria

Political advertising has played a huge role in political campaigns and electoral successes in Nigeria, West Africa. Political parties compete and struggle to outdo one another to market their candidates to the citizenry during election periods. The battlegrounds have always been radio, television, print and digital space. The weapons used range from issue-based campaigns, negative ads, propaganda, hate speech, religious sentiments and other issues that usually involve ethics.

The presidential election held in the country in 2015 was reputed to have been characterised by intense advertising as two major political parties slugged it out with each other. It was the very first time the then People's Democratic Party (PDP)-led government had a very serious challenger in a new party, formed from a merger of other parties, and which seemed to have some kind of acceptability across the north and the south of the country. Thus, every available means was used to outshine each other.

So, it was a shocking experience for Nigerians when they woke up to a shocking newspaper advert about the candidate of the All Progressives Congress (APC), Muhammadu Buhari, on 19 January 2015. The advert, placed in two major national dailies in Nigeria, the *Sun* and the *Punch* newspapers, was insinuating that Buhari would likely die in office. The advert copy warning Nigerians to consider their choice of president placed images of former Nigerian Heads of State who had died in office, all three of them, beside that of candidate Buhari with a question mark. The wordings and the images were insinuating that, because the three former presidents from the same ethnic extraction as Buhari had died while in office, there was a high tendency for Buhari to also die in office if elected.

This advert, sponsored by Mr Ayodele Fayose, a PDP governor in Ekiti State, Southwest Nigeria, stirred up controversy in political circles, academia and advertising regulatory space. People condemned the advert on moral and regulatory grounds. In Africa, and in Nigeria especially, it is not acceptable for a man to wish for the death of a fellow man. Even in the face of any competition, it is still unacceptable to publicly pronounce death on another man. On regulatory grounds, that the advert was splashed on the front pages of two prominent national dailies questions the regulatory powers of the agency established to gate-keep the advertising space.

The Advertising Practitioners' Council of Nigeria (APCON) is the body vested with the powers to regulate advertising practice in Nigeria. Established by the Advertising Practitioners Registration Act No. 55 of 1988, now the Advertising Practitioners Registration Act Cap A7 of 2004, the body is empowered to regulate and control the practice of advertising in Nigeria in all its aspects and ramifications. However, this advertisement found its way to the front page of national newspapers even though the content did not align with the cultural values of the society. It was therefore not surprising that many people found it offensive.

Reflective questions

- Why do you think it is important to reflect cultural values in political advertisements?

- How would you describe the role of the APCON in ensuring the political advertisement is not offensive?
- How would you describe the role of the *Sun* and the *Punch* newspapers in publishing the advertisement? Do you think they should have refused to publish the advertisement?
- Considering this advertisement was sponsored by an individual, do you think he would have consulted an advertising agency to develop the advertisement? If so, what is the role of the advertising agents in ensuring that the advertisement is not offensive?

Rasheed A. Adebiyi, Lecturer of Mass Communication,
Fountain University, Osogbo, Nigeria

Complaints about an advertisement

A complaint is defined as an expression of concern about an advertisement which requires a response. One of the main benefits of advertising self-regulation worldwide is that it provides a cheap (typically cost-free), fast and efficient solution to address consumer complaints about individual ads (Jones & Van Putten, 2008). The complaint may include one or several concerns about the given advertisement by the same complainant. A jury oversees determining whether a personal ad is in breach of self-regulatory standards or not. A jury is group of people who are knowledgeable about laws and principles guiding a certain operation. They are also known as the jurors and, in advertising, they are expected to render an impartial verdict (a finding of fact on a question). They set penalties or judgments based on facts, laws and guiding principles.

Jury members may be advertising industry professionals, independent from the advertising sector or independent experts, lawyers and representatives of civil society organisations depending on the country and the SROs' policy. The structure of the jury should ensure that most members are not employed in, or have a background in the advertising industry. The participation of the independent members ensures the objectivity of the complaint investigation procedure and assures that the system is operated with particular regard to the interests of consumers.

Who can complain?

The following parties may file a complaint to the SROs in their country where the advertisement is created:

- Consumers,
- Consumer organisations, environmental institutions and the related occupational chambers,
- Competitors or advertising agencies.

According to UK ASA, consumers can complain when they think there is something wrong with an advertisement they have seen or heard; if a special offer, competition or prize promotion has been unfairly run; if they want to stop direct mail from companies sent either by post, fax, text message or email or if they think there is something wrong with the marketing on a company's website or their social network site. To complain, this is often done online. It is essential to provide information about the ad, including where and when you saw it, a photo, video or screenshot of the advertisement, a copy of the marketing communication, if possible (i.e. press, magazine, etc.), details of when and where it appeared and the name of the advertiser; in the case of sales promotions, the name of the product and the promoter and copies of labels, leaflets or entry forms; in the case of a direct mailing, a copy of the envelope as well as the mailing. Complainants are also expected to provide the reasons why they consider the advertising to be wrong.

Likewise, companies can make a complaint against a competitor, in case the competitor is bringing the company into disrepute. In South Africa, Reckitt Benckiser Pharmaceuticals (Pty) Ltd raised a complaint about their competitor – Adcock Ingram Healthcare (Pty) Ltd's claim that their product provides symptomatic relief for sore throats, but the advertising, which is found in pharmacies, implies that it has curative properties. This, it submits, is dishonest, misleading and unsubstantiated. Reckitt Benckiser Pharmaceuticals is making an effort to protect their territory by ensuring that competitors are not disrupting the market with misleading advertisements.

In a case several complaints are received for the same ad and handled as a single case, all underlying complaints should be counted. Similarly, in the case of petitions, each signature would be counted as a complaint. In most instances where advertising is found to contravene the Code, the SROs will require the advertisement to be withdrawn or amended.

In the United States, their SRO does not handle consumer complaints because a different body, the Better Business Bureau (BBB) National Programs, does this. In UAE as well, their SRO does not handle consumer complaints. Consumers do not pay fees to complain about an advertisement. However, unlike consumers, companies are often required to pay a fee to file a complaint.

How complaints about advertising are handled

This may vary across different SROs. However here are generic steps often adopted by the SROs.

1. Complaint receipt

According to Canadian Ad standard, one (1) complaint is sufficient for the SRO to activate the process to determine if an advertisement contravenes the Code of Advertising Standards. The number of complaints submitted does not change or influence the rigorous complaint process. Once a complaint is received, it should be acknowledged by the SROs, who then assess if it goes against the advertising codes.

2. Preliminary review

The SRO will carry out an initial review to:

1. Determine whether it comes within the terms of reference of the Code. SROs are not responsible for all marketing communication

    i.   They are not responsible for political advertisement. Claims in marketing communications, whenever published or distributed, whose principal function is to influence voters in a local, regional, national or international election or a referendum are exempt from the Code.
    ii. Editorial content is expressly excluded from the remit of the Code.

iii. They do not investigate marketing communications in foreign media. If marketing communications appear in media based in countries that have self-regulatory organisations (SROs) that are members of EASA or if direct marketing originates from countries that have SROs that are members of EASA, EASA will co-ordinate cross-border complaints, so the SRO in the country of origin of the marketing communication has jurisdiction; consumers need complain only to their SRO.

Code is primarily concerned with the content of advertisements, promotions and direct marketing communications and not with terms of business or products.

2. If they have jurisdiction, they will want to substantiate the supposed problem with the advertisement. The advertisement is checked and assessed against the Advertising Codes.
3. If there appears to be a problem with the advertisement, the SRO will determine if there is a prima facie case for investigation – a cause of action or defence that is sufficiently established by the evidence provided.
4. If there is, the SROs will let the complainant know they are taking up the complaint.
5. If not, they would provide the reasons why it isn't a breach of the Advertising Codes. In some cases, they may be able to suggest another body that can help.

3. Investigation

An investigation is commenced based on the outcome of the preliminary review. There are often two options.

The matter may be resolved by informing both parties about the regulations. In the case of UK ASA, they will write to the advertiser providing appropriate advice and guidance, without seeking an assurance of compliance. Some of these minor complaints can be resolved quickly and informally by working with an advertiser to have an ad changed.

If it can't be resolved informally, the advertiser or promoter (or the advertising/promotional marketing agency involved) is informed of the complaint and invited to comment on it concerning the Code. They are required to respond, and to submit substantiation where necessary, within a stipulated time frame, generally within ten days. The advertiser must defend their advertisement in writing and give evidence to support it. At this stage, the SRO can seek expert advice about the complaint. On receiving the response, the SRO prepares a summary of the case. This will include any facts or advice that the SRO has gathered and recommendations.

The complainant and the advertiser/promoter or agency are provided with a copy of the recommendations and are allowed to express any further views in the matter. Findings are available to the media.

If the rules have been breached, the ad must be changed or withdrawn. In the case of a sales promotion, the promoter may be requested to make the necessary changes to the way the promotion is communicated or conducted and, where appropriate, may also be asked to recompense any consumers who have been adversely affected. If the complaint is "not upheld" no further action is taken.

Appealing the decision

If the consumer or advertiser disagrees with the SRO's decision, the consumer or advertiser can request an appeal. In certain circumstances, advertisers or complainants can request a review of a ruling. Both sides have some days (Canada Ad Standard – 7 days, UK ASA – 21 days) to appeal the decision. They must be able to establish that a substantial flow of process or adjudication is apparent or show that additional relevant evidence is available.

Monitoring

The SRO has to check whether the advertiser has made necessary changes after the rulings. They monitor ads to make sure that the Advertising Codes are being observed.

Enforcement and sanctions

1. There is a press release about advertisements that have been banned, and there are possibilities of negative attitude towards the brand. This could have an impact on the brand's reputation. The UK ASA acknowledges that adverse publicity (from the weekly publication of rulings) can be damaging to most marketers but serves to warn the public.
2. SROs can ensure the withholding of advertising space or time from advertisers. UK ASA uses Ad Alert which is issued at short notice and sent electronically to media houses containing the name and contact details of the non-compliant marketer, a description of the compliance problem and, if possible, a scanned image of the marketing communication in question. In the United Kingdom, Ad Alert may be issued to cover an entire sector if it perceives a widespread problem. Internet search websites may be asked to remove a marketer's paid-for search advertisement if that links directly to a page hosting the marketer's non-compliant marketing communication on its website or in other non-paid-for space under the marketer's control.
3. The member who does not accept the SRO's decisions may be disciplined by the organisation and may be subject to penalties, including fines and suspension of membership. The UK ASA and CAP do not adopt a legalistic attitude towards sanctions. In exceptional cases of noncompliance, members may be expelled.
4. There could be the withdrawal of trading privileges from advertising agencies. For example, agency recognition offered by the print media members of CAP may be withdrawn or the substantial direct mail discounts offered by Royal Mail on bulk mailings withheld.
5. Those persistently break the Advertising Codes and not complying are referred to other bodies for further action, such as Trading Standards or Ofcom. These organisations backed up by law can seek an injunction from the Court to prevent the additional appearance of an advertisement. Anyone not complying can be found to be in contempt of court and liable to be penalised.

Summary

We are all humans. We have a different perception of things, which includes advertisements. The way we process information is changed. Some advertisement may be misleading because the reader is processing it differently. With these challenges, there is a regulator who is serving as a mediator to make sure advertisements are legal, decent, honest and truthful.

While we may assume the regulator is a government organisation, they are instead independent organisations set up by the advertising agencies and other media stakeholders to self-regulate the industry. They have a code of practice which the advertisers abide by and that shapes the creative practice. While there are possibilities to go against the code of practice, the regulatory bodies are there to enforce and support the agencies. There are repercussions for those who continually flaunt the rules.

As an advertising student, there are many benefits in understanding the role of the regulators.

Firstly, you have a better understanding of the working dynamics within the industry. You know the process and the way things should be done. You are better prepared to engage with the legal entities, recognise the input of other professionals and regulators.

Secondly, you have a better understanding of the code of practice as applied in your country and to the brand or sectors you want to work in. While the guide presented in this chapter may be generic, it is essential to know what applies to your country, and perhaps there are some changes or amendments that have been made which you need to recognise.

Thirdly, this understanding will also shape your creative practices. You should be more aware of using claims in advertisements, how to use testimonies and work with protected brands. It would be best if you understood the implication of using images to portray a character without offending people. Regulatory bodies are required to rule against an advertisement while considering a balance between creativity and the advertisers' freedom of expression. The guidelines are there to shape the conscious creative decisions you are making.

Fourthly, you can put yourself in the shoes of the customers – to understand what they may be going through when they see the advertisements, the process they may go through if the advertisement is misleading and they decide to make a complaint. This ensures that, as an advertiser, you provide answers to the anticipated questions and relevant information in order for customers to make an informed choice.

Lastly, you are aware of the repercussions and sanctions if you contravene the rules. You may consider yourself a freelancer but be mindful that the regulators can also rule on advertisements that are on social media. You may find yourself an influencer, so you need to be cognisant of how you position your advertising messages.

Importantly, advertisers need to take responsibility for the content of their messages. This is because people may complain, and even though some advertisements may only invite one complaint, the regulator still has to investigate it. So, have a good understanding of the customers (as discussed in Chapter 7). Ensure you also know their values and the advertising practices that should shape your design, development and dissemination.

Revision questions

1. Why would *you* find an advertisement offensive?
2. What do you understand by the Code of Advertising Practice?
3. What are self-regulatory organisations (SROs)?
4. Do you know the self-regulatory organisation in your country?
5. Why is it essential to have SROs?
6. What are the benefits of advertising pre-clearance?
7. What is your understanding of legal, decent, honest and truthful advertising?
8. Why do you think some industries need a different form of advertising practices?
9. What types of advertisements are not covered under the Code of Advertising Practice?
10. Why would you raise complaints about any advertisement?

Student activities

Identifying and Examining advertisement people found offensive

You are expected to identify advertisements that have been reported as offensive in your country. Remember the fact that if people found an advertisement offensive does not mean it has been ruled offensive by the regulatory organisation. These advertisements are more likely to be available on the website of the regulatory organisation (see Table 8.1) or in the press.

If you cannot find one in your country, here are some examples (from the UK and Australia), be mindful, however, that inherent cultural values, background and insight may influence how you engage with the advertisement.

- In 2018, the KFC rapping and dancing chicken was the most complained about advertisement in the United Kingdom. The advert attracted 755 complaints that it was disrespectful to chickens and distressing for vegetarians, vegans and children. The advertisement was, however, not banned (though people found it offensive) as the ASA decided it did not include any explicit references to animal slaughter and was therefore unlikely to cause serious or widespread offence.
- In 2019, one of the most complained about advertisements in the United Kingdom was from Deliveroo with its "magic bag" TV advertisement, which had 300 complaints. Unlike the KFC advert which the majority of people found provocative, this Deliveroo advert was found misleading because it over promised on the delivery from different restaurants and to different locations. The advert became the most complained about advert in that year to the extent that it was banned. ASA told Deliveroo that it must not broadcast the advert again in its current form.
- In 2020, an advert from Ultra Tune, an Australian-owned franchised automotive servicing and roadside assist company, featuring Pamela Anderson and Warwick Capper in a *Baywatch* theme was the one of the most complained about advertisements in Australia. There were 309 complaints with issues around discrimination, exploitatation, degrading images, violence, sex/sexuality/nudity and health and safety. The complaint was, however, dismissed.

With your selected advertisement,

1. Take the role of a customer, determine the sentiments about the advert. You can do a social media search, read the briefing on the regulatory organisation's website or comments online. What are the general thoughts about the advert?
2. Take the role of a regulatory organisation, decide within your group if the advertisement is truly offensive. You need to provide justifications for your decision.
3. Take the role of an advertising agency; state what you would have done differently.

References

ABG, 2020. *Home*. [Online] Available at: www.abg-me.com/ [Accessed 8.8.2020].
AdStandards.ca, 2020. *Home*. [Online] Available at: https://adstandards.ca/ [Accessed 6.6.2020].
ASA, 2019. *ASA Ruling on Cashino Gaming Ltd t/a Merkur Cashino*. [Online] Available at: www.asa.org.uk/rulings/cashino-gaming-ltd-A19-1022314.html [Accessed 8.8.2020].

ASAS, 2018. *Singapore Code of Advertising Practise*. Singapore: Advertising Standards Authority of Singapore.

Auxtova, K., Brennan, M. & Dunne, S., 2020. To be or not to be governed like that? Harmful and/or offensive advertising complaints in the United Kingdom's (self-)regulatory context. *Journal of Business Ethics*, pp. 1–22.

Beales, H., 1991. What state regulators should learn from FTC experience in regulating Advertising. *Journal of Public Policy & Marketing*, 10(1), pp. 101–117.

Delgado, R. & Foschia, P., 2003. Advertising to children in Brazil. *Young Consumers*, 4(3), pp. 65–68.

Feenstra, R. & Esteban, E., 2019. Autocontrol: A critical study of achievements and challenges in the pursuit of ethical advertising through an advertising self-regulation system. *Journal of Business Ethics*, 154(2), pp. 341–354.

Global SRO, 2018. *Global Factbook of Advertising Self-Regulatory Organizations*. Belgium: Global SRO.

Gwynn, S., 2018. *Clearcast halted Iceland's plans to reuse Greenpeace 'Rang-tan' film*. [Online] Available at: www.campaignlive.co.uk/article/clearcast-halted-icelands-plans-reuse-greenpeace-rang-tan-film/1498487 [Accessed 8.8.2020].

Harker, D. & Harker, M., 2002. Dealing with complaints about advertising in Australia: the importance of regulatory self-discipline. *International Journal of Advertising*, 21(1), pp. 23–45.

Jones, S. & Van Putten, K., 2008. An analysis of consumer complaints about social marketing advertisements in Australia and New Zealand. *Journal of Nonprofit & Public Sector Marketing*, 20(1), pp. 97–117.

Liljedal, K., Berg, H. & Dahlen, M., 2019. Effects of nonstereotyped occupational gender role portrayal in advertising: How showing women in male-stereotyped job roles sends positive signals about brands. *Journal of Advertising Research*, 60(2), pp. 179–196.

Newall, P., 2017. Behavioral complexity of British gambling advertising. *Addiction Research & Theory*, 25(6), pp. 505–511.

Rozendaal, E., Lapierre, M., Van Reijmersdal, E. & Buijzen, M., 2011. Reconsidering advertising literacy as a defense against advertising effects. *Media Psychology*, 14(4), pp. 333–354.

Theme 4

Evaluating the message

9 Evaluating the effectiveness of the advertisement

A considerable amount of money has been spent on creating the brand's message, a lot of effort and manpower has also been invested; it is therefore essential to evaluate how effective the advertisement has been either in terms of sales or the effect on the brand's reputation. This chapter discusses the effectiveness of an advertisement from three perspectives. First, for consumers, advertisement is essential, mainly if it contains a message that relates to them, meets their needs and comes at the right time. Consumers also find advertisement important when it helps them in making decisions and meeting their needs. Second, from the advertisers' perspective, is the importance of highlighting the length of working relationship with the brands and possibly the amount of industry awards and accolades the agency has won. Third, the Brand perspective is vital. They are commissioning the advertisement and therefore they have key expectations in terms of their sales, media and brand mention and a change in behaviour, depending on the aim and objective of the campaign. The chapter concludes with seven strategies for developing an effective advertisement.

Learning outcome

At the conclusion of this teaching, students will be able to:

- Describe what an effective advertisement looks like from the different perspectives;
- Recognise different measures of effectiveness from a brand's point of view;
- Describe high performers advertisement;
- Explain the advertising awards and advertisers' interest;
- Describe the various factors influencing the development of an effective advertisement.

Introduction

A considerable amount of money has been spent on creating the brand's message, much effort and human resources has also been invested in designing and developing the advertisement; it is, therefore, essential to evaluate how effective the advertisement has been.

The main question is: what defines an effective advertisement?

This question will be explored in the context of this lecture to understand what makes an advertisement effective as this knowledge can help in shaping future advertising strategies.

It is also essential to recognise the different stakeholders involved in making this decision. You have the customers who are engaging with the advertisements. The advertiser who had designed and disseminated the advertisements and, importantly, you have the brand, the entity that commissioned the advertisements to be sent out. Each of these stakeholders has its definition of what an effective advertisement is, and it is essential to recognise this. Considering the side you might end up working in – either the agency side or the client-side – it is crucial to understand what success means in terms of advertising strategies.

This chapter gives a general overview of an effective advertisement, and focuses on the consumers' perception of an effective advertisement. Furthermore, the agencies' perspective is further considered with a laser focus on awards and industry recognition for creativity. Brand's definition, in terms of accomplished business objectives, is also explored. The chapter prepares students for a reward of their creative handwork regarding designing and developing an innovative, engaging and effective advertisement.

What defines an effective advertisement?

This is an open-ended question, which means that there are many correct answers, depending on who is answering the question. However, a fundamental approach will be adopted to understand an effective advertisement.

As earlier stated in Chapter 1, advertising is all about communications – communications from a brand to a target audience; communication, which is not limited to marketing purposes, but to pass across a message. An effective advertisement can therefore basically be described as one in which the objective of communication has been achieved. This may not be that simple as many factors are inherent in this process of effectively communicating.

The person who is sending the message – the brand – the way the message has been written or spoken, the creative events, the media in which the advertisement is being shared, the willingness of the receiver to engage with the advertisement all affect the effectiveness of the message. This is important to know because the effectiveness of an advertisement is not just a result or outcome but a combination of many factors which the brand, agencies or the customers may have control over. For an advertisement to be effective, all these factors are expected to align for the effective delivery of the message as intended. This stage – having an effective communication or engagement with concerned parties – is crucial and must be diligently done.

In as much as advertisement is not considered a personal message to a unique individual in public, it is reassuring to know that if an advertisement is deemed ineffective in some quarters, it can be effective somewhere else. If a consumer chooses not to engage with the advertisement, that is a decision which ensures that the message is not delivered as intended, but there could be many customers who will find the advertisement appealing and engage with it. For those individuals, the advertisement can be considered effective because they have received the message as intended.

This highlights implications for advertisers to make sure that their advertisement reach is not all about quantity (of people seeing the advertisement) but rather about the quality of people seeing it (Vardavas et al. 2010). There are those who will engage with the advertisement because it is meeting their needs. This ensures that overall, the advertisement can be considered effective by all stakeholders – the consumer is getting the message that the brand has commissioned the advertising agency to send. And everyone is happy that the objective of the message has been achieved.

Consumers' definition of effective advertisement

For consumers, advertisement is essential, mainly if it contains a message that relates to them, meets their needs and comes at the right time. Consumers also find advertisement important when it helps them in making decisions and meeting their needs. Therefore, they have their understanding of what makes an effective advertisement. For a consumer who is thinking of what to buy for Christmas and finds an advertisement on social media and decides to buy it instantly, the advertisement has been effective.

The fact that the advertisers have researched their target audience, know the right media and the right timing for the advertisement makes the advertisement appealing, but importantly, the idea of saving time to search and buy further complements the effectiveness of the advertisement. While this may be for a low involving product that you can make an instant decision on, advertisement becomes effective for high involving products when it contains the right message, complements the desires of the consumers and meets their needs (Saleem & Abideen, 2011).

It is essential to note that advertisement is not just about selling to a customer. A change of behaviour can be an indication of an effective advertisement; for example, a social campaign to stop people from drinking and driving featuring an advertisement that has been embedded with fear appeal. This is an advertisement, yet it is not aimed at selling a product but facilitating positive change in behaviours of the target audience. An individual who sees that advert feels guilty and decides to change their behaviour. That decision indicates how effective the advertisement has been. The creative effort in the form of encoding and the decoding from a personal point of view ensure the effectiveness of the advertisement.

The effectiveness of an advertisement from a customers' point of view may be relative. What an individual may find effective (because they have received a relevant message), another may not see as compelling (Smith & Yang, 2004). While the advertiser may be blamed for this ineffectiveness, it is essential to recognise human nature as people engage with advertisement. As previously discussed, there is the filtration process which informs how individuals can engage with advertisement.

Case study 9.1

The effective poster

Figure 9.1 is an advertisement I saw in Vancouver when I wanted to rent a bicycle to go through Stanley Park. Even though the advertisement was not on a billboard on the high street, nor on the radio or on social media, I found it useful. It met my need at that time, and I can say the advertisement was effective. Looking at the creative elements, the conscious creative decision of using yellow paper may have paid off; also, looking at the image, merely utilising a line image of a bicycle and the price, I was attracted, and I went in to rent the bicycle. The advertisement provided all the essential information I needed at that point. The effectiveness of an advertisement from a customers' point of view is, however, relative. Many may have seen that advertisement and not trusted it because it looks cheap. Many may have ignored it because they can't cycle and don't consider renting a bicycle. What an individual may find effective (because they have received a relevant message), another may not see as compelling. It is essential to recognise human nature as they engage with the advertisement. The consumer may just not be in the mood to see an advert.

Figure 9.1 Advertisement for bicycle rentals
Source: author.

Reflective questions

1. Why do you think the owner of the bike shop has adopted such a simple design?
2. Would you consider the advertisement creative and effective?
3. If you were to advise the bike shop owner, how could they improve this advertisement to make it more effective?

Advertisers' definition of an effective advertisement

Advertisers are interested in making effective advertisements. That is all they set out to do. To develop an advertisement that will deliver the message as intended by the brand. Their definition of effectiveness can be from two perspectives. Firstly, from the brand's perspective and secondly, from the industry perspective.

Brand's perspective

He who pays the piper dictates the tune. Brands pay advertising agencies to develop the message, and create an effective advertisement. They can decide if the message they intend to communicate has been effectively sent to the intended receivers. This definition of effectiveness can easily be measured by how long the brands and agencies have been working together. It indicates that the relationship has worked because they have achieved great results together; it is working because they are still in partnership and they anticipate making it last longer.

It is therefore not surprising to see brands change their advertising agencies or seeking out a boutique agency to provide a service. Perhaps the working relationship with the current agency has not been very active or productive. Therefore, they want to explore other options. This also allows other agencies to demonstrate what they have to offer; perhaps showcase another effective advertisement they have created in order to win new clients and businesses.

Industry perspective

This is the highlight of creative advertisement. This offers an objective definition of an effective advertisement. This industry perspective is in the form of awards and recognition that the advertising agencies receive for their creative effort. These awards are given to advertisements that are very creative and effective in delivering the message. Winning an award, judged by other creatives, brings a sense of achievement and reassurance, confirming the agency's creative capabilities.

This section discusses how to measure and assess how well the target audience has engaged with the advertisement, offering a sense of feedback to the brand and advertisers on how best to improve for the next campaign.

Brands' definition of an effective advertisement

Brands spend millions of pounds on advertising for a few seconds at the Superbowl. They go all the way to use the most prominent billboard for advertising their products and services to promote their new TV advertisements on social media for everyone to see. The effectiveness of these campaigns is, however, essential. It is a justification for the enormous amount of money they are spending on disseminating their messages. For brands, it is not just about sending the message but knowing that people are engaging with it and are willing to take action.

Sales indication

For brands, there are many definitions for an effective advertisement. However, this depends on the objectives of the advertisements – the purposes of the messages that are being sent. Ultimately, brands want to make sales and improve their share of the market. So, a good indication of an effective advertisement will be the increase in sales based on the advertisements. Irrespective of the size of the company, the return on investment for the advertisement is an essential indication of a successful advertisement. Companies have spent money to advertise, and they want to see an increase in their sales revenue and income. It is, however, essential to recognise that the sales are not solely the outcome of advertisements. For example, the advertisement may bring a customer to a brand's website, but the unresponsive nature of the site can discourage sales. Likewise, an advertisement can get a customer to a store, but the customer services may be poor, and the customer leaves. So, it is important that every party involved plays their roles effectively.

Return on Marketing Investment (ROMI)

According to IPA, Return on Marketing Investment (ROMI) is the financial measure which provides the ratio of profits generated by marketing investment. When looking at ROMI (IPA, 2020b), the two key metrics to have in mind are the incremental net profit generated from the activity (the financial return), versus the cost of campaign (the investment). While measuring the cost of the activity is straightforward, measuring the incremental net profit requires more in-depth investigation. Estimating incremental sales generated by marketing activity is the first step towards calculating financial payback. To do this, the brand needs to compare actual sales with "base sales" – how much they would have sold if they hadn't run the marketing activity in question. Incremental sales can be calculated by subtracting base sales from actual sales. However, it is essential to consider the other factors that may be affecting the brand at the time.

Media metrics

A wide variety of metrics can be used in measuring the effectiveness of an advertisement (Micu & Plummer, 2010). They include media exposure measures like ratings or clicks, attitudinal data like awareness or image or behavioural measures like response rates and actual sales. The number of views on a YouTube video, number of comments or likes on an Instagram post or the number of retweets can also indicate the effectiveness of these advertisements. A survey can also be sent to viewers to see how well they are recognising and engaging with the advertisement.

Brand mention

Besides, the mention of the brand's name on social media can indicate the effectiveness of an advertisement (Dehghani & Tumer, 2015; Gökerik et al., 2018). This, however, depends on the purpose of the advertisement as earlier indicated. Many metrics can be used to evaluate effectiveness. If the advertisement is to create awareness about the brand or to build the brand reputation, the number of impressions, sentiment analysis and social media metrics and mention can indicate how effective the advertisement has become. People have seen the advertisement, they are sharing it and talking about it. As seen with the Burger King advert, there were measurements of number of downloads for the app, number of visitors to the store and number of impressions. These metrics present an objective way to evaluate the success of the campaign. The press coverage around the world can also amplify the message and improve the reputation of the brand.

Change in behaviour

As earlier indicated, not all advertisement is to make sales. It could be for a replacement or behaviour – which could mean to stop a behaviour (like smoking) or to start a new behaviour (saving). The effectiveness of the advertisement can be measured based on how the target audience has changed their behaviours (Tay & Watson, 2002). So, if the UK government pays an advertising agency to develop a campaign for COVID-19 and they found that people engaged with it and stayed at home, the government could say to the agency that their advert worked.

High performers advertisement

High performers are much more likely to be targeting long-term objectives, such as market-share growth, and less likely to be targeting short-term sales activation. Low performers have sacrificed broad effectiveness to push primarily for short-term sales. The over-focus on short-term sales activation is a significant feature of low performers and, as we will see, it leads them to overinvest in the tools of quick response and underinvest in the business of brand building. One observable fact amongst low performers is their weaker focus on primarily emotional advertising; their focus shifts instead to activation prompts in the campaign, which is by nature rational. The difference is not yet great (76% vs 81%), but emotions are such a dominant feature of effective creativity that any dilution has to be a worrying sign. A high-performance advertisement is then the one that helps a brand in achieving both financial and non-financial results that are exceedingly better than what is even expected. High performers are much less likely to make this mistake. They are more likely to take a broader targeting approach to everyone in the market, including non-users of the brand. Some people might think this is a wasteful targeting strategy, but the actual value in creativity lies in its ability to create widely shared popular perceptions of brands. In this context, there is no such thing as wasted reach.

Some examples include the John Lewis Christmas advertisement tradition and Dove's Real Beauty campaign, which prove that brand purpose if communicated creatively can be a force for success, and the Snickers campaign which has been a long-running success story since "You're not you when you're hungry" was born in 2012. Fame and sales have grown relentlessly over the period.

Field (2019) defined high performers' advertisement as:

- A more balanced approach to short and long-term objectives.
- The maintenance of the campaign in the market long enough to embed behavioural change: at least six months typically.

- Broader, earlier targeting of consumers rather than data-driven real-time communications linked to purchase intent.
- Greater use of broad-reach brand-building media, especially TV but also online video and OOH.
- A balanced allocation of media expenditure between brand building and sales activation in line with the latest best practice guidelines.

Advertising awards

There are many awards in which advertising agencies can participate, ranging from small local competitions to prestigious global shows. It has been known that some agencies place much greater importance on winning awards than others. Though winning awards does not necessarily translate into reasonable returns on the client's investment, it is a stamp of creative credibility for the agency.

Awards can be given under these categories (this varies, however, depending on the type of award):

- Branded entertainment
- Creative effectiveness
- Creative use of data
- Design
- Digital craft
- Direct marketing
- Experiential & immersive
- Film
- Health, wellness & pharma
- Integrated
- Interactive & online
- Ip & products
- Mobile
- Moving image craft
- Out of Home
- Print
- Public relations
- Radio & audio
- Social media.

Cannes Lions[1]

Every year, Cannes Lions explores the value of creativity in branded communication: from product and service development to the creative strategy, execution and impact. Since its first outing in 1954, the Cannes Lions International Festival of Creativity has been bringing the creative communications industry together every year at its one-of-a-kind event in Cannes to learn, network and celebrate. The first festival took place in Venice with 187 film entries from 14 countries competing. The Lion of Piazza San Marco in Venice was the inspiration for the Lion trophy. The second festival was held in Monte Carlo and then in Cannes in 1956. After that, the festival took place alternately between Venice and Cannes. In 1984, Cannes became the permanent home of the festival before Roger Hatchuel took the festival into the modern era when he took control of the event in 1987. Over the following 30 years, the festival and awards continued to evolve to reflect the changing face of communications. Today, it continues to serve all marketing communications as a forum for debate and discussions.

D&AD

Since 1962, the D&AD Pencil has represented the very best in design and advertising. Winning a Pencil remains the pinnacle of many careers, and the work it celebrates inspires others to study, debate, copy and reference its excellence, as the industry's finest and most of historic treasures. This organisation was formerly known as British Design and Art Direction (BDAD).

The One Show[2]

The One Show is the world's most prestigious awards show recognising the best creative work in advertising, interactive, design and branded entertainment. The brightest creative minds from advertising agencies, digital agencies, design agencies, production companies, consumer brands and non-profit organisations from around the world enter every year.

The IPA Effectiveness Awards[3]

The IPA Effectiveness Awards were established in 1980 and are recognised by agencies as a robust proof of the payback on marketing communications. They are the world's most rigorous and prestigious awards, attracting a diverse range of entries from around the globe, including Canada, Australia and China. The IPA Effectiveness Awards take place once every two years.

Effie Awards[4]

Effie Worldwide stands for effectiveness in marketing, spotlighting marketing ideas that work and encouraging thoughtful dialogue about the drivers of marketing effectiveness. The Effie Awards are known by advertisers and agencies globally as the pre-eminent award in the industry and recognise any forms of marketing that contribute to a brand's success. For over 50 years, winning an Effie has become a global symbol of achievement. Today, Effie celebrates effectiveness worldwide with over 50 programs, including the Global Effies, regional programmes in Asia-Pacific, Europe, the Middle East/North Africa and Latin America, and national Effie programmes. The Effie Awards were launched in 1968 by the New York American Marketing Association as an awards programme to honour the most effective advertising efforts. The award now honours all forms of effective marketing and the companies and individuals creating effective work across the globe. In July 2008, the New York AMA assigned its rights in the Effie brand over to a separate non-profit organisation, Effie Worldwide, to continue enhancing Effie's mission and educational offerings.

Clio Awards[5]

The Clio Awards is the esteemed international awards competition for the creative business. Founded in 1959 to celebrate high achievement in advertising, the Clios annually and throughout the year recognise the work, the agencies and the talent across advertising, sports, fashion, music, entertainment and health that push boundaries and establish new precedents. Clio's year-round celebration of creativity includes a daily editorial content platform, Muse by Clio, that highlights the best in creativity from the advertising world and beyond with original stories and guest essays from the industry's top talent, and Ads of The World, an international database cataloguing the work of an ever-evolving industry.

Advertisers and advertising awards

The reputation

The reputation of an advertising award is based on the opinion and views of the general public, advertisers and, especially, consumers of a particular product or service. The award given by a recognised and reputable awarding institution validates the reputation and recognition of a brand based on social evaluation and assumption on a set of criteria, such as performance or behaviour. As an advertising agency, winning an award for your creative output enhances your reputation. It is a sign of your creative capabilities. Peer recognition helps distinguish the agency from the herd. Agencies can retain staff. People want to be associated with a successful team; employees who feel like they are part of a successful team are going to do better work. Awards can increase the chances of recruiting new talents. It is a high selling point for recruits. Awards add credibility, which can help an agency win new business. Awards can help an agency (and its clients) build name awareness and generate exposure locally, nationally and even globally. Winning an award can be a motivation to do more good work, continually focusing on great ideas that can benefit their clients. FCB New York won many awards for the Whopper Detour campaign for Burger King, not surprised to see them take pride in their work and have it on the landing page of their website.

The recognition

As an individual who has won an award, there is recognition that follows. There is also a sense of accomplishment. This recognition offers a bragging right and can open doors of more opportunities to move to different agencies and take up new roles (Brazier, 2015). These awards are seeing as the Oscars of advertising. A D&AD Pencil is considered a knighthood for an advertiser's career (D&AD, 2020).

The cost

Previously there were few awards for which agencies could compete, but now there are many. Agencies may have a budget to enter for these creative advertising awards. Therefore, with the rising cost of registration and entering, agencies need to be strategic in their approach. A single campaign entry for the 2020 IPA Effectiveness award was £2460 (including VAT) (IPA, 2020a). This is something some smaller agencies may not be able to afford.

The submissions

With the increasing cost of submission, it is not surprising to see advertising agencies submitting their best works to multiple awards. Even within a single award, they can submit their works to many categories. As seen with the FCB New York submission to the D&AD award, the same campaign was submitted to different categories. This separate submission is an attempt to increase their chances and win as many awards as possible.

The scam

While it is recognised that advertisers are commissioned by brands to develop and disseminate an advertisement, often, when some agencies do not have a client to commission them, they commission themselves to create over-the-top ads that have a better chance of winning an award than selling (Kiefer, 2019). Some agencies have been known to enter creative work that the client never approved or never ran in any media. There have been instances where an agency has developed a fresh concept and paid for it to appear in a local publication – so that it could be entered in a competition. Some agencies enter an advert that has run once, on late-night television, or has only run because they produced a single ad and paid to run it themselves. These are scam or fake advertisements which the awards organisations are aware of and are making an effort to curb. The One Club defines "fake ads" as ads created for non-existing clients, ads made to run without a client's approval and ads created expressly for award shows that are run once to meet the requirements of a tear sheet (One Show, 2020). An agency, the regional office of an agency network, or the independent agency that enters an ad made for non-existing clients, or made and ran without a client's approval, may be banned from entering the awards. Advertisements to be submitted require client contact information to verify the entry.

Students' award

While most awards are for professionals only, there are different awards for students such as the One Show's The Young One's Student Awards. The New Blood Awards from D&AD is open to advertising, design, digital and marketing students, recent graduates and young creatives worldwide.

Case study 9.2

Nike Just Do It "Dream Crazy" (One Show, 2019)

For 30 years, the "Just Do It" mantra has been a motivational call for athletes nationwide, across all sports, and all levels of play. To celebrate that rich diversity, the second film in the JDI series, "Dream Crazy", focuses on a collection of stories that represent athletes who are household names and those who should be. The common denominator: all leverage the power of sport to move the world forward. Along with inspirational pros – LeBron James, Serena Williams, Odell Beckham Jr., Eliud Kipchoge – in this film, you will meet incredible athletes: 31-year-old basketball phenom and wheelchair athlete Megan Blunk, who took gold in Rio in 2016; Isaiah

Bird, who was born without legs, and at ten years old has become the one to beat on his wrestling team; Charlie Jabaley – an Ironman who made over his life by losing 120 pounds, going vegan, and in the process, reversed the growth of a life-long brain tumour; and Michigander Alicia Woollcott, who simultaneously played linebacker and was named homecoming queen during her high school senior season. Additional appearances are made by emerging professional athletes and world champions alike: Canadian soccer star Alphonso Davies; Hawaiian big wave surfer Kai Lenny; American skateboarders Lacey Baker and Nyjah Huston; German champion boxer Zeina Nassar; and US. Soccer's Women's National Team. Narrated by Colin Kaepernick, "Dream Crazy" encourages everyone who has crazy dreams and goals that may seem insurmountable (Nike, n.d.). The advertisement was developed by Wieden+Kennedy/Portland.[6]

Case study 9.3

ReclameAQUI corruption detector[7]

General elections were held in Brazil in October 2018. More than 40,000 candidates favoured by a complex justice system designed to hide their acts of corruption were flooding the country with electoral campaigns. That's why ReclameAQUI, the number one consumer-protection company in Brazil, decided to expand its business to citizens rights. And in a country with over 200 million smartphones, there was no better way to fight corruption than turning their phones into a weapon against corruption. Based on facial recognition, Corruption Detector is a free app that draws on a comprehensive database with all the official records of corruption, previously hidden in hundreds of courts across Brazil. By simply pointing a phone at a candidate, voters can spot the corrupt ones in purple, no matter where they are: TV, papers, internet, outdoors and even in person. All data organised by the app is available for reference at any time. And on Election Day, users received an important notification: a reminder not to vote for a corrupt politician. The strategy was simple: when corrupt politicians show their faces, we drop their masks. In a year when politicians must ask for votes in a country where there is a smartphone for each citizen, we gave a useful weapon to voters that left the corrupt ones no place to hide. The campaign was developed by Grey Brazil.

Developing an effective advertisement

The message

In ensuring an effective advertisement, the message is essential. This is the core of the campaign. This is what the brand wants to communicate; without a message, effectiveness cannot be measured. The message could be designed to nudge, to improve sales, raise awareness or improve the brand's recognition. The message is therefore creatively presented to the audience (Bengtsson 2003). In the case of Project 84, the message was to raise awareness about the much-needed conversation and action around male suicide prevention and bereavement support (Project84 2020). To creatively convey their message, they used the 84 sculptures standing on a skyscraper in London, each representing a man who takes his own life every week in the United Kingdom.

The surprise

Brands and advertisers know the value of creating an effective advertisement, something to stand out from the plethora of advertisements that consumers see every day. When it was time for KFC to apologise for not having chicken, they surprised their customers with their advertisement. They changed their logo in a way that people felt the apology was wholehearted. An effective advert will have a surprise element – something that differentiates it and keeps the customers' attention (Mogaji, Farinloye & Aririguzoh, 2016). This is embedded in the storyline and the creative decisions regarding the advertising appeals that will be used. It is essential to offer consumers something different.

The delivery

The surprise needs to be well delivered at the right time and in the right place for it to be very useful. Burger King has always been known to taunt McDonald's – so far it has been a healthy competition. To take this further, Burger King decides to deliver their advertisement on the doorsteps of McDonald's. They geo-fence McDonald's and expect people to use their app to order the whopper. The creative delivery of the message enhances its effectiveness. Media planning and buying play a crucial role here (Herbst & Allan, 2006). Would the message be starting from a big board with just an image with no words? Would it start from a social media post or a hashtag? Taking the creative approach to the delivery, the message plays a crucial role in ensuring its effectiveness.

The integration

Beyond just one point of delivery, the integration of all the delivery points is essential. This presents an integrated marketing communications approach, to ensure that through all media and touchpoints, the same message is being delivered. As seen with the Nike Just Do It "Dream Crazy" campaign, it started with a tweet from Colin Kaepernick – first point of delivery – but many other athletes were later integrated into the campaign. It was shared on different media and consumers got involved by creating their advertisement. Importantly, the creative elements – white text on the black background – remained consistent throughout all points of integration.

The brand

The brand has a crucial role in ensuring that the message they have commissioned is effectively delivered. Firstly, there are instances when there are negative attitudes towards a brand, and inadvertently there will be some negative attitudes towards the advertisement (Mogaji & Danbury, 2017). This attitude could be due to previous experience with the brand, scandals or reputation damage. Likewise, for some likeable brands, there is a positive attitude towards their advertisement. Secondly, having access to the right team could influence the effectiveness of an advertisement. If the brand is not able to develop a creative advertisement from the in-house team, the brand must make efforts to hire a freelancer or commission an advertising agency. Notwithstanding, there might be a limitation to the effectiveness of the message. Thirdly, the message that the brand wants to send is essential in this context. For a small charity that needs to invite people to their fayre and make boot sales, there is no need for much emphasis on using an advertising agency to design and develop the message. However, for a more prominent charity that is running a campaign for donations, the approach would be different. Understanding the message, the brand sending the message and the extent that the message needs to reach will be crucial in evaluating the effectiveness of the advertisement. Brand communications create enduring memory structures that increase the base level of demand for the brand and reduce its price sensitivity (Field, 2019).

The finance

This builds on the knowledge of the brand sending the message. The financial implications of developing an effective advertisement cannot be overestimated. While it may seem that big brands are spending a considerable amount of money to understand their target audience and develop their marketing campaigns, smaller brands and small enterprises are not exempted from spending money on their campaigns. There could be the cost of hiring a freelancer to design the leaflet for direct mail or the cost of promoting the message on social media. Despite the expenses, effectiveness can be achieved by spending the money on the right media to reach the right people. Buying a full-page advert in a national newspaper may give brand awareness to a brand in a village, but that does not transfer to sales. The message will not be compelling because those seeing the message are not the target audience. Strategically buying media spaces and incurring expenses is essential in ensuring an effective advertisement. As an agency, having the right brands to finance your creative ideas is critical. The knowledge that you have the financial capabilities can be a motivation towards creating an effective advertisement. When the budget is under-allocated to the brand, it affects the creation of an effective advertisement.

The award

There are industry recognitions for effective advertisements. Advertisers strive to get their works recognised. Exploring previous advertisements that have received an effectiveness award can be a motivation for developing a more effective advertisement. Entries for the IPA Effectiveness Awards form part of a permanent database of Effectiveness Case Studies that become a uniquely credible resource for anyone looking for examples of commercial creativity that work (IPA, 2020a). These past works can be a perfect inspiration for advertisers and practitioners.

Creativity drives effectiveness

While many points may have been listed for developing an effective advertisement, it is essential to acknowledge that creativity drives effectiveness. It is the most valuable weapon in the effectiveness arsenal. Practitioners need to recognise the need to be creative, to think beyond the box and find a way to be different. Worryingly, there is less attention on creativity within the industry. Historically, creativity has been the most critical tool we can harness to boost effectiveness. The evidence of this link has been very strong, with enormous effectiveness multipliers evident for the most creative campaigns. So it matters that this link is now critically weakened and perhaps broken.

Peter Field, in his report, found that creative campaigns are now no longer outperforming their less inspired campaigns when it comes to effectiveness. According to his findings, they are less effective than they have been in 24 years of data analysis. Today they are no more effective than non-awarded campaigns. This is described as a crisis in creative effectiveness (Field, 2019). The report found that this collapse in effectiveness can be explained mainly by the shift to short-term activation-focused creativity and the strategic and media trends this has promoted.

This crisis in creative effectiveness could be remedied by learning from creative best practice, exploring high-performing creatively awarded campaigns to learn and understand what made them stand out as these are eight times more effective than their low-performing peers, in terms of the number of business effects they generate, and almost 16 times more likely to bring significant profitability growth.

Summary

While effort has been put into creating an advertisement, understanding its effects is essential for brands (who are sending the message) and advertising agencies (commissioned to develop and send the message). While these evaluations of effectiveness may be relative, it has been considered from three different perspectives. Firstly, from the consumers perspective – who saw, engaged and understood the message at the right time and therefore take action; secondly, from the advertiser – who gets the thumbs up from the Brands and retains the account and also gets accolades from colleagues in the form of awards and recognitions; and thirdly, the brands' perspective – they see an increase in sales, impression and positive mention of the brands, the objectives of the message, as being achieved.

The chapter also considered the value of advertising awards to advertisers, recognising the different types of advertisement awards that are available. Though the list can be inexhaustible as there are many awards both internationally and nationally, advertising agencies need to be strategic on which of these advertising awards to submit. The cost implications and odds of winning (among the competing brands) should be considered. While these awards may be for professionals, there are a few advertising awards for students. They can increase their skills, network and enhance their employability.

Lastly, different strategies and consideration for developing an effective advertisement are offered. Importantly, the role of creativity cannot be ignored. It is the most valuable weapon in the effectiveness arsenal. Advertisers must recognise this and make the best use of it in developing advertisements that will break barriers, engage and make an impact.

Revision questions

1. How would *you* describe an effective advertisement?
2. Describe and illustrate with an example, a high-performer advertisement.

3. Identify five major advertising awards.
4. Why should an advertising agency care about advertising awards?
5. Why should a brand care about advertising awards?
6. How can you develop an effective advertisement? What are the challenges and prospects?
7. What do you understand about the idea that creativity drives the effectiveness of advertisements?

Student activities

Evaluating the effectiveness of a campaign

Ads of the World has a collection of COVID-19 advertisements. The collection showcases the work agencies and brands created around the subject of the COVID-19 global pandemic. As of August 2020, there are over 500 advertisements in this collection.

These collections are available on the Ads of the World website. Visit the website and select four advertisements (the 1st, 3rd, 6th and 9th video advertisements).[8]

Considering they are all addressing the same COVID-19 themes, your task as a group is to examine the effectiveness of the advertisements as a consumer, an advertising agency and an advertising award judge.

Taking the role of a consumer:

- How would you describe the effectiveness of these advertisements? Take note and indicate with key words your answers.
- Would you say you have been impacted by the message and willing to act?
- What do you think makes advertisement effective? Consider the creative elements, the composition and delivery of the message.

Taking the role of an advertising agency:

- What would you have done differently with the advertisement?
- What would you have added or removed?

Taking the role of a judge on an advertising award:

- Which of the four advertisements would you give a Grand Prix Award for the most effective advertisement?

Notes

1 www.canneslions.com/
2 www.oneclub.org/awards/theoneshow/
3 https://ipa.co.uk/awards-events/effectiveness-awards
4 https://www.effie.org/

5 https://clios.com/about
6 www.wk.com/work/nike-dream-crazy
7 www.oneclub.org/awards/theoneshow/-award/33685/corruption-detector
8 www.adsoftheworld.com/collection/covid19_ads

References

Bengtsson, A., 2003. *Towards a critique of brand relationships*. Vol. 30, in *Advances in consumer research*, edited by Punam Anand Keller and Dennis W. Rook, 154–158. Valdosta, GA: Association for Consumer Research.

Brazier, P., 2015. *The importance of advertising awards*. [Online] Available at: https://awardefx.co.uk/the-importance-of-advertising-awards/ [Accessed 4.4.2000].

D&AD, 2020. *The story behind the D&AD Pencil*. [Online] Available at: www.dandad.org/en/d-ad-story-behind-pencils/#:~:text=While%20many%20other%20awards%20organisers,of%20a%20%22career%20knighthood%22 [Accessed 9.9.2020].

Dehghani, M. & Tumer, M., 2015. A research on effectiveness of Facebook advertising on enhancing purchase intention of consumers. *Computers in Human Behavior*, 49, pp. 597–600.

Field, P., 2019. *The crisis in creative effectiveness*. London: IPA.

Gökerik, M., Gürbüz, A., Erkan, I., Mogaji, E. & Sap, S., 2018. Surprise me with your ads! The impacts of guerrilla marketing in social media on brand image, *Asia Pacific Journal of Marketing and Logistics*, 30(5), pp. 1222–1238.

Herbst, K. C. & Allan, D., 2006. The effects of brand experience and an advertisement's disclaimer speed on purchase: Speak slowly or carry a big brand. *International Journal of Advertising*, 25(2), pp. 213–222.

Institute of Practitioners in Advertising (IPA), 2020a. *2020 IPA Effectiveness Awards Entry Pack*. [Online] Available at: https://ipa.co.uk/media/8571/2020_awards_entry_pack_v2.pdf [Accessed 9.9.2020].

Institute of Practitioners in Advertising (IPA), 2020b. *Calculating ROMI*. [Online] Available at: http://romi.ipa.co.uk/index.php/guide/chapter/5 [Accessed 2.2.2020].

Kiefer, B., 2019. *Are scam ads ever awards-worthy?*. [Online] Available at: www.campaignlive.co.uk/article/scam-ads-ever-awards-worthy/1588906 [Accessed 2.2.2020].

Micu, A. & Plummer, J., 2010. Measurable emotions: How television ads really work: Patterns of reactions to commercials can demonstrate advertising effectiveness. *Journal of Advertising Research*, 50(2), pp. 137–153.

Mogaji, E. & Danbury, A., 2017. Making the brand appealing: Advertising strategies and consumers' attitude towards UK retail bank brands. *Journal of Product & Brand Management*, 26(6), pp. 531–544.

Mogaji, E., Farinloye, T. & Aririguzoh, S., 2016. Factors shaping attitudes towards UK bank brands: An exploratory analysis of social media data. *Cogent Business & Management*, 3(1), p. 1223389.

Nike, n.d. Nike's new just do it campaign. [Online] Available at: https://news.nike.com/featured_video/just-do-it-dream-crazy-film.

One Show, 2019. Nike just do it "dream crazy." [Online] Available at: www.oneclub.org/awards/theoneshow/-award/32564/nike-just-do-it-dream-crazy [Accessed 9.9.2020].

One Show, 2020. *Frequently asked questions*. www.oneshow.org/faq/#:~:text=How%20does%20The%20One%20Club,requirements%20of%20a%20tear%20sheet [Accessed 9.9.2020].

Project84, 2020. *Home*. [Online] Available at: www.projecteightyfour.com/ [Accessed 9.9.2020].

Saleem, S. & Abideen, Z., 2011. Effective advertising and its influence on consumer buying behavior. *European Journal of Business and Management*, 3(3), pp. 55–67.

Smith, R. & Yang, X., 2004. Toward a general theory of creativity in advertising: Examining the role of divergence. *Marketing Theory*, 4(1/2), pp. 31–58.

Tay, R. & Watson, B., 2002. Changing drivers' intentions and behaviours using fear-based driver fatigue advertisements. *Health Marketing Quarterly*, 19(4), pp. 55–68.

Vardavas, C., Symvoulakis, E., Connolly, G., Patelarou, E. & Lionis, C., 2010. What defines an effective anti-tobacco TV advertisement? A pilot study among Greek adolescents. *International Journal of Environmental Research and Public Health*, 7(1), pp. 78–88.

10 What lies ahead
The future of advertising

This chapter concludes *Introduction to Advertising* by looking towards the future, and discusses contemporary issues in advertising, asking students about the impact of the General Data Protection Regulation (GDPR) and consumers' data, the role of machines and artificial intelligence and whether robots will take our jobs. The purpose of Big Data will also be discussed. The attention span of consumers is decreasing, there are media spaces everywhere, and advertisers are competing and recognising the impact of new advertising formats on advertising, coupled with emerging digital media. This will inadvertently also shape the industry as some jobs will be lost and new ones created. Students need to be aware of the future of advertising and be prepared for the challenges that lie ahead.

Learning outcome

At the conclusion of this teaching, students will be able to:

- Describe changing consumer behaviour and its implications for advertising practices;
- Recognise the changes within the advertising industry;
- Describe the brand's responsibility in response to evolving consumer behaviour;
- Explain what the future holds for advertising;
- Describe the responsibilities of students for their future careers.

Introduction

This chapter brings us to the end of *Introduction to Advertising*. We have considered advertising as brands' effort to communicate a message to their target audience creatively. The role of advertisers in developing and disseminating truthful, honest and non-offensive advertisement has been explored. Likewise, the diversity within the society which shapes how consumers engage with the advertisement has been considered as well.

This chapter looks at the future of advertising. To identify what the future holds for you as a student of advertising and marketing, the challenges within the industry as you consider your career and prospects, the ever-changing consumer behaviour and brands' effort to continually communicate with their market, it is essential to explore these changing dynamics to prepare you for what lies ahead. Would advertisement be the same by the time you start practising? These are questions worth pondering.

If advertising as a profession or phenomenon changes, how will it affect the teaching and learning of advertising? How will it affect the advertising industry and the stakeholders?

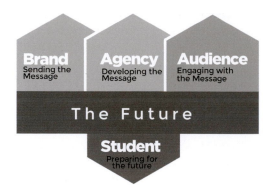

Figure 10.1 Key stakeholders for what lies ahead in advertising
Source: author.

How will the brand communicate and importantly, how will the consumers be aware of options that may appeal to them? Neil Godber, Convenor of Judges and Head of Planning at J. Walter Thompson said now is the time for brand to experiment, engage and excel. The role of technology cannot be ignored in this discussion. It is a double-edged sword that presents the possibilities of adblockers and also provides details about how consumers are engaging with advertisements. Advertisers will have to consider how best they can use technology to complete their creative capabilities as they endeavour to send the message to the audience effectively.

Specifically, this chapter address four key stakeholders illustrated in Figure 10.1:

- The consumers who are being targeted,
- The advertising agencies creating the message,
- The brands commissioning the message and, importantly,
- The students as they venture into advertising education and career progression.

The industry is changing – some jobs will be lost, and new ones created. Ten years ago, there was no role assigned for a social media manager, but who knows what the future holds. Students need to be aware of the future of advertising and be prepared for the challenges that lie ahead.

Changing consumer behaviour

Buying behaviour

Many years ago, if a consumer wanted to buy a dress, they would have been more likely to walk into a brick and mortar shop to see the dress, try it on and buy it there. But now, consumers are increasingly expected to see an advertisement served to them on a screen, maybe TV. They search for it on their mobile phones, read more about it on social media before deciding to buy it. There are many touchpoints of engagement before buying

(Farinloye et al., 2020), and consumers are relying on various sources of information, triangulating their findings before making a choice. This further puts the challenge on advertisers to ensure that consumers are seeing relevant information at each touchpoint, and nudged into acting before leaving the ecosystem (Mogaji & Farinloye, 2017). No one will want to lose a customer because they couldn't provide information and credibility on social media or the information needed on the website is inaccessible.

Media engagement

Consumer behaviour is changing. Not just how they buy things but also how they engage and consume the media. Report from a survey of Chief Marketing Officer confirms that engaging is the most challenging part of the consumer lifecycle for businesses to deliver. There is an increasing level of competition (56%); consumers' intolerance for advertising (46%); and information overload (44%). There are many opportunities to engage with the media. There are multiple screens with different profiles. Advertisers have recognised that reaching consumers across the increasing number of devices they use is key to engaging with them and driving transactions, but it is getting more difficult every day with the advancement and availability of these devices. The attention span of consumers is decreasing, there are media spaces everywhere and advertisers are competing and recognising the impact of new advertising formats on advertising coupled with emerging digital media. As competition intensifies for consumer attention, there are many questions for advertisers to consider. How can brands capitalise on moments of interaction that will be increasingly rare and most often initiated by consumers themselves? How much would this consumer behaviour change in the future? How well are advertisers ready to adapt to these changes? Moving on, as brands expect their messages to be effectively sent across to the target audience, it will be very critical for advertisers to crack this problem.

Data control

Volume, variety and velocity are three defining properties or dimensions of big data. Often referred to as 3Vs, volume refers to the amount of data, variety refers to the number of types of data and velocity refers to the speed of data processing. As part of the changing behaviours and engagement with media and different touchpoints, consumers are generating a vast amount of data, contributing to the volume of big data (Mogaji et al., 2020b). However, consumers are mindful of their data and online footprints. There are growing concerns about security, privacy, ethics and, specifically, accountability. Consumers want to take control of who gets access to them as privacy is of growing concern. With the GDPR, consumers are more mindful about who gets access to their data and how it can be used. This poses challenges for advertisers to make sure these customers are well served with a relevant advertisement at a suitable time based on the information they have provided at different touchpoints.

Advertising agencies are diversifying

According to Greaves (2018), Chief Executive of the Marketing Society, the global network of senior marketers, the industry is beginning to push boundaries, tackle taboos, have uncomfortable conversations and think about the humanity in everything we do. This new narrative is changing something else. Marketing leaders aren't just trying to grow their brands, but also working out how to make the world a better place.

New players onboard

Agencies are under pressure from other players coming on board. Management consultancies are entering the ad industry through the high-profile acquisition of several marketing services agencies (Dentsu Report, 2018). For the first time, in 2017, four management consultancies entered the Ad Age ranking of the ten largest advertising companies in the world – Accenture Interactive (no. 6), PwC Digital Service (no. 7), IBM iX (no. 8) and Deloitte Digital (no. 9). They had a combined revenue of $13.2 billion. Ad Age noted that IBM iX was the first to make the list of the world's biggest advertising companies in 2008 and cracked the top 10 in 2014. These new players can benefit from their global consulting ventures and shake up the industry as they make an effort in fuelling innovation, uncovering insights and advancing brands. Besides, there are smaller boutique agencies, specifically in digital marketing, that are also coming on board to provide unique services for brands. The Dentsu Aegis Network report noted that digital technologies have helped erode barriers to entry and create the conditions of near-perfect competition between producers and consumers. In this demand-led economy, growth is emerging from unexpected quarters as brands step out of their traditional industry (Dentsu, 2018). Adtech startups are also making their presence felt, with many developing competitive, niche value propositions. Besides, some freelancers may not necessarily be called agencies but can design and disseminate campaigns.

Influence of technology

Technology has the possibilities and potentials for enabling the effective communication of advertisements. Technology is continuing to expand, connect and complicate advertising. Advertisers are recognising the opportunities of delivering value for their clients using technology. Ibrahim (2018) noted that advertising agencies are under pressure to evolve to keep up with the exponential rise of advertising technologies (AdTech) and marketing technologies (MarTech). A report of Dentsu Aegis Network's global survey of 1,000 CMOs and senior-level marketers from across ten markets and industry sectors reveals that digital technologies may be arming marketers with new tools to deliver their strategy (Dentsu, 2018). But it is the more profound shift towards a digital economy that demands a more fundamental resetting of a brand's long-term strategy than many appreciate. Besides, the working relationship between technology and creativity is essential. The AdBlocker, as a form of technology, is also changing how consumers engage with advertisements. All these highlight practical implication for advertisers and advertising as we move into the future.

Data-driven marketing

This is about turning consumer insight into the next commercial opportunity, extracting data to develop advertisement, digitally serving it across all media and yet not offending the customers. Data is the enabler that allows businesses to identify new growth opportunities (Dentsu, 2018). If you have the data, you have the advantage. However, CMOs globally recognised a data breach or misuse of consumer data as the most significant strategic risk. Furthermore, 60% of CMOs believe that the European Union's General Data Protection Regulation (GDPR) will make it harder to build a direct relationship with consumers. According to IBM (2019), there are growing needs for effectively using data to identify unmet customer needs, integrating data from multiple sources and effectively translating data into actionable insights (Dwivedi et al., 2019; Mogaji et al., 2020a).

Human resources

Human touch is still vital for an advertisement to engage consumers. In addition to the challenges of technical and financial resources to implement data-driven marketing, human resources needed to champion these projects might also pose a problem. The level of knowledge about artificial intelligence (AI) in digital marketing is not keeping pace with the development in AI as it becomes increasingly sophisticated. AI developers and data scientists might prefer to work with AI companies and start-ups instead of advertising agencies; therefore recruiting and retaining developers may be challenging. The changing dynamics around the marketing industry and growth in tech-enabled platforms and startups are recognised. The insufficiency of skilled individuals may be a barrier to exploring the full capabilities of data-driven digital marketing.

Diversity within the team

Advertising agencies are thinking of expanding their workforce to meet growing demands. Advertising Diversity Taskforce research reveals that 31% of senior leaders are privately educated and only 8% are from BAME backgrounds. Diversity is not just about race, but also includes the support available for the mothers and even the gender pay gap across the industry. Working mothers are not seeing a path to thrive in their careers and, at the same time, be hands-on parents, and many women are leaving the industry once they start a family – a trend that points to the lack of compatibility with family life. The research also highlighted the industry's ageism problem, with only 10% of the sample being over 45. This issue is particularly acute among women, with only a third of over-45s in the industry being female. The ad industry is also failing to represent and reflect disabled people within the workforce, and the research suggests that only 1% are registered disabled. Diversity remains a critical discussion point as we move on. As the industry is not advertising to a unified audience, diversity will always remain relevant. Organisations must rebuild themselves from within, changing recruitment policies, overcoming unconscious bias and embracing people's differences. It is recognised that diverse teams, talents and skills produce better financial results. Diversity is not optional if advertising, marketing and media are to grow and thrive. Trade bodies are taking it seriously, as a diversity survey is to become a compulsory part of IPA membership and brands are asking questions about the diversity of the agencies working with them.

The evolving media

The definition of media is changing, and the media space is evolving to accommodate the growing demand for an effective avenue to engage with the audience. According to Credit

Case study 10.1

The battle of the Jo – John Boyega dumps Jo Malone

John Boyega is a British Actor and was the first male global ambassador for Jo Malone, a perfume company. Mr Boyega conceived, created and starred in an after-shave advertisement for Jo Malone, entitled London Gent. The advertisement was a celebration of his personal story, showing him enjoying the company of his family and friends in Peckham, London, where he grew up. The advertisement showed the actor on a white stallion, friends on bicycles within an estate, a visit to the local market and dancing in a club. The advertisement went on to win the Fragrance Foundation Virtual Awards 2020 for Best Media Campaign.

Jo Malone subsequently released an advertisement for Chinese audiences, which used the concept and idea that had been created by Mr Boyega. The crux of the matter, however, was that, first, Mr Boyega was replaced by another actor, Liu Haoran, in the re-shot advertisement. Second, the original version, showing Mr Boyega enjoying time with his friends and family in Peckham, was removed for Chinese audiences. Third, all these creative decisions were made without Mr Boyega's consent or prior notice.

Beyond the abuse of the intellectual property and the idea of Mr Boyega, there was a racial undertone as his creative contribution as a black man was ignored and never considered or appreciated. This revelation made Jo Malone London promptly tender an apology, saying "We deeply apologise for what, on our end, was a mistake in the local execution of the John Boyega campaign". This made Mr Boyega step down as an ambassador for the company in protest over their decision.

Though in line with congruency theory which suggests that brands should reflect the inherent cultural values of their target audience in their advertisements, Jo Malone could have created a new advertisement for the Chinese audience if they felt it was not necessary to use the one created by Mr Boyega. Instead, they decided to re-shoot the advertisement without consulting or starring the originator of the idea. This mistake has had a significant impact on their brand reputation, and the creative decision made was a mistake which has put a blemish on their brand and also made them lose money, at least the cost of creating that advert.

It is crucial to consider that one person does not decide on an advertisement. The advertising process involves different stakeholders. These are people and organisations deciding on the advertisement to use, how to conceptualise the campaign, the storyline and also selecting the cast to feature in the advertisement. This mistake showed that possibly no one within that team raised a concern about the error they were about to make. Perhaps they all felt it was right to use the advertisement; not to seek Mr Boyega's consent; not to cast him again for the advertisement because it was for the Chinese market and to remove any indication into his heritage.

This mistake further raises concerns about diversity within the advertising industry, either within the agencies or the in-house team. It highlights challenges brands may be facing with regard to how they effectively engage with their audience by working with a diverse group that can recognise diversity in the real world and reflect it in their advertisements. Consumers are now more expectant, demanding that brands avoid any stereotypical portrayal and reflect a diverse society.

Reflective questions

1. Why do you think it was important for Jo Malone to create an advertisement specifically for the Chinese audience?
2. Why do you think Jo Malone may have recreated that advertisement for the Chinese market without consulting Mr Boyega?
3. Considering the advertisement was negatively received, with a backlash, what are the implications of this for the Jo Malone brand?
4. What are the implications of having a diverse team working on an advertisement?
5. Would you expect Jo Malone to withdraw the advertisement they created for the Chinese Market?

Suisse, Facebook and Google now account for one-fifth of all global ad spend. However, beyond digital media, the traditional media are evolving. There are bigger and more interactive billboards. In 2015, Clear Channel UK installed 1,200 of Ultravision's Master Series UltraPanels at the iconic Cromwell Road advertising site creating six LED digital displays as part of the revitalisation of the area. Advertisers now can add dynamic content to their messages to attract even more attention from the thousands of people who pass the site each week. Media owners can deliver even more flexible campaigns across their inventories. Billboards use beacons to provide metrics and data about how people are engaging with it. There are possibilities of using real-time data to change the advertising context. Contextual creatives can be played at specific locations and at specific times to increase the relevance of a brand's campaign. Radio stations are being integrated into smart speakers to allow better and broader delivery of advertisements. Like in print media, there is development as the *Guardian*, *News UK* and *Telegraph* have launched a joint advertising business called The Ozone Project which allows advertisers to buy online ad space across news titles from one site. The Ozone Project has been launched in response to demand from advertisers for a one-stop-shop to purchase digital adverts across multiple leading news sites.

Brands are taking responsibilities

Brands are aware that their customers' behaviours are changing. They are aware of the challenges advertising agencies are facing in reaching these diverse audiences and they are taking responsibilities to stay ahead of the game and be better prepared to remain commercially viable. Brands now have access to resources to make an informed decision. Technology has offered tremendous assistance to help brands manage a massive set of tasks. There are new offerings in customer data platforms and dynamic creative optimisation is emerging. Brands can therefore further question the role of advertisers in the context of message delivery. Can brands do without advertising agencies?

Bringing agency in house

As brands seek greater control for their marketing communication, there is a growing interest in having in-house agency/creative teams instead of working with an advertising agency. The in-house agencies vary in size and scope depending on the size of the organisation. While there are advantages to this approach, there are also disadvantages. As an advantage, companies exercise greater control over their data and reduce their risk. The ANA (2018) in-housing survey showed that 78% of large US advertisers have some in-house agency, a percentage that has increased from 58% in 2013. In-house agencies work for only one client, their employer. They don't have to pitch for new business and the approval process moves quicker with in-house agencies. It can be financially more sustainable to have an in-house team than an advertising agency on a retainer fee. Working with an in-house agency brings a limitation to the level of exposure and experience of the team. Agencies work on different brands at different times and on diverse projects; they are often very versatile and experienced. Creative people love challenges, and some may find it too dull to work on a single brand; therefore in-house advertising agencies may not be able to attract creative individuals and this will have an implication on their creative output and the diversity within their team. To balance the advantages and disadvantages of having an in-house agency, the hybrid model is considered more appropriate. This is when an in-house team partners with a specialist or professional advertising agency. It is the best of both worlds. Many organisations see the hybrid approach as the best advertising approach. Most already have at least a core nucleus of in-house marketing professionals, yet their range of expertise or resources is limited. It can be highly cost-effective to aid this team by outsourcing critical services to agency specialists.

Staying "woke"

Brands are recognising issues concerning social and racial justice. Still, the question remains how well can they integrate this awareness with an advertising campaign? Brands are making woke advertisements which are not aimed at promoting products, but at addressing social issues.

In 2017, Procter & Gamble released an advertisement titled "My Black is Beautiful" in the United States. It features scenes of black parents openly sharing truths about bias their children experience or are likely to experience. The same year, the brand released another advertisement titled "We See Equal" to address gender bias, equal representation and an equal voice for women.

In 2017, Pepsi decided to jump on the woke advertisement bandwagon. The brand wanted to align with the #BlackLivesMatter protests by releasing an advertisement featuring reality star/model Kendall Jenner. Though they joined the conversation, they received much criticism, and the advertisement was withdrawn. In their apology statement, Pepsi claimed to be "trying to project a global message of unity, peace and understanding". They missed the mark and had to apologise.

Nike released an advert starring Colin Kaepernick in 2018. The advert, titled "Dream Crazy", featured the former NFL quarterback and the slogan: "Believe in something. Even if it means sacrificing everything. Just do it." Donald Trump, the American president, was among those who attacked the advert at the time of its release. The advert has won many awards, including outstanding commercial at the Creative Arts Emmys.

In 2019, Gillette also released a socially charged advertisement titled "We Believe: The Best Men Can Be". The advertisement created quite a buzz online, generating over 30 million views on YouTube. The ad explores the topic of toxic masculinity and #MeToo movement and encourages men to support women, and each other, to truly be the "Best a Man Can Be".

Woke advertisement can be very engaging but risky, as seen with Pepsi and Gillette. It can be very divisive as consumers try to establish the brand's balance between capitalism and activism. It is often considered a shrewd business move, but it galvanises those who have been preaching about those social issues. It often sparks dialogue on special media, thereby generating brand awareness. The backlash cannot be ignored, however, especially when there is a call for boycotts. Nike shares dropped when they released their advertisement but later picked up.

Consumers are more socially aware than ever before, and they want to associate with brands that are socially responsible as this can boost brand's values, loyalty and trust. More so, social media provides immediate feedback. It is essential to see whether brands will want to go through this route. Bernard (2019) asked if brands should try doing it at all since they struggle to make it work. Looking into the future, would woke advertisement be for more prominent brands? Who will gain more prominence and perhaps, can smaller brands attempt such?

Diversity in deed and indeed

Brands need to ensure that advertising has a broader appeal. Not just about making woke advertisements but by reflecting diversity in their offerings. Nick Easen wrote that Generation Z is leading the way and redefining gender, making a traditional binary understanding feel outdated and out of touch (Easen, 2019). Brands need to be aware of the diversity and work with the agency to present and represent this. Consumers are more informed and can call out brands that are being insensitive. Exercise bike brand, Peloton, lost a staggering $1bn in market value in just three days because of claims their Christmas advert was "sexist". Peloton's share price tumbled by more than 15%, no thanks to online backlash about their Christmas advert that featured a woman receiving a bike.

What the future holds

Data drive market

This is expected to grow and become more sophisticated. As consumers keep generating more data when engaging with brand touchpoints, brands and advertising agencies are enhancing how they can explore the data to effectively service customers with relevant advertisements. With the changing dynamics in digital marketing, brands are having unprecedented access to information about their customers, and they can use this technology to influence consumer behaviour (Dwivedi et al., 2019). Personal data and information legitimately collected online by companies can be used to design and personalise advisements that appeal to consumers' emotions and are shared online (Gökerik et al., 2018). There are challenges for collecting and using the data, especially considering the European Union General Data Protection Regulation (GDPR). Data is essential in understanding the customers, their journeys, and in developing the advertising campaigns. Companies have been collecting information about their customers for many years, and they must start considering the information with regard to AI, making it structured enough for digital marketers to use.

Artificial intelligence

The vast amount of data being generated, increased use of a mobile device, cloud computing and internet have contributed to the significant development of artificial intelligence (AI). AI is having a double-edged impact – constituting a significant source of innovation yet threatening human jobs (Huang & Rust, 2018). Artificial intelligence offers opportunities to enhance campaign creation, planning, targeting and evaluation, using advanced data analytics to optimise multiple channels continuously. Three key stakeholders are identified as the opportunities for AI in digital marketing are being explored. Firstly, brands, who need to understand their customers and communicate with them on a very personal and emotional level. Secondly, the advertisers and marketing agencies, who are responsible for digital marketing strategies. They need AI to bridge the gap between the brands, the customers and data (Bell, 2019), and thirdly, the customers, who need to engage with the brands' marketing communications. They are the recipient of the information and the generators of the data which is being used for targeting. With this understanding, the opportunities for these stakeholders are presented, especially for digital marketers. With AI being able to do what humans typically do, there are opportunities for more innovated and relevant content creation. With consumers' demand for appropriate content, advertisers can explore the prospects of AI to develop pertinent materials for the customers because they now have a better understanding through the analysed data. Content here includes advertisement, social media posts and email campaigns. Information such as past purchases, interests and browsing behaviours can be used to create automated campaigns that can enhance the customers' purchase intention. AI can identify the consumer's pattern about lifestyle choices, including music, favourite celebrities and location to create unique content.

To illustrate some practical examples and possibilities, in November 2018, Lexus launched an advertisement which was scripted entirely using artificial intelligence (AI) and directed by Oscar-winner Kevin Macdonald. The 60-second feature is entitled "Driven by Intuition" (Lexus, 2018). The production process involved developing bespoke AI and training it with data. This included 15 years of award-winning luxury adverts, emotional intelligence about what connects most strongly with viewers and specially commissioned information about human intuition.

Bidalgo recently introduced "Creative AI" as part of its self-serve advert automation platform (Bidalgo, 2018). It uses image and video recognition technology to analyse every component of an advertiser's creatives, down to each pixel, to then develop ad creatives that drive campaign goals. Creative AI uses Bidalgo's proprietary AI-based algorithms to break down the DNA of successful ad creatives by analysing dozens of variables including images, colours, promotions, contrast, concepts, copy and more (Takahashi, 2018).

Persado offers AI software to instantly generate better performing email subject lines through emotional language (Persado, 2018). Their new tool uses deep learning algorithms to create an emotional profile for individual users based on previous campaigns, then generates the corresponding language to personalise the message. This step includes options for email, display advertising, social advertising, landing pages, SMS and push notifications in as many as 23 languages. Phrasee also offers a similar tool. They use advanced end-to-end

Deep Learning to optimise engagement results on an on-going basis. Phrasee AI learns from customers' response metrics, quantifies and optimises a language that makes the audience engage with their messages. They promised that using a better language in marketing communications will lead to more customer engagement and make brands more money (Phrasee, 2018).

AI integration with OBA and MLBA

There are enormous possibilities for the integration of AI with online behavioural advertising (OBA) and mobile location-based advertising (MLBA). Currently, behavioural targeting mostly occurs when using computers or smartphones (Gutierrez et al., 2019). Scholars argue that it offers personalised and targeted advertisement, providing a precise way of targeting customers (Kumar & Gupta, 2016) and contributing to the growth in online advertising revenues (Chen & Stallaert, 2014). Likewise, MLBA offers consumers benefits such as personalised communications that are tailored to the mobile user's real-time geographic location (Krishen et al., 2017). These two concepts are emerging marketing strategies, and involve collecting data either online or offline and using it to develop advertising campaigns. With AI offering data collection and processing at a faster rate, a better understanding and effort towards triangulating these online and offline data for better understanding of consumers' needs are essential. This helps in providing practical implications for marketing researchers and practitioners.

Metrics and evaluation

The relationship between advertisement and sales should be revisited. How are the parameters resulting in sales? This is towards ensuring an effective advertisement. It is not about the number of likes, comments or retweets but how effectively the advertisement has been able to achieve the campaigns aims and objectives. Tom Goodwin, marketing thought leader and author of *Digital Darwinism: Survival of the Fittest in the Age of Business Disruption* wrote that the modern internet has provided the worlds of advertising and marketing with abundance, in terms of tools, techniques, data and possibilities (Goodwin, 2019). Human beings may be challenging to monitor and observe when it comes to advertisement (Mogaji et al., 2018). Their browsing history may not be a true reflection of their personality and what appeals to their emotions. Therefore, the metrics and form of evaluating the effectiveness of the campaign should be further explored. There is a need to develop and test the practicality of the campaign – whether it has increased sales for brands and enhanced consumers' choice-making process.

Marketing fraud

As we recognise the values in metrics and evaluation, the dark sides of these things should be explored as well. Fraudulent marketing, ranging from fake news disseminated by robots, to fraudsters syphoning off advertising cash, is coming under increasing scrutiny; as well as fake websites and internet domains, fake accounts, and bot farms that generate fake views by robots, not people. Marc Pritchard, P&G Chief Brand Officer said brands are "wowed by shiny objects, overwhelmed by big data, and intimidated by algorithms" (Pritchard, 2019). Spanier (2019) wrote that the awkward truth for brands is that the digital ecosystem is complex and fragmented, and they can't tackle marketing fraud in isolation. How real are the likes on a video, how real are the followers of an Instagram influencer? Are they bots or fake followers? While the emphasis is placed on these metrics, it further raises concerns about how they can be manipulated for financial gains. An influencer may buy thousands of fake followers to appear credible and influential to prospective brands. The lack of independent verification of ads on platforms such as Google and Facebook is becoming worrisome as well; that's where companies like DoubleVerify become relevant. DoubleVerify (DV) authenticates the quality of each digital media impression, ensures that brands only pay for ads that are viewable and provides real-time metrics on-demand.

The *Guardian*, *News UK* and *Telegraph* have launched a joint advertising business called The Ozone Project. The venture allows advertisers to buy online advertising space across news titles from one site. This initiative was in response to concerns about brand safety, data governance, lack of transparency in the supply chain and ad fraud following many online advertising scandals. There is also the Conscious Advertising Network (CAN). Launched in 2019 as a voluntary coalition of over 70 organisations, it was set up to adhere to six key ethical principles, which are Anti Ad-Fraud, Informed Consent, Diversity, Fake News, Hate Speech and Children's Wellbeing. The coalition aims to assist brands to produce communication that is engaging, truthful and can be trusted. A report from Juniper Research found that advertisers will lose an estimated $19 billion to fraudulent activities next year, equivalent to $51 million per day (Juniper, 2017). This figure, representing advertising on online and mobile devices, will continue to rise, reaching $44 billion by 2022. Not surprising therefore to see brands taking ownership of their marketing activities.

Bernard (2019) noted that big brands are taking responsibility for their data to avoid these metrics scams. They are investing in their data platforms and analytics. P&G recognises that the next great revolution in using technology to make people's lives better is under way. They recognised the potential pitfalls that can't be ignored: data misuse and privacy breaches, transparency lapses, fraud, brand safety and more. Marc Pritchard called on the industry to unite and act now to create a New Media Supply Chain grounded in quality, civility, transparency and privacy. The Brand Officer iterated that P&G is taking control of their destiny, reinventing agency models to bring more media planning and buying in-house – when and where it makes sense – gathering data on their platforms, using their data to accelerate performance analytics and hiring their individual data scientists. They plan to reduce overall media waste by 20%, while increasing media reach by 10%. The brand has not only saved nearly $1 billion in agency fees and production costs, they are also getting closer to their consumers.

Influencer marketers

Considering the exponential growth of expenditure on influencer marketing (Lou & Yuan, 2019), connecting online personas with brands or services that target a selected audience (Childers et al., 2019), the role of social media and influencer marketing and marketers cannot be ignored, moving forward into the future. Beyond fashion and beauty products, there will be many more brands using social media celebrities and influencers to advertise their products and services (Xiao et al., 2018). The concern, however, will remain around the source trustworthiness, brand attitude, social presence and the need for disclosure (Jin et al., 2019; Stubb et al., 2019). An example is the Scarlett Dixon (aka Scarlett London) post in 2018 for Listerine which created a tonne of attention for the wrong reasons because people were certain that the post was not real but staged and did not reflect the everyday life of people (Guthrie, 2018). Advertisers therefore need to recognise the growing prospects of influencer marketers and be strategic in using them to communicate their brand messages.

Case study 10.2

Anglia Ruskin University paid Instagram influencer

Influencer marketing has become an integral part of brands marketing and advertising strategies. Brands are paying social media influencers and celebrities to endorse their products and share them with their vast number followers. Influencer marketing has often been adopted and associated with fashion and beauty products; but recently, it was revealed that the UK Government paid social media influencers to promote the NHS Test and Trace service. This approach, therefore, suggests influencers can be used for any marketing communication campaign.

Though recognising the competition for prospective students in the UK higher education system, it came as a surprise to see Anglia Ruskin University in Cambridge paid Instagram influencer graduates to promote their degrees – despite them not attending the university. The university revealed that they paid several lifestyle, fashion and travel influencers to promote the institution on Instagram in the weeks leading to the release of the A-Level results. Many of these Instagram influencers shared how well they enjoyed their time at university, albeit not at Anglia Ruskin.

It is essential to recognise that these influencers can offer an effective marketing channel provided they are used correctly. A brand (like Anglia Ruskin University) wants to communicate a message (about their university) to an audience (prospective students), and they have found that influencers have a suitable channel to disseminate this message to their audience.

No doubt, this has raised many questions. There are questions about the suitability of the channel for the brand – should a university pay influencers on Instagram to endorse their programmes and appeal to students. Questions about the attitude of the audience towards the brand and message – how would students engage, considering they are conversant with influencers endorsing beauty products and now university. Also, there are concerns around the effectiveness of the message – would it make student consider Anglia Ruskin University? The university has set a pace, and it will not be surprising to see many other universities adopt the same strategies. This further highlights what lies ahead for advertisers and brands.

Reflective questions

1. Should Anglia Ruskin University pay influencers on Instagram to endorse their programmes and appeal to students?

2. How would you engage with a post from your favourite influencer endorsing Anglia Ruskin University?
3. Do you think many other universities pay influencers on Instagram to endorse their programmes?

Advertising teaching and learning

While this chapter brings us to the end of *Introduction to Advertising*, it is essential to note that there are still many areas of advertising that have not been covered in this module. To have an all-round perspective as an advertising student ready for the industry, some key topics in advertising are presented. You are expected to build these topics on your knowledge of *Introduction to Advertising*. Figure 10.2 presents a summary of advertising teaching and learning.

Customer insight and research

It will be essential for brands to have a good understanding of their customers. The theoretical knowledge of consumer insight through research is necessary for advertising students. The integration of consumer behaviour and marketing research to have a better understanding of the consumer will surely enhance your marketing knowledge as an advertising student. It would help if you understood who the customers are, how they engage with media and how they make everyday decisions. Before developing any advertisement, understanding the target audience is vital and imperative if one is to succeed in the marketplace. You need to understand consumer behaviour for effective development and implementation of the campaigns.

Contemporary issues in marketing

With the understanding of the individual customer, a holistic understanding of the market is also essential. This is integrated into the contemporary issues of marketing. It is about understanding the broader role that marketing communications play in modern culture. At this stage, you should recognise the issues that affect the market you are targeting, their shared values, what appeals to them or what may insult them. The country context is also relevant. As the example of Volvo in the United Kingdom and Poland, same-sex relationship, which is recognised in the United Kingdom, is reflected in the UK advertisement, but this was not same in Poland. It would be best if you understood the broader impacts that marketing communications' campaigns could have on consumers and society at local, national and global levels.

Content creation

Content creation in advertising has to do with the process involved in an advertiser or advertising agency generating the right themes or ideas that have necessary characteristics that can appeal to the brand's buyer persona or target audience. This, furthermore, deals with creation of either visual or written content around those generated themes and ideas, and pushing the intended message to the right audience or target consumers. Therefore, content creation should offer practical insight into creating appealing advertising content. This should give you valuable practical experience of creating visual and written content for different media and monitoring engagement and ROI. You should be able to outline and discuss the key components and creative elements for contents on the different media platforms; understand the role of content in driving traffic to other media and channels and subsequently in developing engagement; demonstrate familiarity with content management tools for two or more platforms and use examples of metrics that help optimise the effectiveness of content marketing. Importantly, this should not just be limited to digital media; an understanding of creating content for print or TV will be relevant. It is important to note here that traditional media is evolving, so also are its content creation strategies.

Integrated marketing communications

With the ability to create different content, it is essential to be able to integrate this content across various media and to send coherent marketing communication. You should be able to identify different media channels and how they can be integrated. Understanding tools, techniques and tactics associated with the application of these marcom activities in the context of promotional campaigns is essential for students. It would be best if you understand how different marketing communication content and activities could be integrated, coordinated and synchronised.

Media planning and buying

With many media channels and content, it can be a challenge to identify which media channel to choose for dissemination of the marketing communications to the targeted audience. With your understanding of media planning and buying, you should be able to develop abilities to critique and select a range of planned media channels – appropriate for different market sectors and organisational contexts. You should understand the fundamental metrics of audience measurement and media accounting; be able to allocate a media budget across multiple media platforms; understand the relative strengths of a range of media including traditional printed media, broadcast, online and interactive; access and use secondary sources of media data and develop strategic and measurable media objectives.

Advertising campaign management

This topic should take a more comprehensive view of advertising and promotion in the business context and consider its integration into the overall marketing plan to achieve corporate objectives. This topic recognises that marketing research has been done to understand the consumers, creative and engaging contents have been created and shared through appropriate media. This topic brings a management perspective to ensure that the project is completed. A critical understanding of the dynamics within the creative team is essential, either within the agency team, in-house or freelancers. This topic should give you an understanding of how advertising fits within the corporate communications mix and its role in helping to achieve the company's overall objectives.

Marketing metrics

Evaluating the performance of an advertising campaign is essential. Both quantitative and qualitative techniques that can be used to evaluate the effectiveness of a campaign are worth exploring. A range of metrics can be used to assess marketing performance and establish whether marketing objectives are being achieved. Findings will be relevant in developing future campaigns.

Marketing integration

This topic should provide insight into how advertising practices can be used for marketing integration in different contexts. This could be for many reasons, including:

Social marketing

This is where marketing tools and principles can be effectively used to create and implement social change (Wymer, 2010). This allows students to bring their knowledge about content creation, integrated marketing communications and media planning and for social cause and change in behaviour. This may involve addressing ethical, social and environmental problems.

Global marketing management

The knowledge of advertising can also be integrated towards global marketing (Potgieter et al., 2012). This enables students to widen their knowledge and understanding of

Figure 10.2 Summary of advertising teaching and learning
Source: author.

international marketing and global marketing and the role advertisement can play. It recognises the role of the global agencies network, the advertising practices in different countries and how best to engage with a diverse audience. The student should understand the complexity of developing a campaign that can appeal to a global audience.

Non-profit and charity marketing

These groups of clients may not have the financial resources to hire an advertising agency, yet they have messages that need to be communicated. Recognising these limitations is essential in integrating their marketing strategies (Dolnicar & Lazarevski, 2009).

For the student: now and future

This is not the end of learning. As iterated above, there are still many grounds to cover. Now, the focus should be on understanding the working principles of advertising, getting to know how things work, acquiring the knowledge and getting engaged. You want to be open to opportunities, try your hand at something and keep yourself mentally alert.

For the future career,

Where would you like to work?

Think about this from now. Be conversant with the advertising agencies. Understand the agency culture. What do they need? How is the recruitment process? Do they have an entry-level role? How diverse is the team? There are many questions you need to be asking. Would you want to start your boutique agency, be a freelancer or work on the client's side? There are many opportunities for you.

What type of role do you want?

You need to see the credit list of an advertisement. It will open your eyes to the opportunities that abound. You need to start thinking about the type of role you want in your career. Are you good with words – copywriter – or good with design – Junior Art Director or Designer. There are opportunities for account management, media planners or marketing analysis. You know, be open to possibilities and explore.

What skills do you need?

No doubt, you know about advertising, but you need to start looking at the skills that you need to excel in the industry. For creatives, Adobe Creative Cloud is essential. However, improving your skill could begin with enhancing your proficiency level on Microsoft Excel. You may be considering becoming a data scientist and learning computer programming languages. You could also improve your Photoshop design skills. Be aware of what is needed and work towards improving yourself.

What can you offer?

Your portfolio is essential. Make sure it is readily available to highlight what you have done, your potentials and the values you can add to brands and the agency. Demonstrate your skills and what you bring to the team. Remember, quality is essential. It is not about the quantity of work but the quality. How well it stands out. Be modest, not arrogant; remember you are engaging with people who are also creative and even with many years of experience.

When do you reach out?

You can reach out as soon as you are ready! You may not be ready for your full-time role, but you can work as an Intern, work during the holidays or work part time. Put yourself out there. Your social media presence is essential. Make sure you are well projected. Have and maintain your profile on key social media sites (like Behance, YouTube and LinkedIn). If you are entrepreneurial, thinking of starting your agency, networking is critical – to have the right team and the right clients. You can't be an island.

Summary

Now you have an understanding of the basic principles of advertising. Over the past chapters, we have explored the functions and processes of advertising, recognising that advertising is about creatively communicating with the target audience. Not only from big brands but also perhaps from charities and non-profit organisations. The creative elements developing the advertisements, the channels and consumer engagement with the advertisements have all been explored.

This final chapter brings the module to an end and highlights the practical implications for consumers as they change their behaviours, making it more challenging to serve them with advertisements. The agencies are trying to develop innovative ways to reach out on behalf of the brands and the brands are taking responsibility – bringing the design process in-house and taking control of their data. These highlight the dynamics of the industry. It is changing and we should be prepared for it. Advertising has had to change as consumer behaviour shifts.

The future looks exciting with what the technology offers. We have experienced the prospects of the technology. Coupled with the vast amount of data being generated, increased use of mobile devices, cloud computing and internet, we can be confident of what it can achieve in the future. However, despite various ethical, financial and human limitations, there are prospects and it should be recognized, in advertising, many jobs will be lost and yet many more will be created. AdTech and MarTechs are here to stay.

In conclusion, students need to be aware of the precarious nature of the industry, and they need to recognise the agency culture and be prepared for their career. However, before then, they need to have the theoretical understating of different topics in advertising and marketing and then be ready for the industry. Skills and talents are essential, but the student must take responsibility for their career progress. Whether working in an agency, the client's side or running your business, opportunities abound.

Revision questions

1.   What is your understanding of woke advertising? Do you expect brands to take a stance for social injustices?

2. Describe the changing consumer behaviour and its implications for advertising practices.
3. Put yourself in the place of an advertiser. How would you engage with your audience differently?
4. What is the future of advertising with Ad blockers?
5. Do you see a future where you get paid to watch an advertisement?
6. What is the future with data in advertising? Would advertisers get more data to shape their designs or would consumers stop sharing their data?
7. What is the future of smart speakers in advertising?
8. Can you identify an advertising agency you would like to work with and the role you may be applying for?
9. What is the prospect of social media influencer? Will everyone become an influencer or will there always a selected few who are influencers?
10. Would machines take over the job of advertisers? Discuss the growing role of artificial intelligence in the advertising industry.

Student activity

Conceptualising a social campaign

OptimumVentures is a relatively young and growing FinTech start up. They are considering creating a social campaign – they want to be "woke". They have seen many brands do the same and feel it is the right time for them to take a stand; however, they have seen Gillette and Pepsi advertisements that backfired and they are being mindful of the methods they use to engage with the consumers. They have never done any of this type of campaign before and they need some advice.

Your task is to create a brief, conceptualise some ideas and present a short business report to the founder. Present your findings under these seven key points. For this task, any other facts that are not indicated can be assumed.

1. The form – What form of social injustices would you want a FinTech to address? (there are many examples out there, check out "Elevator – Racism", "It Stops With M", "Always #LikeAGirl" and "The Look" from P&G; recently there are more campaigns for the Black Lives Movement.)
2. The message – What would you consider the key message of the campaign?
3. The research – What information would you suggest for OptimumVentures to develop this campaign? What do they need to understand?
4. The creative element – What creative elements would you advise for this campaign? Remember the "Nike Just Do It "'Dream Crazy'" was predominantly in black colour, featuring sport celebrities.
5. The dissemination – How would you advise the campaign to be shared? Think beyond social media.
6. The data – How can technology and data be integrated into the campaign development?
7. Your role – What role can you play as a student (and as a group) in helping OptimumVentures develop this campaign?

References

Bell, A., 2019. *Waiting on hold will soon become a thing of the past.* [Online] Available at: https://whatsnext.nuance.com/customer-experience/artificial-intelligencebridges-gaps-between-consumer-demands-and-contact-centers/ [Accessed 9.2019].

Bernard, J., 2019. *Brands struggle to make "woke" marketing work.* [Online] Available at: www.raconteur.net/marketing/brands-woke-marketing/ [Accessed 9.9.2020].

Bidalgo, 2018. Home. [Online] Available at: https://bidalgo.com/ [Accessed 2.2.2018].

Chen, J. & Stallaert, J., 2014. An economic analysis of online advertising using behavioral targeting. *MIS Quarterly*, 38(2), pp. 429–447.

Childers, C., Lemon, L. & Hoy, M., 2019. # Sponsored# Ad: Agency perspective on influencer marketing campaigns. *Journal of Current Issues & Research in Advertising*, 40(3), pp. 258–274.

Dentsu, 2018. *CMO Survey 2018*, Japan: Dentsu.

Dolnicar, S. & Lazarevski, K., 2009. Marketing in non-profit organizations: An international perspective. *International Marketing Review*, 26(3), pp. 275–291.

Dwivedi, Y. K. et al., 2019. Artificial Intelligence (AI): Multidisciplinary perspectives on emerging challenges, opportunities, and agenda for research, practice and policy. *International Journal of Information Management.* https://doi.org/10.1016/j.ijinfomgt.2019.08.002.

Easen, N., 2019. *Calling time on sexist stereotypes in advertising.* [Online] Available at: www.raconteur.net/marketing/stereotypes-advertising-ban/ [Accessed 9.9.2020].

Farinloye, T., Mogaji, E. & Kuika Watat, J., 2020. Social media for universities' strategic communication. In: E. Mogaji, F. Maringe & R. E. Hinson, eds. *Strategic marketing of higher education in Africa.* London: Routledge.

Gökerik, M. et al., 2018. Surprise me with your ads! The impacts of guerrilla marketing in social media on brand image. *Asia Pacific Journal of Marketing and Logistics*, 30(5), pp. 1222–1238.

Goodwin, T., 2019. *Five mistakes marketers should avoid in 2019.* [Online] Available at: www.raconteur.net/marketing/marketers-mistakes-2019/ [Accessed 8.8.2020].

Greaves, G., 2018. *Bravery at the heart of new marketing leaders' mission.* [Online] Available at: www.raconteur.net/c-suite/cmo/brave-new-marketing-mission/ [Accessed 9.8.2020].

Guthrie, S., 2018. *Listerine influencer marketing debacle: Who's really at fault?.* [Online] Available at: https://sabguthrie.info/listerine-influencer-marketing-debacle/ [Accessed 2.2.2020].

Gutierrez, A., O'Leary, S., Rana, N. P., Dwivedi, Y. K., & Calle, T., 2019. Using privacy calculus theory to explore entrepreneurial directions in mobile location-based advertising: Identifying intrusiveness as the critical risk factor. *Computers in Human Behavior*, Volume 95, pp. 295–306.

Huang, M. H., & Rust, R. T., 2018. Artificial intelligence in service. *Journal of Service Research*, 21(2), pp. 155–172.

IBM, 2019. *The modern marketing mandate*, Armonk: IBM.

Ibrahim, M., 2018. *How you can get the best out of adtech.* [Online] Available at: www.raconteur.net/marketing/adtech-creativity/ [Accessed 9.9.2020].

Jin, S., Muqaddam, A. & Ryu, E., 2019. Instafamous and social media influencer marketing. *Marketing Intelligence & Planning*, 37(5), pp. 567–579.

Juniper, 2017. *Ad fraud to cost advertisers $19 billion in 2018, representing 9% of total digital advertising spend.* [Online] Available at: www.juniperresearch.com/press/press-releases/ad-fraud-to-cost-advertisers-19-billion-in-2018 [Accessed 2.2.2020].

Krishen, A., Raschke, R., Close, A. & Kachroo, P., 2017. A power-responsibility equilibrium framework for fairness: Understanding consumers' implicit privacy concerns for location-based services. *Journal of Business Research*, 73, pp. 20–29.

Kumar, V. & Gupta, S., 2016. Conceptualizing the Evolution and Future of Advertising. *Journal of Advertising*, 45(3), pp. 302–317.

Lexus (2018). *Lexus Es launches with advert scripted by artificial intelligence.* [Online] Available at: https://blog.lexus.co.uk/lexus-es-launched-with-advert-scripted-by-artificial-intelligence/ #:~:text=Lexus's%20reputation%20for%20pushing%20the,by%20Oscar%2Dwinner%20 Kevin%20Macdonald.

Lou, C. & Yuan, S., 2019. Influencer marketing: How message value and credibility affect consumer trust of branded content on social media. *Journal of Interactive Advertising*, 19(1), pp. 58–73.

Mogaji, E., Czarnecka, B., & Danbury, A., 2018. Emotional appeals in UK business-to-business financial services advertisements. *International Journal of Bank Marketing*, 36(1), pp. 208–227.

Mogaji, E. & Farinloye, T., 2017. Attitudes towards brands and advertisements: qualitative and thematic analysis of social media data. In: B. Rishi & S. Bandyopadhyay, eds. *Contemporary issues in social media marketing.* London: Routledge., pp. 206–216.

Mogaji, E., Olaleye, S. & Ukpabi, D., 2020a. Using AI to personalise emotionally appealing advertisement. In: *Digital and Social Media Marketing.* Cham: Springer, pp. 137–150.

Mogaji, E., Soetan, T. & Kieu, T., 2020b. The implications of artificial intelligence on the digital marketing of financial services to vulnerable customers. *Australasian Marketing Journal.* https://doi.org/10.1016/j.ausmj.2020.05.003.

Persado, 2018. *Home.* [Online] Available at: www.persado.com/ [Accessed 9.9.2020].

Phrasee, 2018. *Home.* [Online] Available at: https://phrasee.co [Accessed 2.2.2020].

Potgieter, A., Adamovic, D. & Mearns, M., 2012. Knowledge sharing through social media: Investigating trends and technologies in a global marketing and advertising research company. *South African Journal of Information Management*, 14(1), pp. 1–7.

Pritchard, M., 2019. *Marc Pritchard on 5 actions P&G is taking to improve the media supply chain.* [Online] Available at: https://us.pg.com/blogs/PritchardANA2019/ [Accessed 2.2. 2020].

Spanier, G., 2019. *How to tackle marketing fraud.* [Online] Available at: www.raconteur.net/ legal/fraud/tackle-marketing-fraud/ [Accessed 8.8.2020].

Stubb, C., Nyström, A. & Colliander, J., 2019. Influencer marketing: The impact of disclosing sponsorship compensation justification on sponsored content effectiveness. *Journal of Communication Management*, 23(2), pp. 109–122.

Takahashi, D. (2018). *Bidalgo uses AI to make mobile advertising more creative.* [Online] Available at: https://venturebeat.com/2018/07/26/bidalgo-uses-ai-to-make-mobile-advertising-more-creative/ [Accessed 8.8.2018].

Wymer, W., 2010. Rethinking the boundaries of social marketing: Activism or advertising?. *Journal of Business Research*, 63(2), pp. 99–103.

Xiao, M., Wang, R. & Chan-Olmsted, S., 2018. Factors affecting YouTube influencer marketing credibility: A heuristic-systematic model. *Journal of Media Business Studies*, 15(3), pp. 188–213.

Index

Note: Page numbers in *italic* refer to Figures; those in **bold** refer to Tables

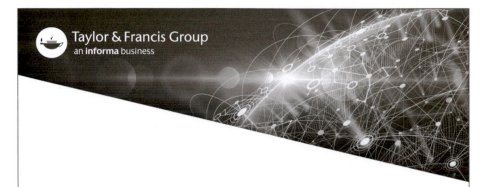